Migration Policy in Crisis

"Migration has become an everyday topic in the last years, and the arrival of persons fleeing for their lives or human rights or in search of a better life has been deemed as a "crisis". In reality, though, Politics are creating a crisis of protection. This book flashes out this scenario in Europe, pointing to the crisis of policies towards migrants in the EU. To face the challenges in the current international setting balancing the interests of States and the needs of human beings is essential. This requires analysis a commitment to being comprehensive, propositional and analytical and this book delivers this."
– *Liliana Lyra Jubilut, Professor in International Law, Member of the IOM Migration Research Leaders' Syndicate, Brazil*

"Whenever we hear the voices of irresponsible populists trying to destroy the European project, we should never forget that we live in and have to fight for an age of enlightenment. The volume at hand provides a superb reminder."
– *Markus Kotzur, Chair of European and International Law and Vice Dean for Studies and Teaching, Universität Hamburg, Germany*

Migration Policy in Crisis

Edited by

Ibrahim Sirkeci

Emília Lana de Freitas Castro

Ülkü Sezgi Sözen

POLICY SERIES

TRANSNATIONAL PRESS LONDON

2018

Migration Policy in Crisis
Edited by Ibrahim Sirkeci, Emília Lana de Freitas Castro, Ülkü Sezgi Sözen

First Published in 2018 by TRANSNATIONAL PRESS LONDON in the United Kingdom, 12 Ridgeway Gardens, London, N6 5XR, UK.
www.tplondon.com

Transnational Press London® and the logo and its affiliated brands are registered trademarks.

Requests for permission to reproduce material from this work should be sent to: sales@tplondon.com

Paperback
ISBN: 978-1-910781-85-2

Cover Design: Gizem Çakır
Cover Photo: migrants to the state border by Photobank gallery, ID: 317688476, https://www.shutterstock.com/image-illustration/migrants-state-border-317688476?src=JjsP5KHPDCIDd0Q9r0QVlQ-1-17.

www.tplondon.com

ABOUT THE EDITORS AND CONTRIBUTORS

Ibrahim Sirkeci is Professor of Transnational Studies & Marketing and Director of Centre for Transnational Studies at Regent's University London, UK. After his BA in Political Science at Bilkent University, he received his PhD in Geography in 2003 from the University of Sheffield and completed his PGCE from the Institute of Education, University College London in 2007. Before joining the Regent's University London in 2005, he worked at the University of Bristol. His research on migration journey started over two decades ago with the International Migration Survey headed by NIDI. His main areas of expertise are remittances, integration, conflict, labour markets, minorities, and segmentation. Sirkeci is known for his extensive work on insecurity and human mobility as well as his conceptual work on conflict model of migration. He has also coined the term "transnational mobile consumers" as he examines connected consumers and the role of mobility in consumer behaviour within a transnational marketing context. He is the editor of several journals including *Migration Letters* and *Remittances Review*. Sirkeci is author and editor of several books including *Turkey's Syrians: Today and Tomorrow* (2017), *Turkish Migration Policy* (2016), *Conflict, Security and Mobility* (2016), *Little Turkey in Great Britain* (2016), *Migration and Remittances during the Global Financial Crisis and Beyond* (2012), and *Cultures of Migration, the global nature of contemporary mobility* (2011).

Professor Sirkeci can be contacted at sirkecii@regents.ac.uk and @isirkeci

Emília Lana de Freitas Castro is doctoral researcher at the Law School of Universität Hamburg, Germany, and since 2015 holds a scholarship from Coordination for the Improvement of Higher Level Personnel (CAPES - *Coordenadoria de Aperfeiçoamento de Pessoal de Nível Superior*), a scholarship from the Brazilian Ministry of Education. Her Ph.D. research project is titled "The free movement of persons and the freedom of settlement of migrants in Brazil and within MERCOSUL: taking Germany and the European Union as possible legal and policy models for the freedom of migration", which is supervised by Prof. Dr. Markus Kotzur, LL.M. (Duke). Emília Castro holds a Bachelor Degree in Law from the Universidade do Estado do Rio de Janeiro (UERJ) and a Master of Laws in International Law from the same University. She is a qualified lawyer in Brazil and has also worked as an Assistant Lecturer for Private International Law at UERJ in 2013 and 2014. In 2017 and 2018, Emília Castro is also a Lecturer for Brazilian Private International Law at Universität Hamburg.

Emília Castro can be contacted at Emilia.Castro@studium.uni-hamburg.de

Ülkü Sezgi Sözen is a research fellow and PhD student at the Law Faculty, Albrecht Mendelssohn Bartholdy Graduate School of Law, Universität Hamburg (UHH). After graduating her bachelor's degree as the third-best in 2012 at the Law Faculty of Istanbul Kültür University with a state scholarship, she received in

October 2013 her LL.M. degree in European Legal Studies at Europa-Kolleg Hamburg with a full scholarship from Schulze-Fielitz Stiftung. Currently, in her research project she deals with the association law and migration policy with special reference to Mediterranean countries. Besides her ongoing academic projects, she gives lecture on Turkish migration law and policy at the law faculty of UHH.

Ülkü Sezgi Sözen can be contacted at uelkue.sezgi.soezen@uni-hamburg.de

Maciej Stepka, MA, MSc is a PhD candidate at the Institute of European Studies, Jagiellonian University in Krakow, Poland. He earned his Master degrees in Political Science from University of Amsterdam (2011) and European Studies from Jagiellonian University in Krakow (2009). His research interests revolve around European policy-making, critical security studies, as well as migration and border studies. Address: Institute of European Studies, Jodlowa 13, 30-252 Krakow, Poland, email: maciek.stepka@uj.edu.pl

Axel Kreienbrink is Head of Unit "International Migration and Migration Management" at the "Research Centre Migration, Integration and Asylum" of the Federal Office for Migration and Refugees in Nuremberg (Germany). After graduating in History and Political Science he made his PhD in Migration Research on the topic of "Immigration policy in Spain" at the University of Osnabrück. He entered the Federal Office in 2005 and became Head of Unit in 2007. His research topics cover international migration, irregular migration, return migration, migration and development, Muslims in Germany, and research for the European Migration Network EMN. He has several publications on migration history and migration policy in Germany, Spain and Europe, see: www.axel-kreienbrink.de

Johanna C. Günther is a PhD candidate at the Centre for Area Studies, Friedrich-Alexander-University Erlangen-Nuremberg. She holds a PhD scholarship of the Studienstiftung des Deutschen Volkes. Her dissertation investigates how judgments of the European Court of Human Rights affect EU policy making processes in the area of asylum. Johanna Günther has contributed to studies and reports of the German Institute for Human Rights concerning the protection of migrants' rights in Germany. Previously, she was a member of an EU-funded research consortium analyzing the perceptions of the EU in its strategic partner countries. Johanna Günther completed a traineeship at the European Network of National Human Rights Institutions (ENNHRI) in Brussels, a postgraduate programme in European Studies at Freie Universität Berlin, and an undergraduate degree in cultural studies and political science at Leuphana Universität Lüneburg.

Barbora Olejárová is a PhD Candidate at the Faculty of Political Science and International Relations, Matej Bel University, Slovakia. Her research expertise includes the issues of international migration covering the Middle Eastern Region and the Eastern Mediterranean. She was a visiting researcher at the Department of Sociology, University of Vienna (2016) and at the Trinity College, Dublin (2017) and she joined the Globsec Academy Centre as a Conference Project Coordinator in 2017. She is a former trainee at the Representation of the European Commission in Slovakia (2014) and she was active on behalf of the Institute for Cultural Diplomacy in Berlin (2014) as well. Barbora also spent some time during her early career and studies travelling China (2012) while working for the non-governmental sector to raise cultural and language awareness of the local population. Her latest policy publications focus on security concerns over the third-countries' migration in the EU; Turkish migration policy and coercive-engineered migration waves.

Vasiliki Kakosimou is the head officer of the Regional Asylum Office (RAO) of Piraeus, Athens (Greek Asylum Service). He deals with cases of international protection from Afghanistan and Bangladesh. Before his current position, Vasiliki used to work in RAO Attica for international protection cases from sub-Saharan countries and Europe. He is a PhD candidate in asylum management and holds a Master degree in public management. Graduated from National School of Public Administration (ENA), the author has published many journal and conference papers. His research interests are: refugee law, asylum management, new public service, among others.

Katarzyna A. Morawska holds a doctoral degree in law from Gdańsk University, Faculty of Law and Administration. Her PhD thesis was of an interdisciplinary character, being devoted to circular migration in the European Union. She completed her post-graduate studies in European Studies at Gdańsk University, as well as her MA studies in European Studies at the Institute for European Studies in Brussels and in International Relations at Łódź International Studies Academy. Since 2010 she has been working as a researcher and academic lecturer at several Universities (e.g. Sopot University of Applied Science, WSB University in Gdańsk, Pomeranian Academy in Starogard Gdański). Since 2016 she holds the function of a research officer in the Gdynia Emigration Museum. Over the last few years, the area of her research has focused mainly on the European immigration law and policy. E-mail: k.morawska@muzeumemigracji.pl

Maria Psoinos is a social psychologist with expertise in the field of migration, health and psychosocial wellbeing. She holds a PhD and an MPhil from Cambridge University, UK and a BSc from Aristotle University of Thessaloniki, Greece. Maria has worked as a researcher and lecturer in the UK (University of Cambridge, St George's University of London, Kingston University) and in Greece (Aristotle University of Thessaloniki, American College of Thessaloniki, National School of Public Health). She has held an Honorary Research fellowship at Kingston University (2009-2014) and is currently a Visiting Research Fellow at Canterbury Christ Church University. She is also Adj. Psychology Professor at the American College of Thessaloniki. Maria has published a number of articles and book chapters on the concept of migrant integration; skilled migrants' and refugees' professional experiences and psychosocial wellbeing; health and social care services for migrants and refugees; qualitative research principles in health and social care. Address: Faculty of Health and Wellbeing, Canterbury Christ Church University, North Holmes Road, Canterbury, Kent, CT1 1QU, United Kingdom. E-mail:

m.psoinos471@canterbury.ac.uk.

Orna Rosenfeld is a housing expert and urban strategist specializing in affordable housing policy and provision, including housing migrants, housing governance and finance as well as urban and city development. She is an adjunct professor at the Sciences Po – Paris Institute of Political Studies, France. Orna holds a PhD from Westminster University, UK, MA from Sheffield University, UK and BArch from Technion Israel Institute of Technology. Since 2016, Dr. Rosenfeld is serving the European Commission as an independent senior housing expert. She also works with the United Nations Economic Commission for Europe (UNECE), the World Bank and Council of Europe Development Bank advising them on the matters of housing migrants among others. Orna has published of a number of articles and book chapters on housing migrants in the UK, Spain and Italy. She believes in connecting scientific fields focusing on migrant integration, wellbeing and housing for best policy results. She is an author of the UNECE flagship publication 'Social housing in the UNECE region: models, trends and challenges' published by the United Nations.

Address: Sciences Po – Paris Institute of Political Studies, Urban School, 117 Boulevard Saint-Germain 75006, FRANCE. E-mail: orna.rosenfeld@sciencespo.fr

Panagiotis Chasapopoulos is a joint PhD candidate at the Antwerp Centre of Evolutionary Demography (ACED) of the Faculty of Applied Economics at the University of Antwerp in Belgium and at the Tilburg Shool of Economics and Management (TiSEM) of Tilburg University in the Netherlands.

Arjen van Witteloostuijn holds a PhD in Economics from Maastricht University (1990) and currently is a Full Professor of Business and Economics at the VU University Amsterdam. He is also Dean of the VU School of Business and Economics (SBE) in Amsterdam.

Christophe Boone holds a PhD in Applied Economics from the University of Antwerp (1992) and currently is a Full Professor of Organization Theory and Behavior at the same university. He is also co-founder and co-director of the Antwerp Centre of Evolutionary demography (ACED).

CONTENTS

2

PREFACE

Markus Kotzur [1]

Prof. Ibrahim Sirkeci, who is well known for his extensive conceptual work on human mobility, conflict, insecurity and cultures of migration, Emília Castro and Ülkü Sezgi Sözen, two younger legal scholars working in the same field and applying a distinctly comparative approach, present their latest book on the crisis of migration policies within the EU. The endeavour could not be more topical. Since 2015, increasing numbers of migrants arrive in the European Union either risking a dangerous journey across the Mediterranean Sea or traveling overland through Southeast Europe via the so-called Balkan Routes. The malfunctions of the Dublin system became obvious when the Member States could not agree how to distribute the refugees amongst themselves. In particular solidarity is at stake when fear-driven anxieties built a new integration-sceptic narrative and provokes strong tendencies of re-nationalization in sovereignty-centered "splendid isolation". The willingness or reluctance towards burden-sharing might indeed become the litmus test for European integration in times of solidarity-crises? Facing this recent challenges one should, however, not forget that migration is by no means a new phenomenon. From the perspective of global history, migratory movements present a continuum in human socialisation; at the same time, they are always tied to ever-changing social, political and economic conditions – in short the real world context. The relevant real world conditions, though, have, what can be seen as another continuum, always taught the lecture that conflicts occur when migratory movements become encounters of people and when these encounters of people turn into confrontations between people. It is exactly this conflictual potential of migration which became most obvious in Europe during the recent "refugee crisis" – wrongly labelled so since the European public is not facing a "crisis of refuges" but rather a crisis of its political communities regarding the question how to adequately deal with refugees approaching their borders.

In a situation like that the need for managing migratory movements is evident. The very idea of an effective migration management has at its heart two components: the reactive aim of defining a framework within which processes of social change can be processed; and the proactive aim of bringing about social change. The overall aim is to comprehensively secure the rule of law in questions of migration, without opening avenues for an overhasty retreat into those exceptional situations that lie beyond the law. The management of migration in both European and Public International law involves the horizontal integration of

---

[1] Prof. Dr. Markus Kotzur, LL.M. (Duke Univ.) is Chair of European and International Law, Vice Dean for Studies and Teaching at Universität Hamburg, Germany.

state and non-state actors alike, whilst making use of all vertical mechanisms typical of multi-level governance, including the establishment of "international benchmark norms" as a normatively binding guide for regulation and enforcement at the supranational European as well as national level.

A second preliminary remark concerns terminology questions. The use of the phrase "migration" requires semantic sensitivity: whilst "migration" in everyday usage implies an exception to the norm of a settled existence, "movement" rather connotes the constitutive norm for the globalised world of the 21st Century and its mobile societies. Migration refers to the movement of persons across borders with the aim of taking up permanent, or at least temporary, residence in a country other than the country of origin. International migration law has no unified institutional framework, remaining instead highly fragmented. It lacks coherent governance structures. And yet, the management of migration requires cooperation. International migration law should become international law of cooperation par excellence and European migration law the supranational should achieve effective implementation of the cooperation model. Especially human rights can provide a normative means of directing cooperation on the international and the European plane as well. All actors being bound by human rights are obliged to establish a minimum level of infrastructure, without which basic human rights would in their substance be empty. This at least has to be achieved by European migration law and brings us back to the notion of solidarity, too. As the great European Jacques Delors said: "Solidarity mechanisms are not based on pure generosity but on enlightened self-interest". Whenever we hear the voices of irresponsible populists trying to destroy the European project, we should never forget that we live in and have to fight for an age of enlightenment. The volume at hand provides a superb reminder.

INTRODUCTION

Ibrahim Sirkeci, Emília Lana de Freitas Castro, Ülkü Sezgi Sözen

Migration and challenges associated with human mobility are here to stay. We, as migration scholars, reiterate, rethink, reconsider what we do know and identify areas for further investigation constantly. Every year we get intrigued by volumes of research and scholarship presented at the Migration Conferences (TMC) since 2012. At the fifth conference in 2017 held at Harokopio University in Athens, about 400 papers were disseminated by researchers covering different aspects, approaches, methods, and takes on human mobility. This edited volume in hand here, although inspired and shaped by the contributions initially presented at the TMC 2017, is more than a conference proceedings book. The volume includes not only more experienced and distinguished academics but also new researchers committed to high quality scholarship in this field.

Our intent was to bring together a selection of papers complementing each other and covering legal studies as well as other social sciences to offer useful material for informed and effective migration policy. The chapters included can also be considered as concentrated on Europe and European approaches on migration. Alluding to the premises of the conflict model of migration, these chapters reflect both conflicts and cooperation between state level actors as well as reflecting at the cross-cutting issues at micro and mezzo levels (Sirkeci, 2009). Individual and group level insecurities reflect the perceived impact of conflicts, tensions, discomforts, disagreements and upsets at micro level and these are moderated by mismatches of policies and practices at state levels. Recent experiences of migration policy in Europe offer both cases of cooperation and conflict as countries' interests do not always complement. The deal(s) with Turkey is probably the reason for a mass outpouring of refugees from Turkey in the later part of 2015. This was a clear display of conflict between the interests at state level (i.e. Turkey and the EU agreed on a scheme) and individual level (i.e. refugees did not want to stay in Turkey). A more recent incident came after a shift in Italian cabinet towards extreme right wing: rescue boats were refused and directed towards Spanish coast (i.e. a clear conflict between EU policies and Italian interpretation). Despite the fact that this edited book was not conceived as a set of cases to exhibit conflicts in migration policy across borders, it turned out a good collection of chapters critically discussing such cases.

In the first chapter titled *"Humanitarian Securitization of the 2015 'Migration Crisis": Investigating Humanitarianism and Security in the EU Policy Frames on Operational Involvement in the Mediterranean"*, Stepka investigates the process of the so-called humanitarian securitization, focusing on dynamics between humanitarian and security-oriented rhetoric and policy actions embedded in the EU policy frames produced in response to the 2015 "migration crisis". Looking at the Mediterranean borders of the EU, the author focuses on the nature of the humanitarian framing of the crisis within the EU policy discourse and its relation to the development of operational and militarized responses to increased migratory flows.

Kreienbrink also focuses on the "refugee crisis", in the second chapter titled *"Restriction, Pragmatic Liberalisation, Modernisation: Germany's Multifaceted Response to the "Refugee Crisis"*. He outlines the German political, legislative and administrative reactions to the "refugee crisis" in 2015 and 2016 and traces expected outcomes of a series of restrictive regulations. The author also comments and analyzes some liberal regulations the country developed in the area of integration, as well as some administrative modernizations occurred lately in Germany.

The following chapter by Günther, titled *"Communicating Refugees and Human Rights: the German Government's Assessment of the Role of the European Court of Human Rights"* expands the critique to European level as she investigates the German government's assessment of the role of the European Court of Human Rights concerning matters of asylum and refugee policy. Through a qualitative analysis of 30 documents released by the German government including transcripts of press conferences, interviews, op-eds, speeches, legislative drafts, reports, and information material, Günther presents and discusses some of the characteristics and contexts of the extracted statements about the ECtHR and/or its judgments.

Olejárová, in her chapter titled *"Solidarity vs. Sovereignty: Perspective on the Slovak Foreign Policy Reactions to the Migration Crisis"* reflects on the so-called "migration crisis". She evaluates legal and political implications of the Slovak government's foreign policy reactions to the "migration crisis". She offers an informative account of the Slovak Republic's position on the migration crisis and the EU solutions with reference to the mandatory quota system and the deal with Turkey.

The European asylum procedures and integration challenges are revisited in the remaining chapters. Kakosimou's chapter titled *"Asylum under Pressure: International Deterrence and Access to Asylum"* explores the ways in which the EU States' deterrence strategies fail to conform with States' obligations under International Human Rights Law, especially because they prevent refugees from having access to asylum. When referring to the EU's migration policy in relation to third countries, Morawska, in the following chapter titled *"Legal and Circular Migration in the European Union Mobility Partnerships"*, examines the mobility partnerships, which aim at promoting legal migration to the EU, including circular migration. She examines the already signed mobility partnerships and also tries to show to what extent these measures support legal migration within the region.

Psoinos' and Rosenfeld takes us into the integration debate with their paper titled *"Developing the Understanding of Migrant Integration in the EU: Implications for Housing Practices"*. They examine how the concept of migrant integration has been theoretically developing in social sciences and suggest applying this new conceptualization to assessing and improving housing practices in Europe. The authors underline that housing issues as part of the integration debates have been an understudied topic. Therefore, they believe that reviewing and critically discussing the evolution of the concept of migrant integration could also trigger more well-informed housing policies and practices for migrants.

The last chapter by Chasapopoulos, van Witteloostuijn and Boone empirically examines the impact of international migration on political outcomes in the Netherlands. In their article, the authors investigate how the stock of immigrants and the immigrant inflows to Dutch municipalities affect the electoral support for the radical right parties of the country. They reveal several interesting findings, including that the share of second-generation immigrants negatively affects anti-immigrant votes, and also that increasing immigrant inflows have a positive and statistically significant effect on voting for radical right parties.

We hope this book will be of use and enhance audience's understanding of political and legal challenges regarding migration in Europe and possibly elsewhere. We have been fortunate enough to have genuinely committed colleagues who contributed to this book. We would like to thank our authors, reviewers and our team that, despite a tight schedule and several parallel projects, have always enabled us a very friendly and pleasant working environment.

HUMANITARIAN SECURITIZATION OF THE 2015 "MIGRATION CRISIS": INVESTIGATING HUMANITARIANISM AND SECURITY IN THE EU POLICY FRAMES ON OPERATIONAL INVOLVEMENT IN THE MEDITERRANEAN

Maciej Stępka [1]

Introduction

The 2015 "migration crisis" has stimulated the European political imagination with an image of migration and border control as based on a mixture of humanitarianism and security. Indeed, the European borders and migratory routes have been increasingly framed in the media and political debates as the sites of a humanitarian and security emergency (see Dekker & Scholten, 2017; Greussing & Boomgaarden, 2017; Ibrahim & Howarth, 2017). The accounts of children dying in the Mediterranean have been reproduced together with images of uncontrollable crowds gathering at the borders, and again with overburdened reception centres with deplorable humanitarian conditions (see BBC, 2018; The Guardian, 2018; Reuters, 2018). All these framings have been (re)merging in the public debate, building a sense of humanitarian crisis, but also insecurity and uncertainty regarding the most suitable course of action at the European level. Regardless the European Union's (EU) attempts to respond to the increased migratory flows, the humanitarian situation has been getting more severe, generating a political momentum for mobilization of more decisive, security-oriented and even militarized measures in dealing with the crisis. Consequently, the EU has decided to increase its operational and military presence in the Mediterranean with Frontex-led[2] Joint Operations (JO) (i.e. Triton, Poseidon and Themis) and Common Security and Defence Policy (CSDP) naval mission (i.e. EUNAVFOR MED Sophia), explicitly framing the mobilization of security capabilities as search and rescue and "live saving" operations.

In this chapter, I will investigate the process of humanitarian securitization,

---

[1] This chapter was financed by the Preludium project number UMO-2015/19/N/HS5/01229 (National Science Centre, Poland) and written within the scope of the Etiuda scholarship number UMO-2016/20/T/HS5/0024 (National Science Centre, Poland).

Maciej Stepka, MA, MSc is a PhD candidate at the Institute of European Studies, Jagiellonian University in Krakow, Poland. Address: Institute of European Studies, Jodlowa 13, 30-252 Krakow, Poland, email: maciek.stepka@uj.edu.pl.

[2] The name Frontex has remained popular in the academic and policy discourse while referring to the European Border and Coast Guard Agency (see Carrera, Blockmans, Cassarino, Gros, & Guild, 2016; Carrera & Hertog, 2016; Moreno-Lax, 2018; Niemann & Speyer, 2018; Paul, 2017).

focusing on the dynamics between humanitarian and security-oriented rhetoric and policy actions embedded in the EU policy frames produced in response to the 2015 "migration crisis". In doing so, I will focus on the nature of the humanitarian framing of the crisis within the EU policy discourse and its relation to the development of operational and militarized responses to increased migratory flows. The chapter focuses predominantly on the Mediterranean border of the EU, which, given the dangerous nature of irregular border crossing and the number of fatalities, occupies the central role in conceptualization of the humanitarian features of the "migration crisis" (IOM, 2018). In this approach I do not treat humanitarianism and security as opposite or mutually exclusive, but concentrate on the way these two logics coincide and intertwine in the framing process. In this respect, the chapter aims to contribute to less-studied branch of securitization, analysing how human referent object and the idea of humanitarianism changes and/or prevails when confronted with security and how this dynamic has been unravelling in the course of the "migration crisis".

The chapter is structured as follows. The first part is devoted to conceptualization of humanitarian securitization approach, focusing on its distinctive features and relation to the so-called humanitarian borders. The second part discusses the conceptual framework and methods, focusing on application of frames and framing in analysis of securitization process and outlining the applied methodological approach. Further, the chapter proceeds to the discussion on the nature of humanitarian rhetoric applied in the framing of the "migration crisis", focusing on its main characteristics. The fourth part of the chapter, analyses conceptualization of remedial action in reference to the humanitarian rhetoric produced by the EU, tracing how the elements of humanitarianism and security have been marginalized and/or empowered at this stage of the framing process. The chapter ends with conclusions.

Securing Human Referent Object: Conceptualizing Humanitarian Securitization

Securitization theory has made a significant impact on the way academics and practitioners have been studying and conceptualizing security (Buzan & Waever, 1997; C.A.S.E., 2006; Fierke, 2013; Peoples & Vaughan-Williams, 2015). It departures from thinking about security in terms of an objective "truth" or a condition and turns into its inter-subjective nature, conceptualizing security as a process of establishment of existential threats with sufficient saliency to have a political effect (Buzan, Waever, & de Wilde, 1998, p. 25). To this extent security can be construed as a *sustained strategic practice aimed at convincing a target audience to accept, based on what it knows about the world, the claim that a specific development or an issue is threatening enough to socially valued referent object to warrant an extraordinary security response* (Balzacq, 2005, p. 173). In this vein, successful securitization creates a threatening representation of an issue allowing to remove it from "normal politics" and subject it to restrictive security measures (Buzan & Waever, 1997; Waever, 1995). As argued by Moreno-Lax, the essence of securitization lies in its ability to catalyse and mobilize fears, placing the public and political realm in the state of continuous vigilance to anticipate and minimize risks, legitimizing restrictive policies of *permanent control and exceptionality* (2018, p. 121).

Migration constitutes one of the most popular objects of securitization, as based on a security-centred narrative and institutional framework around migrants, framing them as a threat to national identity (Ceyhan & Tsoukala, 2002), economic security (Burgess & Gutwirth, 2012), or simply the homogeneity of the State (Bigo, 2002), to name a few. In this respect, securitization of migration at the EU level has been driven by the introduction of the Schengen zone which liberalized internal border checks between member states (Huysmans, 2000, pp. 756–757). In this respect, the security-oriented framing of (especially irregular) migration has been commonly applied in the EU policy discourse, becoming a normal and institutionalized form of problematization of migration-related challenges (Huysmans, 2006; van Munster, 2009).As pointed by van Munster, the main mode of securitization at the EU level has not been based on the idea of dramatic events or exceptional security measures, but rather on mundane practices and discourses that have been gradually incorporating migrants into the frameworks of control and surveillance (2009, pp. 11–13). In the EU policy discourse non-EU migrants, specifically those who irregularly cross the EU border, are framed as objects of risk that need to be controlled in order to avoid breaches of security and trans boundary flows that might amount to migratory invasion (de Haas, 2008). Under this optic, the EU has deployed a wide net of instruments devoted to coordinated risk management and threat identification. In this respect the EU border policing, migrant profiling and restrictive surveillance policies carried out or coordinated by the EU bodies such Frontex or Europol are commonly defined as "securitizing practices" or "moves" pertaining to the incorporation of migration into the EU security framework (Leonard, 2015; Neal, 2009; Perkowski, 2016; Rijpma & Vermeulen, 2015; Rozée, Kaunert, & Léonard, 2013). In this way, securitization of migration is a process that not only defines and creates security around the phenomenon of mobility, but also claims control over it while protecting valued referent objects such as identity, the state, society, and in the case of humanitarianism, human life and dignity (Sjöstedt, 2013; Vaughn, 2009; Watson, 2011).

The concept of humanitarianism is organized around the ideas of human security and human rights, referring to the promotion of welfare and the alleviation of human suffering (Weiss, 2011, pp. 21–23). It reflects the obligation for preservation and protection of human life and dignity with respect to such principles as *humanity, impartiality, neutrality, independence, voluntary service, unity, and universality* (ICRC, 2015). Such a characterization of humanitarianism has been often juxtaposed with the notions of international security, peace, development and international obligations to protect those whose life is at risk (Thomas & Tow, 2002; Weiss, 2011; Wheeler, 2000). This has increased with a wide endorsement of the 2001 *Responsibility to Protect* report, promoting the idea of international obligation to intervene and mobilize military resources in order to alleviate human suffering and protect human life even if it means non-consensual intervention (Weiss, 2011, pp. 100–101). The use or rather misuse of humanitarian justification for the purposes of military interventions in the conflict zones has been widely commented and criticized throughout the academic spectrum. For instance, the realists argue that the use of military force should be limited to the matters of national security (traditionally understood) (Wolfers, 1952, p. 490), while critical scholars challenge the idea of humanitarian action pointing towards imperialist character of the interventions and accompanying misappropriation of humanitarian principles for the legitimization of violence (Ayoob, 2002; Slim, 2001; Welsh, 2004). There are also academic voices, which are not completely dismissive of the use of security measures for humanitarian purposes, as long as they are governed by a clear set of parameters that ensure compliance with the humanitarian values and goals (Fiott, 2013; Weiss, 2011; Weiss & Campbell, 1991). Regardless the standpoint in this debate, it has become increasingly evident that the elements of security and humanitarianism have become closely intertwined in the academic and practice-oriented discourses becoming an instrument for extraordinary mobilization of substantial resources and measures in the name of humanity and humanitarian values (Gasper, 2005; Watson, 2009, 2011).

As noted by Watson, in the context of securitization process humanitarianism can be construed as a type of new security, having powerful effect on generating a sense of urgency and mobilizing security discourses and practices for the purpose of protection of human life and dignity (2011, p. 5). As he argues, this humanitarian securitization or human securitization reflects a security sector of its own governed by a distinctive *logic of threats and vulnerability, a historical set of practices in which certain actors are empowered to speak security, and its own set of rules that define the normal and exceptional practices of humanitarianism* (Watson, 2011, p. 5). To this extent, humanitarian securitization builds explicitly on the narratives of human misery and large-scale loss of human life, claiming the state of exceptionality, which is supposed to warrant mobilization of significant resources and immediate deployment of remedial actions (Watson, 2011, p. 9). In this vein, humanitarian discourses introduce a sense of extreme urgency, imposing a powerful, morally charged diagnosis of the situation, introducing a distinctive imperative for collective action (Calhoun, 2008). As noted by Watson, humanitarian securitization might lead to rapid military response or suspension of specific policies (e.g. immigration policies), but also remain within more institutionalized spectrum mobilizing a plethora of mundane security and non-security practices designed to protect human life and alleviate human suffering (e.g. through specialized NGOs and state agencies) (2011, p. 11).

Humanitarian securitization is inherently complex and often interlocked between elements of security and humanitarianism, which gain or loose prominence in this process leading to different policy outcomes (Watson, 2011, p. 12). On the one hand, humanitarian securitization builds on the humanitarian principles of protection and responsibility, but on the other, it entails the element of security and distinctive elements of control (Waever, 1995, p. 55; Watson, 2011, pp. 4–5). In a sense these two logics do not stand in opposition, but correspond or even complement each other, playing different roles in mobilization of extraordinary measures in the name of humanity. As noted by Pallister-Willkins, even explicitly humanitarian motivations and discourses may not be completely free from security, as they share interest in governance of populations, territories and entities, which arc believed to be at risk (2015, pp. 59–60). In a similar sense, Agier describes the relation between humanitarianism and security and control as symbiotic (2011). As he argues, *there is not care without control* and there is a *functional relationship between the humanitarian realm (the hand that cares) and the realm of security and control (the hand that strikes)* (Agier, 2011, pp. 4–5) . Indeed, mobilization of humanitarian narratives invites a possibility of mobilization of security measures that introduce the elements of protection, but also policing, filtering, channelling and surveillance of what is defined as referent objects within the humanitarian space (Walters, 2011, p. 142).

The intersection of those specific elements is distinctively visible on the example of humanitarian borders, which constitute a specific space of humanitarian securitization in relation to border management and human mobility (Williams, 2016, p. 13). Indeed, the development of humanitarian borders is often attributed to militarization and fortification of borders, as well as increased securitization of migration broadly in different policy sectors (Walters, 2011, p. 147). In this respect, humanitarian borders constitute a space where humanitarian governance and practices of security and control overlap with the territorial edges of the nation-states (Williams, 2015, p. 12). Here, the humanitarian engagement (e.g. humanitarian aid and services located in border regions) is stimulated by life-threatening character of border crossing and negotiated with violence inherent to restrictive border policies and processes of state territorialisation (Walters, 2011, p. 147). In this respect, Walters defines humanitarian borders as a *complex assemblage, comprising particular forms of humanitarianism, specific forms of authority but also certain technologies of government* (Walters, 2011, p. 142). In this context, in order to truly understand the nuanced and complex character of mobilization of humanitarian and security narratives and practices, it is important to remember that these two logics do not necessarily cancel each other out or stand in opposition to one another. Paraphrasing Williams, they interlock, change and shift over time being framed into various forms and modes of discourses and governance introducing a sense of humanitarian urgency but also imperative for regaining security and control over the crisis situation (Williams, 2015, p. 13). Thus, what is most challenging and interesting in this interplay between humanitarianism and security, is how they coincide, overlap and feed on each other in the deployed policy frames and policy responses to tragic and large-scale loss of human life.

Humanitarian Securitization as the Work of Framing

Securitization as the work of framing has been applied in critical security studies to investigate mobilization of *a particular security oriented mind-set that would change the perception of both the nature of the problem and the adequate instruments to deal with it* (Huysmans, 2006, p. 24). Indeed, from the point of view of securitization theory, the framing approach offers an interesting insight into how different notions and interpretations of a given problem (security and/or humanitarian) intertwine and coincide in its political contestation, reflecting different diagnoses, evaluations, and ideas for policy responses (see Carvalho Pinto, 2014; Peoples, 2014; Rychnovská, 2014). In this paper I employ a policy-oriented perspective which defines framing as an contextually embedded process of production and communication of frames by policy actors who attempt to promote specific interpretations of the problem, making a *normative leap from what 'is' to what 'ought to be'* (Rein & Schön, 1996, p. 124). As explained by Entman, to frame is *to select some aspects of a perceived reality and making them more salient in a communicated text, in such a way as to promote a particular problem definition, causal interpretation, moral evaluation, and/or treatment recommendation* (Entman, 1993, p. 52). In this sense, policy framing can be construed as a strategic play of power, where the winning frame shapes the perception of reality, defines the problem and more importantly decides about the type of corrective steps to be taken (Stone, 2012, p. 253). In this sense, framing should be understood as a complex process reflecting a variety of interpretations, ideas and notions about different aspects of socially contested issues. It allows to look into the way policy actors socially construct problems by *culling a few elements of perceived reality, assembling a narrative that highlights connections among them to promote a particular interpretation and remedial action* (Entman, 2007, p. 167).

Building on the conceptualization of policy framing presented by Rein and Schön I propose to split up the framing process into two phases, namely rhetoric- and remedial action-oriented (1996, p. 90). This approach allows for a more accurate isolation of different logics and interpretations applied in the framing process and focus on the logical and sequential representation of a problem and remedial action (Matthes & Kohring, 2008). Here, the rhetoric phase of the framing process comprises primarily of diagnosis and (moral) evaluation of the problem *serving the function of persuasion, justification and symbolic display* (Schön & Rein, 1994, p. 32). The diagnostic part focuses on answering the question of the nature of the problem (Boräng et al., 2014, p. 191). Thus, it concentrates on elements related to problem definition, its root causes and main characteristics (Entman, 2007, p. 164). The evaluation-oriented part of the rhetoric phase focuses on causal agents and effects of the problem at hand (Entman, 1993, p. 52). In this vein, it focuses on perceived consequences of the problem (risks, threats and benefits), attributing blame or merit (David, Atun, Fille, & Monterola, 2011). The rhetoric phase of the framing process is often driven by ideal-type concepts such as social justice, gender equality (Rein & Schön, 1996, p. 92), or as in the case of this chapter humanitarianism or security. This is dictated by its specific function, which is to win allegiances of large groups of people and secure support of specific problem definition (Schön & Rein, 1994, p. 32). That is why the rhetorical frames frequently include abstract concepts which describe a problem, proposing a general, often ideal, direction for policy actions (Meier, 2008). The action-oriented phase of the framing process focuses on propositions of specific solutions, ideally corresponding with the diagnosis and evaluation of the problem (Rein & Schön, 1996, p. 92). This stage of the framing process is concerned with concrete proposals of *laws, regulations, allocation of resources, institutional mechanisms, sanctions, incentives and procedures* that are supposed to manage, mitigate or even remove the problem from public space (Schön & Rein, 1994, p. 32). As Rein and Schön point out, the action in question refers to specific policy design practices through which policy professionals enact policies but also review them and adjust to the changing nature of the problem (Rein & Schön, 1996, p. 91).

Method and analysis

The chapter draws on the official EU policy texts and media materials concerned with the framing of the "migration crisis" and the EU operational involvement in the Mediterranean. The analysed material builds on the texts produced between 2014-2017 by the main EU policy actors involved in the problematization of the crisis and conceptualization of the joint policy responses, namely External Action Service (EEAS), European Commission, Council of the European Union, European Parliament, and Frontex. The selection of documents was carried out in accordance to the methodology of text selection outlined by Buzan and his colleagues, where the core analysis of security discourses in based on policy texts understood as seminal policy or political documents and strategic communications (Buzan et al., 1998, pp. 163–164). In this way, the selected documents include only those texts, which have a capacity to meaningfully impact the framing of an item in question (i.e. "migration crisis") and are representative of discourses produced in response to a specific security problem. This strategy also allows for selection of additional sources, if there is a strong inter-textual link that substantiates this decision (see Daviter, 2007; Princen & Rhinard, 2006).

The analysis of the EU policy framing is text-based and utilizes, Computer Assisted Qualitative Text Analysis (CAQTA) to study how security and humanitarianism underlie and intertwine in the EU policy framing of the "migration crisis" and its operational involvement in the Mediterranean (Boräng et al., 2014; Eising, Rasch, & Rozbicka, 2015; Rozbicka, 2016). I use MAXQDA12 software for initial-automated and manual coding and analysis of policy texts. CAQTA method allows investigating latent contextual meanings, which can be extracted from large portions of text (Boräng et al., 2014). The coding of the texts relies on the codebook, which was developed on the basis of both pre-defined categories (deductive) and/or as a result of in vivo coding, where categories emerge in the process of text analysis (inductive) (Miles, Huberman, & Saldana, 2014, p. 80).

Building the Humanitarian Rhetoric of the "Migration Crisis"

The first stages of the framing process are often characterized with a high level of contention and conflict between policy actors, who struggle over the dominant interpretation of the nature of the problem, the definition of referent objects, threats and responsible parties (Aukes, Lulofs, & Bressers, 2017). The central idea in this phase is to impose a specific type of rhetoric that is acceptable among the actors, compatible with the social, legal and cultural context, and ideally actionable within the existing policy framework (Eising et al., 2015). In regards to the "migration crisis", the humanitarian rhetoric centred on the protection of migrants' lives has quickly gained resonance in the first stages of the framing process, mobilizing a rather unified front among the EU policy actors, who have been producing, reproducing and internalizing the humanitarian perspective into their discourses (see Council of the European Union, 2015a; European Commission, 2015b; European Council 2015a; European Parliament 2015b). One of the major focusing events and starting points for the humanitarian rhetoric was the tragic death of approx. 300 migrants off a small Italian island of Lampedusa in 2013 (Kington, 2013) The framing of the Lampedusa events has to some extent intersected the traditionally securitized EU policy discourse on irregular migration with more humanitarian-centred perspective, recognizing the humanitarian nature of sea borders and dangers related to irregular crossing of the Mediterranean,. Consequently, the EU has started to frame itself not only as a guardian of its borders but also as a more humanitarian actors, pledging to do *everything possible to save the lives of people in danger* (European Parliament, 2013, para. B; see also Council of the European Union, 2014; European Council, 2013).

This explicit humanitarian framing of migrants and irregular migration was later applied in relation to the 2015 "migration crisis" which has quickly become known in the public discourse as "refugee crisis" (Dekker & Scholten, 2017; Greussing & Boomgaarden, 2017). Given the spiralling fatalities among the migrants attempting to cross the Mediterranean into Europe (IOM, 2018), the humanitarian rhetoric has structurated[3] the EU policy discourse, leading to a mainstreaming of humanitarian narratives on the "migration crisis" focusing the attention on *human tragedy* (European Parliament 2015g) , *tragic loss of lives* (European Council 2015g; European Commission 2015b; European Parliament 2015c), and *tragic events in the Mediterranean* (European Parliament 2015g), to name a few. In this regard, the EU's policy framing has been building up a sense of humanitarian urgency, placing the centre of the crisis predominantly in the Mediterranean, which witnessed the highest numbers of fatalities, amounting to the toll of 15 865 migrant deaths recorded between 2014 and 2018 (IOM, 2018). This has consequently turned the Mediterranean and its border crossings into the humanitarian border, requiring control and intervention in the name of humanity and protection of migrants' lives (European Commission, 2016a; 2016c; European Parliament 2016a). In this sense, the EU policy framing aligned with humanitarian securitization, explicitly depicting irregular migrants and refugees fleeing into Europe as the ultimate referent objects, threatened, vulnerable and in need of rescuing. As stated in the Valletta Summit Political Declaration: *We are deeply concerned by the sharp increase in flows of refugees, asylum seekers and irregular migrants which entails suffering, abuse and exploitation, particularly for children and women, and unacceptable loss of life in the desert or at sea (...).* (European Council, 2015c, p.1).

As in this interpretative scheme migrants are construed as the referent object, trans-border organized crime is defined as a direct and main threat to their lives (Council of the European Union, 2016b; European Commission, 2015a, 2015b, 2017d, 2017e; European Parliament, 2016b) . In this respect, the EU policy framing is filled with depictions of human smugglers and traffickers as the main perpetrators and facilitators of violence towards migrants, exploiting human desperation and feeding on degradation of human security environment in the EU neighbourhood (European Parliament, 2016a, p.2). The EU framing of human smugglers puts much emphasis on the inhuman and degrading mode of their operations, often iterating that *scores of migrants drown at sea, suffocate in containers or perish in deserts, while being squeezed onto unseaworthy boats – including small inflatable boats or end-of-life cargo ships*

---

[3] In this chapter so called "structuration" refers an interpretation that becomes powerful and dominant enough to be acknowledged as a "common sense", without which the document or speech would be considered unreasonable, irrelevant or less applicable in describing and conceptualizing challenges related to, in this case the "migration crisis" (Hajer, 2002, pp. 60–61)

- *or into trucks* (European Commission 2015b:1). In this respect, the EU policy actors have been emphasizing the fact that *migrant smuggling has become an increasingly violent form of crime, which may involve serious physical or psychological violence and human rights abuse, exposing women and children to particular risk* (Council of the European Union 2016b:1). The EU policy texts consistently frame smuggling and trafficking as part of the same industry feeding on structural deficiencies of the European and national security and tragic situation of migrants, who often seek services of trans-border criminal groups out of desperation (Council of the European Union, 2016b; European Commission, 2015a, 2015b; European Parliament, 2016a). This type of security framing is consistent throughout the EU policy discourse, defining human smugglers and traffickers as the enemies to the EU and the primary threat to irregular migrants.

The EU has embraced the humanitarian nature of the crisis, centring the attention on the life-threatening character of irregular crossing of the Mediterranean and voicing the imperative for action. The EU's humanitarian framing proposes a clear and broad conceptualization of referent objects, which includes both refugees and economic migrants, recognizing the violent as well as economic push factors driving them to seeking refuge in Europe. At the same time, the humanitarian framing of the migrants employs a very narrow understanding of humanitarianism, focusing predominantly on their survival and removal from life-threatening situations. As often reiterated in the EU policy discourse, *the first priority in this context is to save lives and do everything necessary to rescue and protect the migrants whose lives are at risk* (European Council, 2015c, p.1).This type of framing, on the one hand generates a sense of extreme urgency, building on the narrative of the tragic loss of life, while on the other hand leaves little space for discussion on wellbeing or broader protection of those who are rescued at sea (see Council of the European Union, 2015a; European Commission 2015d, 2015e, 2016a, 2017b,). Consequently, it opens the framing process to more securitized narratives, allowing for mobilization of extraordinary measures in the name of saving lives. This distinctive framing of the Mediterranean borderland in terms of crisis, tragedy or emergency has generated a strong imperative for humanitarian actions, concentrating on "here and now" of the sinking dinghies, dying children, and migrants who would cross any barrier and border, trying to flee war and barbarism of the so-called Islamic State (European Commission, 2015e, p.3). The EU policy framing directly connects this situation with human smugglers and traffickers, who are consistently framed as not only violently exploiting but also representing a holistic threat to the lives of migrants and the stability of the EU external borders. This interpretation of the crisis calls for an urgent and decisive response, which would allow governing the Mediterranean humanitarian borderland, here constituting a focal point of the crisis and a space of interactions between the referent objects and the threat.

Conceptualizing remedial actions. Between "Search and Rescue" and "Seek and Destroy"

Given the purpose of the rhetoric part of the policy framing stated above, the broadly applied humanitarian-centred narrative did exactly what it was supposed to do. As outlined above, it has produced a straightforward and commonly acceptable definition of the humanitarian referent object that requires protection, and the enemy, here personified as a human smuggler and trafficker. Taking this rhetoric into account, the EU has generated a complex network of different and intertwining external and internal policy responses and, frameworks[4] that aspire to become a holistic approach to the challenges related to migration (Carrera & Hertog, 2016; Niemann & Speyer, 2018; Niemann & Zaun, 2018). Within this framework of policy responses, the explicitly humanitarian thread is distinctively continued in a particular conceptualization of remedial actions, namely humanitarian border and naval interventions, blending the search and rescue, border control and security measures into a coordinated policy action. This humanitarian and securitizing approach is explicit in the European Commission's *Agenda on Migration*, where rhetoric of humanitarianism is intertwined with calls for security-oriented and powerful measures. As stated in the Agenda, *Europe cannot stand by whilst lives are being lost,* but in order to step up in its humanitarian commitment it needs to mobilize extraordinary resources, taking up what supposed to be a "shield" (i.e. Frontex-led operations) and a "sword" (i.e. naval CSDP operations) to protect migrants' lives at sea (European Commission, 2015b, 2017d, 2017e). In the EU's framing of the humanitarian-security remedial action this combination of "search and rescue" and "seek and destroy" capabilities is presented to be the most suitable course of actions and most importantly *a powerful demonstration of the EU's determination to act* (European Commission, 2015b, p.3).

In this respect, the EU's involvement in the Mediterranean can be narrowed down specifically, but not exclusively, to Frontex-led joint border operations Triton[5], Poseidon[6] and Themis[7] and EUNAVFOR MED Operation Sophia. The EU's framing of joint border operations has been utilizing a "here and now" imperative for action, fulfilling a "dual role", as an instrument for regaining control over the EU borders and more prominently strengthening search and rescue activities. In this respect, covering Central (Joint Operation Triton, since 2018 Themis) and Eastern (Joint Operation Poseidon) Mediterranean the Frontex-led border operations have been tasked with strengthening the capacity for border

---

[4] Reform of the Common European Asylum System, relocation and resettlement schemes, return operations, new readmission agreements and trust funds with Third countries, developed of European Border and Coast Guard Agency, to name a few (for overview see Niemann & Zaun, 2018).

[5] Joint Operation Triton was launched in November 2014 on request of the Italian authorities covering the area of the Central Mediterranean, specifically search and rescue zones of Italy and Malta. It was a continuation of the Italian naval-humanitarian operation "Mare Nostrum" deployed after tragic events off Lampdusa. Triton's operational mandate was initially based on border control and surveillance, search and rescue activities, and later expanded to include forms of cross-border crime. Triton officers were also tasked with debriefing of rescued migrants and collection of intelligence on human smuggling networks operating in Libya and other African countries. The Operation was concluded in 2018 (Frontex, 2018e).

[6] Joint Operation Poseidon-Sea was launched in 2011 on request of the Greek authorities and a multipurpose operation covering the area of Eastern Mediterranean, including the Greek islands in the Eastern Aegean Sea. The main tasks of the Operation include border surveillance, search and rescue, registration identification of the migrants, and assistance to the Greek authorities in returns and readmissions activities (Frontex, 2018c).

[7] Joint Operation Themis was launched in February 2018 as a replacement of Operation Triton, assisting Italian authorities in border control of the Central Mediterranean. It has remained search and rescue components but its mandate has been additionally strengthened with law enforcement and security tasks, focusing on intelligence gathering and detection of terrorist threats among rescued migrants. (Frontex, 2018d)

control, surveillance, and search and rescue activities carried out by the Italian and Greek authorities respectively (Frontex 2018c, 2018e). With increased air-surveillance capabilities (including 4 aircrafts and 4 helicopters), 28 coast guard vessels, 1190 guest officers and access to the European Border Surveillance System, the joint operations in the Central and Eastern Mediterranean were supposed contain the crisis and do *everything possible to prevent further loss of life at sea* (European Parliament, 2015e, para. 1). Nonetheless, this assemblage of technical, operational and humanitarian support was missing an explicit security measure that could contribute not only to control and retrieval of migrants at risk, but also address the threats to their lives, here framed a trans-border organized crime. In this respect, the EU has decided to mobilize the CSDP naval operation, tasked with *preventing further loss of life at sea and to tackle the root causes of the human emergency* (European Council, 2015a, para. 1). EUNAVFOR MED, later renamed as Operation Sophia, was launched in June 2015 and was designed as a crisis management mission with an explicit focus on enforcing and sustaining security in the Mediterranean by *targeting criminal networks which exploit vulnerable migrants by systematically identifying, capturing and destroying vessels used by smugglers (*EEAS, 2017b, p. 28). The operation was planned to unfold in three phases: 1) information gathering on human smuggling models and detection of migration networks; 2) search, seizure and diversion of naval vessels suspected of being used for human smuggling or trafficking purposes; 3) disposal of the vessels confirmed to be used by the smugglers or rendering them inoperable (Gruszczak, 2017, p. 38; Council of the European Union, 2016a, 2017).

The humanitarian undertone in both types of missions has quickly gained prominence within the EU policy discourse, giving space for a wider coalition between Council of the European Union, European Commission, and European Parliament who, invoking humanitarianism, promoted further development of the EU's operational engagement in the Mediterranean (Council of the European Union, 2015a; European Commission, 2015d, 2016d; European Parliament 2015b, 2015c). Even European Parliament, which has been traditionally employing a cautious approach to securitization of migration policies in the EU (Huber, 2015; Karamanidou, 2015), has become a supporter of *aims of navy operations such as Operation Sophia, stressing the need to protect life, emphasising that all aspects of the operation should ensure that migrant lives are protected* (European Parliament, 2016b, para. 9). Nonetheless, as already outlined in the previous section of this chapter, this humanitarian rhetoric was far from inclusive and reflected a rather narrow understanding of humanitarian obligation. In terms of operational tasks of the missions it has been concentrating the attention on the activities related to retrieval and rescue of migrants at risk allowing the EU policy actors to freely focus on the most straight-forward and tangible aspect of humanitarianism and potentially use it as an instrument for legitimization of further increase of operational resources, budget, operational capabilities and geographical scope of the EU's operations[8].

---

[8] For instance in 2015 as a result of the expansion of the mandates by search and rescue activities, Joint Operations Triton and Poseidon-Sea have been granted additional EUR 26,25 million and another EUR 45 million in 2016 (Frontex, 2015). As stated often reiterated by the EU officials, between 2015-2017 the EU has tripled the operational budgets of its Mediterranean border operations (European Commission, 2015b,

It has become very important for the framing of the EU's involvement in the Mediterranean to sustain its humanitarian connotations directly linking the increase of resources and capabilities with life saving activities. As stated by Frontex Executive Director on the occasion of the expansion of Operations Triton and Poseidon: *we have to dramatically increase the deployment levels in the Central Mediterranean to support the Italian authorities in controlling its sea borders and in saving lives, too many of which have already been tragically lost this year* (Frontex, 2015). In this respect, the element of search and rescue has been continuously publicized throughout the EU policy discourse with factsheets and media materials explaining step by step how Frontex uses border security measures to save migrants' lives and exhibiting visual and statistical[9] proofs of its successful operations (European Commission, 2017f, 2018). The case of EUNAVFOR MED constitutes yet another example of how the humanitarian framing was used in order to increase the life-saving undertone of essentially a military operation. Here, the renaming of the operation from its original codename to Operation Sophia (after a baby girl born on board of the EU vessel), was framed by the European Action Service as an act *to honour the lives of the people we are saving, the lives of people we want to protect, and to pass the message to the world that fighting the smugglers and the criminal networks is a way of protecting human life* (EEAS, 2016a). Thus, regardless the explicit security orientation of the operation, the general undertone of Sophia has remained humanitarian, strongly promoting its capacity for saving migrants' lives at sea as one of its most successful and material accomplishment (EEAS, 2017a, 2017b; European Parliament, 2018). During the debate on the future of the mission, its humanitarian aspect has proven to be one of the key arguments for its extension, pointing out that it *saves lives by disrupting criminal networks* (European Parliament, 2018) and has already assisted in rescuing over 40 000 lives at sea (EEAS, 2017a).

This humanitarian framing has provided a powerful political drive in the conceptualization of the EU's operational engagement in the Mediterranean elevating it to a widely acceptable humanitarian intervention in the EU borderlands. However a critical investigation of the EU's operations also reveals their security-oriented and securitizing nature, which in the course of the "migration crisis" has started to dominate in the conceptualization of the EU's remedial action towards the crisis (Council of the European Union, 2017; European Commission, 2017a, 2016c; European Council, 2017a). The most visible symptom of (re)mergence of security in the EU's engagement in the Mediterranean was a gradual reconceptualization of the referent object. Here, the migrant as the humanitarian referent object has been reframed from an object of protection to an object of control, surveillance and finally a potential risk. In fact, this process has started as early as the deployment of the Operation Sophia, which has visibly shifted the attention from search and rescue to proactive combating of human smugglers and trans-border organized crime that facilitates illegal transit (Council of the European

---

2017c).

[9] Statistics reflecting the numbers of rescued migrants during joint border operations have been continuously reproduced for the benefit of public hearings in the European Parliament, (for example LIBE, 2017, 2016; 2015) or to underline the humanitarian commitment of the EU in the State of the Unions (European Commission, 2015e, 2016d, 2017c)

Union, 2015, 2017). As pointed out by Moreno-Lax, while built on the humanitarian narrative, the operational plan of the mission was in fact designed not so much to rescue the migrants but contain their irregular flows by seeking and destroying smuggling vessels (Moreno-Lax, 2017, p. 10). In this sense, the rescue component of Sophia was not so much "by design" but rather "on occasion".

This decline of humanitarian features has also been visible on the example of joint border operations, which in the course of the "migration crisis" have been distancing from proactive search and rescue (Gruszczak, 2017; Niemann & Zaun, 2018). While joint border operations have been continuously promoted as a humanitarian measure, they have not lost border control features, being additionally responsible for assistance in migrant registration, identification (Operation Poseidon), and intelligence gathering on human smuggling networks (Operation Poseidon and Operation Triton) (Frontex, 2018c, 2018e). As indicated by the Executive Director of Frontex in reference to the review of the Triton operation in the Central Mediterranean, joint operations should not overly concentrate on humanitarian goals as *stepping up search-and-rescue operations would only encourage desperate migrants to risk the passage* (Kingsley & Traynor, 2015). Indeed, the Joint Operations Poseidon, Triton and its successor Themis have been gradually marginalizing their humanitarian components, focusing predominantly on border security, surveillance and assistance in management of migratory flows (Frontex, 2018d, 2018e). In this regard, the most recent Frontex initiative - Joint Operation Themis, which replaced Triton in 2018, can be considered as a new type of border operations, which explicitly diverts from humanitarian goals to predominantly security and law enforcement operational tasks (Frontex, 2018b). The Operation has been equipped with extensive security components specifically tailored for combating and tracing illicit and illegal trans-border activities, including terrorism and detection of foreign fighters (Nielsen, 2018). As stated by Frontex executive director: *We need to be better equipped to prevent criminal groups that try to enter the EU undetected. This is crucial for the internal security of the European Union* (Frontex, 2018b) Together with this change of approach, the migrant referent object ultimately loses its dominance, being replaced by the protection of borders and internal security of the EU. Some observers point out that with the Operation Themis, the securitization of operational responses in the Mediterranean has become evident, as the EU has officially exposed its *refocusing on people rescued at sea as potential threats* (Nielsen, 2018).

Conclusions

The concept of humanitarian securitization allows for better understanding of mobilization of extraordinary measures in the situations of humanitarian crisis when life and wellbeing of human beings are defined as the ultimate referent object requiring protection from structural and pervasive threats. The EU policy framing of its operational engagement in the Mediterranean during the "migration crisis" constitutes such a situation, in which the policy actors have built up a humanitarian rhetoric around increased irregular migratory flows into Europe and consequently have proposed to mobilize exceptional security measures to address the loss of life on the Mediterranean route. However, this case of humanitarian securitization does not fall under the purely humanitarian framework, which consistently focuses on the protection of human beings and alleviating their suffering in the name of humanity. Here, the analysis of the policy framing of the "migration crisis" has revealed a rather dynamic mode of humanitarian securitization, reflected in a shifting conceptualization of referent object and an interplay between humanitarian and security-oriented logics.

The analysis of the EU's policy framing of the "migration crisis" has indicated that the humanitarian rhetoric has had a prominent role in mobilization and further securitization of the remedial actions. Firstly, the rhetoric part of the EU's framing process has distinctively humanitarised the crisis outlining a narrative of pity and protection over the suffering irregular migrants. It has proposed a clear set of objects and actors interacting and coinciding in the Mediterranean humanitarian borderland, generating a sense of humanitarian urgency and imperative for action. In this respect, the rhetoric part has outlined the human referent object, in this case an irregular migrant, whose life is threatened by the organized crime that feeds on his/her misery and exploits his/her desperation. In turn, human smugglers and traffickers are framed as the ultimate enemies being both the threat to migrants and the root cause of the crisis. In this respect, they need to be handled with decisive and swift security measures, combated and dismantled for the sake of migrants' lives and stability of the Mediterranean borderland. However, the EU's humanitarian optics has created a certain type of path dependency for conceptualization of the remedial actions. It has imposed a very narrow definition of the humanitarian obligation, reflected in the retrieval of migrants from life threatening situations at sea, extensively elaborating on their right to be searched and rescued, but little beyond that. This type of rhetoric has accommodated the expectations regarding the EU's humanitarian involvement in the crisis, generated a powerful imperative for humanitarian intervention and also opened further conceptualization of the remedial actions to a plethora of decisive and security-oriented measures that would alleviate the crisis, but also impose a specific security regime of the humanitarian borderland.

The conceptualization of the remedial actions towards the Mediterranean has indeed introduced distinctive security features into the humanitarian securitization process. With Frontex-led operations and CSDP naval Operation Sophia, the EU has deployed a plethora of instruments allowing to control, surveil and engage the situation in the humanitarian borderlands, be it for the purposes of "search and rescue" of irregular migrants or "seek and destroy" of smuggling vessels. However, in the course of the crisis, the policy reviews of the remedial actions have visibly marginalized the humanitarian migrant-centred features that have already served its purpose legitimizing and creating momentum for mobilization of extraordinary measures. Here, the framing of the policy responses has shifted its attention from the life saving and humanitarian nature of the missions and reoriented it to the modes of border security, counter-organized crime, and counter-terrorism. This trend can be observed on the example of the latest generation of border operations deployed in the Mediterranean (i.e. Operation Themis), which have lost its search and rescue orientation for the benefit of security components. Thus, its mandate is currently focused on combating organized crime and detecting terrorist and foreign fighters attempting to exploit the crisis and gain access to the EU. In this respect, the EU's mode of humanitarian securitization of the "migration crisis" reveals an interesting characteristic and at the same time may be symptomatic for further securitizations of the migration at the EU level. It shows how humanitarian and human security centred rhetoric may carry securitizing practices, however only to a specific end, which is institutionalization of the security measures within the humanitarian setting, and in this case militarization and securitization of the Mediterranean humanitarian borderland.

References

Agier, M. (2011). Managing the Undesirables: Refugee Camps and Humanitarian Government. Cambridge: Polity Press.

Aukes, E., Lulofs, K., & Bressers, H. (2017). Framing mechanisms: the interpretive policy entrepreneur's toolbox. Critical Policy Studies, 0(0), 1–22. http://doi.org/10.1080/19460171.2017.1314219

Ayoob, M. (2002). Humanitarian Intervention and State Sovereignty. The International Journal of Human Rights, 6(1), 81–102. http://doi.org/10.1080/714003751

Balzacq, T. (2005). The Three Faces of Securitization: Political Agency, Audience and Context. European Journal of International Relations, 11(2), 171–201. http://doi.org/10.1177/1354066105052960

BBC, (2018), Migrant crisis: Migration to Europe explained in seven charts. Retrieved from http://www.bbc.com/news/world-europe-34131911. Accessed: 28.03.2018.

Bigo, D. (2002). Security and Immigration: Toward a Critique of the Governmentality of Unease. Alternatives, 27(1), 63–92. http://doi.org/10.1177/03043754020270S105

Boräng, F., Eising, R., Klüver, H., Mahoney, C., Naurin, D., Rasch, D., & Rozbicka, P. (2014). Identifying Frames: A comparison of Research Methods. Interest Groups & Advocacy, 3(2), 188–201. http://doi.org/10.1057/iga.2014.12

Burgess, J. P., & Gutwirth, S. (2012). A Threat Against Europe?: Security, Migration and Integration. Asp / Vubpress / Upa.

Buzan, B., & Waever, O. (1997). Slippery? contradictory? sociologically untenable? The Copenhagen school replies. Review of International Studies, 23(2), 241–250.

Buzan, B., Waever, O., & de Wilde, J. (1998). Security: A New Framework for Analysis. Boulder, London: Lynne Rienner Publishers.

C.A.S.E. (2006). Critical Approaches to Security in Europe: A Networked Manifesto. Security Dialogue, 37(4), 443–487. http://doi.org/10.1177/0967010606073085

Calhoun, C. (2008). The imperative to reduce suffering: charity, progress, and emergencies in the field of humanitarian action. In M. Barnett & T. G. Weiss (Eds.), Humanitarianism in Question: Politics, Power, Ethics (pp. 73–97). Ithaca: Cornell University Press.

Carrera, S., & Hertog, L. Den. (2016). A European Border and Coast Guard: Fit for purpose? (CEPS Commentary). Brussels.

Carrera, S., Blockmans, S., Cassarino, J., Gros, D., & Guild, E. (2016). The European Border and Coast Guard. Brussels.

Carvalho Pinto, V. (2014). Exploring the interplay between Framing and Securitization theory: the case of the Arab Spring protests in Bahrain. Revista Brasileira de Política Internacional, 57(1), 162–176. http://doi.org/10.1590/0034-7329201400109

Ceyhan, A., & Tsoukala, A. (2002). The Securitization of Migration in Western Societies: Ambivalent Discourses and Policies. Alternatives: Global, Local, Political, 27(1), 21–39. http://doi.org/10.1177/03043754020270S103

Council of the European Union. (2014). Council conclusions on "Taking action to better manage migratory flows". Retrieved from http://www.consilium.europa.eu/uedocs/cms_data/docs/pressdata/en/jha/145053.pdf. Accessed: 15.03.2018.

Council of the European Union. (2015a). Council Conclusions on Measures to handle the refugee and migration crisis. Retrieved from http://www.consilium.europa.eu/en/press/press-releases/2015/11/09/jha-council-conclusions-on-measures-to-handle-refugee-and-migration-crisis/. Accessed: 17.03.2018.

Council of the European Union. (2015b). Luxembourg Presidency report - Managing migration flows. State of play - implementing solutions and remaining gaps. Retrieved from http://www.consilium.europa.eu/media/23778/20151216-migration-presidency-report-implementation.pdf. Accessed: 18.03.2018.

Council of the European Union. (2016a). Council conclusions on EUNAVFOR MED operation Sophia. Retrieved from http://www.consilium.europa.eu/pl/press/press-releases/2016/05/23/fac-eunavfor-sophia/. Accessed: 27.03.2018

Council of the European Union. (2016b). Council conclusions on migrant smuggling – Council conclusions (10 March 2016). Retrieved from http://www.consilium.europa.eu/en/press/press-releases/2016/03/10/council-conclusions-on-migrant-smuggling/. Accessed: 15.03.2018.

Council of the European Union. (2017). EUNAVFOR MED Operation Sophia: mandate extended until 31 December 2018. Retrieved from http://www.consilium.europa.eu/en/press/press-releases/2017/07/25/eunavformed-sophia-mandate-extended/. Accessed: 18.03.2018.

David, C. C., Atun, J. M., Fille, E., & Monterola, C. (2011). Finding Frames: Comparing Two Methods of Frame Analysis. Communication Methods and Measures, 5(4), 329–351. http://doi.org/10.1080/19312458.2011.624873

Daviter, F. (2007). Policy Framing in the European Union. Journal of European Public Policy, 14(4), 654–666. http://doi.org/10.1080/13501760701314474

de Haas, H. (2008). The Myth of Invasion: the inconvenient realities of African migration to Europe. Third World Quarterly, 29(7), 1305–1322. http://doi.org/10.1080/01436590802386435

Dekker, R., & Scholten, P. (2017). Framing the Immigration Policy Agenda. The International Journal of Press/Politics, 22(2), 202–222. http://doi.org/10.1177/1940161216688323

EEAS. (2016a). About EUNAVFOR MED Operation SOPHIA. Retrieved from https://eeas.europa.eu/csdp-missions-operations/eunavfor-med-operation-sophia/36/about-eunavfor-med-operation-sophia_en. Accessed: 23.03.2018.

EEAS. (2016b). EU Operations in the Mediteterranean Sea, Retrieved from https://eeas.europa.eu/sites/eeas/files/5_euoperationsinmed_2pg.pdf. Accessed: 17.03.2018.

EEAS. (2017a). EUNAVFOR MED Operation Sophia: mandate extended until 31 December 2018. Retrieved from http://www.consilium.europa.eu/en/press/press-releases/2017/07/25/eunavformed-sophia-mandate-extended/. Accessed: 27.03.2018.

EEAS. (2017b). European Union Common Security and Defence Policy Missions and Operations. Annual Report 2017. Retrieved from https://eeas.europa.eu/sites/eeas/files/csdp_annual_report_2017_web_en_2.pdf. Accessed: 19.03.2018.

Eising, R., Rasch, D., & Rozbicka, P. (2015). Institutions, policies, and arguments: context and strategy in EU policy framing. Journal of European Public Policy, 22(4), 516–533. http://doi.org/10.1080/13501763.2015.1008552

Entman, R. M. (1993). Framing: Toward Clarification of a Fractured Paradigm. Journal of Communication, 43(4), 51–58. http://doi.org/10.1111/j.1460-2466.1993.tb01304.x

Entman, R. M. (2007). Framing bias: Media in the distribution of power. Journal of Communication, 57(1), 163–173. http://doi.org/10.1111/j.1460-2466.2006.00336.x

European Commission. (2015a). Communication from the Commission to the European Parliament, the Council, the European Economic and Social Committee and the Committee of the Regions. EU Action Plan against migrant smuggling (2015 - 2020). Retrieved from https://ec.europa.eu/anti-trafficking/sites/antitrafficking/files/eu_action_plan_against_migrant_smuggling_en.pdf. Accessed: 18.03.2018.

European Commission. (2015b). Communication from the Commission to the European Parliament, the Council, the European Economic and Social Committee and the Committee of the Regions. The European Agenda on Migration. Retrieved from http://eur-lex.europa.

eu/legal-content/EN/TXT/?uri=celex%3A52015DC0240. Accessed: 19.03.2018.

European Commission. (2015c). Communication from the Commission to the European Parliament, the Council, the European Economic and Social Committee and the Committee of the Regions. The European Agenda on Security. Retrieved from http://eur-lex.europa.eu/legal-content/EN/TXT/?uri=COM:2015:185:FIN. Accessed: 19.03.2018.

European Commission. (2015d). Meeting on the Western Balkans Migration Route: Leaders Agree on 17-point plan of action. Retrieved from http://europa.eu/rapid/press-release_IP-15-5904_en.htm. Accessed: 18.03.2018.

European Commission. (2015e). State of the Union 2015: Time for Honesty, Unity and Solidarity. Retrieved from http://europa.eu/rapid/press-release_SPEECH-15-5614_en.htm. Accessed: 18.03.2018.

European Commission. (2016a). Communication from the Commission to the European Parliament, the European Council and the Council. Back to Schengen - A Roadmap.. Retrieved from https://ec.europa.eu/home-affairs/sites/homeaffairs/files/what-we-do/policies/borders-and-visas/schengen/docs/communication-back-to-schengen-roadmap_en.pdf. Accessed: 17.03.2018.

European Commission. (2016b). Communication from the Commission to the European Parliament and the Council. Action plan to strengthen the European response to travel document fraud. Retrieved from http://eur-lex.europa.eu/legal-content/EN/TXT/?uri=CELEX:52016DC0790. Accessed: 17.03.2018.

European Commission. (2016c). Securing Europe's external borders: Launch of the European Border and Coast Guard Agency. Retrieved from http://europa.eu/rapid/press-release_IP-16-3281_en.htm. Accessed: 29.03.2018.

European Commission. (2016d). State of the Union 2016 by Jean-Claude Juncker, President of the European Commission. Retrieved from http://europa.eu/rapid/attachment/SPEECH-16-3043/en/SOTEU%20brochure%20EN.pdf. Accessed: 19.03.2018.

European Commission. (2017a). Future-proof migration management: European Commission sets out way forward. Retrieved December from europa.eu/rapid/press-release_IP-17-5132_en.pdf. Accessed: 18.03.2018.

European Commission. (2017b). Joint Communication to the European Parliament, the European Council and the Council Migration on the Central Mediterranean route. Managing flows, saving lives. Retrieved from http://eur-lex.europa.eu/legal-content/EN/TXT/?uri=CELEX%3A52017JC0004. Accessed: 18.03.2018.

European Commission. (2017c). President Jean-Claude Juncker's State of the Union Address 2017. Retrieved from europa.eu/rapid/press-release_SPEECH-17-3165_en.pdf. Accessed: 19.03.2018.

European Commission. (2017d). Remarks by Commissioner Avramopoulos at the LIBE Committee meeting on the delivery of the European Agenda on Migration. Retrieved from https://ec.europa.eu/commission/commissioners/2014-2019/avramopoulos/announcements/remarks-commissioner-avramopoulos-libe-committee-meeting-delivery-european-agenda-migration_en. Accessed: 19.03.2018.

European Commission. (2017e). Report from the Commission to the European Parliament, the European Council and the Council. Progress report on the European Agenda on Migration. Retrieved from https://ec.europa.eu/home-affairs/sites/homeaffairs/files/what-we-do/policies/european-agenda-migration/20171114_progress_report_on_the_european_agenda_on_migration_en.pdf. Accessed: 17.03.2018.

European Commission. (2017f). Saving Lives: Central Mediterranean Route and Commission Action Plan to Support Italy and Stem Migration Flows. Retrieved from https://ec.europa.eu/home-affairs/sites/homeaffairs/files/what-we-do/policies/european-agenda-migration/20170704_factsheet_-_central_mediterranean_route_commission_action_plan_to_support_italy_and_stem_flows_en.pdf. Accessed: 10.03.2018.

European Commission. (2018). How does Frontex Joint Operation Triton support search and rescue operations?. Retrieved from https://ec.europa.eu/home-affairs/sites/homeaffairs/files/what-we-do/policies/european-agenda-migration/background-information/docs/frontex_triton_factsheet_en.pdf. Accessed: 17.03.2018.

European Council. (2015a). Special meeting of the European Council Thursday 23 April in Brussels. Background note. Retrieved from http://www.consilium.europa.eu/media/23741/150322-background-euco-final.pdf. Accessed: 19.03.2018.

European Council. (2015b). Valletta Summit on Migration, 11-12 November 2015 Action Plan. Retrieved from http://www.consilium.europa.eu/media/21839/action_plan_en.pdf. Accessed: 19.03.2018.

European Council. (2015c). Valletta Summit on Migration, 11-12 November 2015 Political Declaration. Retrieved from http://www.consilium.europa.eu/media/21841/political_decl_en.pdf. Accessed: 19.03.2018.

European Council. (2017a). Leaders' Agenda. Migration: way forward on the external and internal dimension. Retrieved from https://www.consilium.europa.eu/media/32143/en_leaders-agenda-note-on-migration_.pdf. Accessed: 19.03.2018.

European Council. (2017b). Malta Declaration by the members of the European Council on the external aspects of migration: Addressing the Central Mediterranean route. Retrieved from http://www.consilium.europa.eu/en/press/press-releases/2017/02/03/malta-declaration/. Accessed: 18.03.2018.

European Parliament. (2013). Migratory flows in the Mediterranean, with particular attention to the tragic events off Lampedusa (2013/2827(RSP)). Retrieved from http://www.europarl.europa.eu/sides/getDoc.do?pubRef=-%2f%2fEP%2f%2f TEXT%2bTA%2bP7-TA-2013-0448%2b0%2bDOC%2bXML%2bV0%2f%2fEN&language=EN. Accessed: 20.03.2018.

European Parliament. (2014). Situation in the Mediterranean and the need for a holistic EU approach to migration (2014/2907(RSP)). Retrieved from http://www.europarl.europa.eu/sides/getDoc.do?pubRef=-%2f%2fEP%2f%2fTEXT%2bTA%2bP8-TA-2014-0105%2b0%2bDOC%2bXML%2bV0%2f%2fEN&language=EN. Accessed: 17.03.2018.

European Parliament. (2015a). Humanitarian crisis in Iraq and Syria, in particular in the IS context (2015/2559(RSP)). Retrieved from http://www.europarl.europa.eu/sides/ getDoc.do?pubRef=-%2f%2fEP%2f%2fTEXT%2bTA%2bP8-TA-2015-0040%2b0%2bDOC%2bXML%2bV0%2f%2fEN&language=EN. Accessed: 18.03.2018.

European Parliament. (2015b). Migration and refugees in Europe (2015/2833(RSP. Retrieved from http://www.europarl.europa.eu/sides/getDoc.do?pubRef=-%2f%2fEP%2f%2f TEXT%2bTA%2bP8-TA-2015-0317%2b0%2bDOC%2bXML%2bV0%2f%2fEN &language=EN. Accessed: 19.03.2018.

European Parliament. (2015c). Proposal for a Council decision establishing provisional measures in the area of international protection for the benefit of Italy and Greece (COM(2015)0286 — C8-0156/2015 — 2015/0125(NLE)). Retrieved from http://www.europarl.europa.eu/sides/getDoc.do?pubRef=-%2f%2fEP%2f%2fTEXT%2bTA%2bP8-TA-2015-0306%2b0%2bDOC%2bXML%2bV0%2f%2fEN&language=EN. Accessed: 19.03.2018.

European Parliament. (2015d). Situation in Libya (2014/3018(RSP)). Retrieved from http://www.europarl.europa.eu/sides/getDoc.do?pubRef=-%2f%2fEP%2f%2fTEXT%2bTA%2bP8-TA-2015-0010%2b0%2bDOC%2bXML%2bV0%2f%2fEN &language=EN. Accessed: 19.03.2018.

European Parliament. (2015e) The latest tragedies in the Mediterranean and EU migration and asylum policies (2015/2660(RSP)). Retrieved from http://www.europarl.europa.eu/sides/getDoc.do?pubRef=-%2f%2fEP%2f%2fTEXT%2bTA%2bP8-TA-2015-0176%2b0%2bDOC%2bXML%2bV0%2f%2fEN&language=EN. Accessed: 19.03.2018.

European Parliament. (2016a). Implementation of the Directive 2011/36/EU of 5 April 2011 on preventing and combating trafficking in human beings and protecting its victims from a gender perspective (2015/2118(INI)). Retrieved from http://www.europarl.europa.eu/sides/getDoc.do?pubRef=-%2f%2fEP%2f%2fTEXT%2bTA%2bP8-TA-2016-0227%2b0%2bDOC%2bXML%2bV0%2f%2fEN&language=EN. Accessed: 18.03.2018.

European Parliament. (2016b). The situation in the Mediterranean and the need for a holistic EU approach to migration (2015/2095(INI)). Retrieved from http://www.europarl.europa.eu/sides/getDoc.do?pubRef=-%2f%2fEP%2f%2fTEXT%2bTA%2bP8-TA-2016-

0102%2b0%2bDOC%2bXML%2bV0%2f%2fEN&language=EN. Accessed: 19.03.2018

European Parliament. (2018). Legislative Train Schedule Towards New Policy on Migration: European Union Naval Force- Mediterranean Operation Sophia. Retrieved from http://www.europarl.europa.eu/legislative-train/theme-towards-a-new-policy-on-migration/file-eunavfor-med-operation-sophia. Accessed: 19.03.2018.

Fierke, K. M. (2013). Critical Approaches to International Security. Cambridge, Malden: Policy Press.

Fiott, D. (2013). Realist Thought and Humanitarian Intervention. The International History Review, 35(4), 766–782. http://doi.org/10.1080/07075332.2013.817466

Frontex. (2015). Frontex expands its Joint Operation Triton. Retrieved from https://frontex.europa.eu/media-centre/news-release/frontex-expands-its-joint-operation-triton-udpbHP. Accessed: 29.03.2018.

Frontex. (2018a). Mission and Tasks. Retrieved from http://frontex.europa.eu/about-frontex/mission-and-tasks/. Accessed: 19.03.2018.

Frontex. (2018b). Frontex launching new operation in Central Med. Retrieved from https://frontex.europa.eu/media-centre/news-release/frontex-launching-new-operation-in-central-med-yKqSc7. Accessed: 18.03.2018.

Frontex. (2018c). Joint Operation Poseidon (Greece). Retrieved from https://frontex.europa.eu/media-centre/focus/joint-operation-poseidon-greece--3ImFxd. Accessed: 16.03.2018.

Frontex. (2018d). Joint Operation Themis. Retrieved from https://frontex.europa.eu/media-centre/videos/joint-operation-themis-i9pnjL. Accessed: 19.03.2018.

Frontex. (2018e). Joint Operation Triton (Italy). Retrieved from https://frontex.europa.eu/media-centre/focus/joint-operation-triton-italy--ekKaes. Accessed: 19.03.2018.

Gasper, D. (2005). Securing Humanity: Situating "Human Security" as Concept and Discourse. Journal of Human Development, 6(2), 221–245. http://doi.org/10.1080/14649880500120558

Greussing, E., & Boomgaarden, H. G. (2017). Shifting the refugee narrative? An automated frame analysis of Europe's 2015 refugee crisis. Journal of Ethnic and Migration Studies, 43(11), 1749–1774. http://doi.org/10.1080/1369183X.2017.1282813

Gruszczak, A. (2017). European Borders in Turbulent Times: The Case of the Central Mediterranean "Extented Borderland." Politeja, 50(5), 23–45.

Hajer, M. (2002). The Politics of Environmental Discourse. Oxford, New York: Oxford University Press.

Huber, K. (2015). The European Parliament as an actor in EU border policies: its role, relations with other EU institutions, and impact. European Security, 24(3), 420–437. http://doi.org/10.1080/09662839.2015.1028188

Huysmans, J. (2000). The European Union and the securitization of migration. Journal of Common Market Studies, 38(5), 751–777. http://doi.org/10.1111/1468-5965.00263

Huysmans, J. (2006). The Politics of Insecurity: Fear, Migration and Asylum in the EU. London, New York: Routledge. http://doi.org/10.1057/palgrave.jird.1800148

Ibrahim, Y., & Howarth, A. (2017). Communicating the "migrant" other as risk: space, EU and expanding borders. Journal of Risk Research, 1–22. http://doi.org/10.1080/13669877.2017.1313765

ICRC. (2015). The Fundamental Principles of International Red Cross and Red Crescent Movement. Retrieved from https://www.icrc.org/sites/default/files/topic/ file_plus_list/4046-the_fundamental_principles_of_the_international_red_cross_and_red_crescent_movement.pdf . Accessed: 19.03.2018.

IOM. (2018). Missing Migrants. Tracking Death Along Migratory Routes. Retrieved from https://missingmigrants.iom.int. Accessed: 16.03.2018.

Karamanidou, L. (2015). The Securitisation of European Migration Policies: Perceptions of Threat and Management of Risk. In G. Lazaridis & K. Wadia (Eds.), The Securitisation of Migration in the EU (pp. 37–61). Houndmills, New York: Palgrave Macmillan.

Kingsley, P., Traynor, I.,(2015). EU borders chief says saving migrants' lives 'shouldn't be priority' for patrols. Retrieved: https://www.theguardian.com/world/2015/apr/22/eu-borders-chief-says-saving-migrants-lives-cannot-be-priority-for-patrols. Accessed: 28.03.2018.

Kington, T. (2013). Lampedusa shipwreck: Italy to hold state funeral for drowned migrants, Retrieved from https://www.theguardian.com/world/2013/oct/09/lampedusa-shipwreck-italy-state-funeral-migrants. Accessed: 18.03.2018.

Leonard, S. (2015). Border Controls as a Dimension of the European Union's Counter-Terrorism Policy: A Critical Assessment. Intelligence and National Security, 30(2–3), 306–332. http://doi.org/10.1080/02684527.2014.988447

LIBE. (2015). Respecting human rights in the context of migration flows in the Mediterranean. Retrieved from http://www.europarl.europa.eu/committees/en/libe/events-hearings.html?id=20150915CHE00021. Accessed: 18.03.2018.

LIBE. (2016). Securing the External Borders of the EU. Retrieved from http://www.europarl.europa.eu/committees/en/libe/events-hearings.html?id=20160420CHE00191. Accessed: 29.03.2018.

LIBE. (2017). Exchange of views on Search and rescue activities in the Central Mediterranean. Retrieved from http://www.europarl.europa.eu/committees/en/libe/events-hearings.html?id=20170705CHE02221. Accessed: 17.03.2018.

Matthes, J., & Kohring, M. (2008). The Content Analysis of Media Frames: Toward Improving Reliability and Validity. Journal of Communication, 58(2), 258–279. http://doi.org/10.1111/j.1460-2466.2008.00384.x

Meier, P. (2008). Critical Frame Analysis of EU Gender Equality Policies. Representation, 44(2), 155–167. http://doi.org/10.1080/00344890802079656

Miles, M. B., Huberman, M. A., & Saldana, J. (Eds.). (2014). Qualitative data analysis: a methods sourcebook. Los Angeles, London, New Delhi, Singapore: SAGE Publications.

Moreno-Lax, V. (2017). The EU Humanitarian Border and the Securitization of Human Rights: The "Rescue-Through-Interdiction/Rescue-Without-Protection" Paradigm. JCMS: Journal of Common Market Studies, 56(1), 119–140. http://doi.org/10.1111/jcms.12651

Moreno-Lax, V. (2018). The EU Humanitarian Border and the Securitization of Human Rights: The "Rescue-Through-Interdiction/Rescue-Without-Protection" Paradigm. JCMS: Journal of Common Market Studies, 56(1), 119–140. http://doi.org/10.1111/jcms.12651

Neal, A. W. (2009). Securitization and risk at the EU border: The origins of FRONTEX. Journal of Common Market Studies, 47(2), 333–356. http://doi.org/10.1111/j.1468-5965.2009.00807.x

Nielsen, N. (2018). Frontex naval operation to look for 'foreign fighters'. Retrieved from https://euobserver.com/migration/140806. Accessed: 17.03. 2018.

Niemann, A., & Speyer, J. (2018). A Neofunctionalist Perspective on the "European Refugee Crisis": The Case of the European Border and Coast Guard. JCMS: Journal of Common Market Studies, 56(1), 23–43. http://doi.org/10.1111/jcms.12653

Niemann, A., & Zaun, N. (2018). EU Refugee Policies and Politics in Times of Crisis: Theoretical and Empirical Perspectives. JCMS: Journal of Common Market Studies, 56(1), 3–22. http://doi.org/10.1111/jcms.12650

Pallister-Wilkins, P. (2015). The Humanitarian Politics of European Border Policing: Frontex and Border Police in Evros. International Political Sociology, 9(1), 53–69. http://doi.org/10.1111/ips.12076

Paul, R. (2017). Harmonisation by risk analysis? Frontex and the risk-based governance of European border control. Journal of European Integration, 39(6), 689–706. http://doi.org/10.1080/07036337.2017.1320553

Peoples, C. (2014). New nuclear, new security? Framing security in the policy case for new nuclear power in the United Kingdom. Security Dialogue, 45(2), 156–173. http://doi.org/10.1177/0967010614521840

Peoples, C., & Vaughan-Williams, N. (2015). Critical security studies : an introduction (2nd ed.). London, New York: Routledge.

Perkowski, N. (2016). Deaths, Interventions, Humanitarianism and Human Rights in the Mediterranean "Migration Crisis." Mediterranean Politics, 21(2), 331–335. http://doi.org/10.1080/13629395.2016.1145827

Princen, S., & Rhinard, M. (2006). Crashing and creeping: agenda-setting dynamics in the European Union. Journal of European Public Policy, 13(7), 1119–1132. http://doi.org/10.1080/13501760600924233

Rein, M., & Schön, D. (1996). Frame-critical policy analysis and frame-reflective policy practice. Knowledge & Policy, 9(1), 85–104. http://doi.org/10.1007/BF02832235

Reuters, (2018). Flight to Europe. Retrieved from https://www.reuters.com/subjects/migrant-crisis. Accessed: 29.03.2018.

Rijpma, J., & Vermeulen, M. (2015). EUROSUR: saving lives or building borders? European Security, 24(3), 454–472. http://doi.org/10.1080/09662839.2015.1028190

Rozbicka, P. (2016). Policy ideas through the prism of knowledge regimes and framing. Interest Groups & Advocacy, 5(1), 107–112. http://doi.org/10.1057/iga.2015.11

Rozée, S., Kaunert, C., & Léonard, S. (2013). Is Europol a Comprehensive Policing Actor? Perspectives on European Politics and Society, 14(3), 372–387. http://doi.org/10.1080/15705854.2013.817808

Rychnovská, D. (2014). Securitization and the power of threat framing. Perspectives, 22(2), 9–31.

Schön, D., & Rein, M. (1994). Frame reflection: towards resolution of intractable policy controversies. New York: Basic Books.

Sjöstedt, R. (2013). Ideas, Identities and Internalization: Explaining Securitizing Moves. Cooperation and Conflict, 48(1), 143–164. http://doi.org/10.1177/0010836712445023

Slim, H. (2001). Violence and Humanitarianism. Security Dialogue, 32(3), 325–339. http://doi.org/10.1177/0967010601032003005

Stone, D. A. (2012). Policy paradox: the art of political decision making (3rd ed.). London, New York: W.W. Norton & Company. http://doi.org/10.1017/CBO9781107415324.004

The Guardian, (2018). Migration crisis: the new routes to Europe. Retrieved from https://www.theguardian.com/world/series/migration-crisis-the-new-routes-to-europe. Accessed: 19.03.2018.

Thomas, N., & Tow, W. T. (2002). The Utility of Human Security: Sovereignty and Humanitarian Intervention. Security Dialogue, 33(2), 177–192. http://doi.org/10.1177/0967010602033002006

van Munster, R. (2009). Securitizing immigration. The Politics of Risk in the EU. Houndmills, New York: Palgrave Macmillan.

Vaughn, J. (2009). The Unlikely Securitizer: Humanitarian Organizations and the Securitization of Indistinctiveness. Security Dialogue, 40(3), 263–285. http://doi.org/10.1177/0967010609336194

Waever, O. (1995). Securitization and Desecuritization. In R. D. Lipschutz (Ed.), On Security (pp. 46–76). New York: Columbia University Press.

Walters, W. (2011). Foucault and Frontiers: Notes on the Birth of the Humanitarian Borders. In U. Bröckling, S. Krasmann, & T. Lemke (Eds.), Governmentality: Current Issues and Future Challenges (pp. 138–164). New York: Routledge. http://doi.org/10.4324/9780203846476

Watson, S. (2009). The Securitization of Humanitarian Migration. Digging moats and sinking boats. London, New York: Routledge. http://doi.org/10.14288/1.0099879

Watson, S. (2011). The "human" as referent object?: Humanitarianism as securitization. Security Dialogue, 42(1), 3–20. http://doi.org/10.1177/0967010610393549

Weiss, T. G. (2011). Humanitarian Intervention. Cambridge, Malden: Polity.

Weiss, T. G., & Campbell, K. M. (1991). Military humanitarianism. Survival, 33(5), 451–465. http://doi.org/10.1080/00396339108442612

Welsh, J. M. (2004). Taking Consequences Seriously: Objections to Humanitarian Intervention. In J. M. Welsh (Ed.), Humanitarian Intervention and International Relations (pp. 52–70). Oxford: Oxford University Press.

Wheeler, N. J. (2000). Saving Strangers. Humanitarian Intervention in International Society. Oxford, New York: Oxford University Press.

Williams, J. M. (2015). From humanitarian exceptionalism to contingent care: Care and enforcement at the humanitarian border. Political Geography, 47, 11–20.

http://doi.org/10.1016/j.polgeo.2015.01.001

Williams, J. M. (2016). The safety/security nexus and the humanitarianisation of border enforcement. The Geographical Journal, 182(1), 27–37. http://doi.org/10.1111/geoj.12119

Wolfers, A. (1952). "National Security" as an Ambiguous Symbol. Political Science Quarterly, 67(4), 481–502.

RESTRICTION, PRAGMATIC LIBERALISATION, MODERNISATION: GERMANY'S MULTIFACETED RESPONSE TO THE "REFUGEE CRISIS"

Axel Kreienbrink [1]

Introduction

In 2015 and 2016, Germany faced an influx of asylum seekers on an unprecedented scale. How did the country react to this so-called "refugee crisis"? The response was a major effort at all levels of the federal state: the federal level, the Länder, the local authorities, but also civil society, welfare associations and NGOs. There have been countless measures in the most diverse fields of action (Grote, 2018). This article will specifically deal with the question of how and which legislative and administrative changes were put in place at the federal level in order to better manage the changing influx.

A simple assumption would be that the policy approach here has been above all a restrictive one. This would fit with the patterns of the past decades of German policy on foreigners and asylum. Ever since the first German law on foreigners was passed in 1965, a restrictive approach dominated the law: foreigners should be controlled for reasons of public security and permanent immigration should be avoided (Schönwälder, 1999). Asylum seekers from socialist but non-aligned Yugoslavia (and Hungary) were met with mistrust. At that time, the term "economic refugee" appeared first (Münch, 1993: 59-60) and already in 1966 "unfounded asylum applications" were the subject of an inquiry in the Bundestag (Kimminich, 1982: 24). This gave rise to the argumentation patterns that were to play a central role in the discussion about asylum policy in the following decades (Poutrus, 2009: 173). With the increase in the number of asylum seekers since the late 1970s and reaching 100,000 per year (1980), measures were taken to reduce this influx. These included the introduction of visa requirements, an employment ban for asylum seekers during the asylum procedure, measures to speed up asylum procedures and to streamline legal remedies (Fullerton, 1989; Kreienbrink, 2013: 399ff.). This pattern continued in the early 1990s, when the highest number of asylum seekers until then arrived in Germany in 1992: more than 438,000.

[1] Axel Kreienbrink is Head of Unit "International Migration and Migration Management" within the Research Centre Migration, Integration and Asylum of the Federal Office for Migration and Refugees (BAMF), Frankenstrasse 210, 90461 Nuremberg, Germany. E-mail: axel.kreienbrink@bamf.bund.de.

Views expressed in this article are exclusively those of the author. The author would like to thank Tabea Rösch, Dana Wolf, Janne Grote and the anonymous reviewer for their valuable comments and suggestions.

Politicians reacted with the so-called "asylum compromise" in 1992 (Hailbronner, 1994; Bosswick, 2000: 49f). Among other things, it included an amendment to the Basic Law introducing the concept of safe third countries and safe countries of origin. At the same time, a separate right to benefits for asylum seekers was created, the Asylum Seeker Benefits Act (AsylbLG), which contained reduced benefits compared to social assistance (Fijalkowski, 1993).

This restrictive pattern, according to the hypothesis, also continued in the course of the recent "refugee crisis". At the same time, however, developments could also be observed which can be labelled as "liberalisation". These legislative developments were accompanied by processes of modernisation at the administrative level, as they had already been observed in the course of the previous "refugee crises" of the early 1980s and early 1990s (Kreienbrink, 2013: 403-404, 406).

Setting the scene: Unprecedented asylum migration

Asylum migration in 2015 and 2016 was the highest ever registered since asylum procedures began in Germany in 1953. Between 1953 and 2017, some 5.6 million people applied for asylum in the Federal Republic of Germany (first time and subsequent applications), of which over 1.2 million applied in 2015/2016 (BAMF 2017a: 11). Since the low level of asylum applications in 2007 (below 20,000 applicants), the number of asylum seekers saw a strong increase already in 2013 and 2014, especially of applicants from the Western Balkan states. However, the origin of the applicants shifted, as civil war refugees from Syria became the largest group of applicants, followed by persons from Afghanistan, Iraq and Iran. From the conflict zones in the Middle East, migration routes led via Turkey, then mostly via the Aegean to Greece or by land, further via the states of the Western Balkans (the so-called "Balkan Route" - Macedonia (FYROM), Serbia, Croatia), Hungary, Austria to Germany and partly further to Switzerland, Sweden or the Netherlands (Frontex, 2016a, b). However, Germany was the main country of destination within the EU.

The number of asylum seekers arriving rose steadily throughout the spring and summer of 2015, especially from the beginning of September onwards when the Federal Government and Austria "agreed to admit several thousand asylum seekers from Hungary in order to put an end to the 'emergency situation' facing Hungary" (Grote, 2018: 22). The opening of the border was based on the right of self-entry under the discretionary clauses of the Dublin III Regulation. However, this triggered an even greater rush to Germany and partly uncontrolled entry, so that border controls at the German-Austrian border were introduced just one week later in order to re-establish an orderly entry procedure. It was not until the end of that year and due to the efforts of the countries along the Balkan route to increasingly close their borders that the arrival figures declined significantly. With the official closure of the Balkan route and the EU-Turkey Agreement in March 2016, arrival figures dropped significantly to remain at a low level (Grote, 2018: 22-24), although the route cannot be regarded as completely closed (Weber, 2017).

In 2015, 476,649 asylum applications (first time and subsequent applications) were registered in Germany alone (compared to 202,834 in 2014). This marked an increase of 135.0% compared to the previous year and represented a third of all applications in the EU. The main country of origin was Syria, followed by Albania, Afghanistan and Iraq. However, the capacities of the administration in Germany were not geared to immigration of this scale and therefore not all arriving persons were able to file their asylum applications immediately after their initial registration. This lead to a gap of almost 650,000 between the registration figures of the system for initial distribution of asylum seekers (1.092 million) and the number of filed applications for asylum (441,899). Even if the number of initial registrations after adjustments in the course of subsequent registrations in 2016 (e.g. due to missing and double registrations as well as onward and return migration) was stated at 890,000, the difference remained considerable (Konar et al., 2017).

Despite the decline in the number of arriving asylum seekers in 2016, the number was still around 321,000. By contrast, due to the necessary race to catch up for those who were unable to file their application in 2015, in 2016 altogether 745,545 first time and subsequent applications were registered, the highest number ever achieved in Germany (1992: 438,191). Compared internationally, Germany was also the country with the highest number of applications worldwide in 2016, followed by the United States (262,000), Italy (123,000) and Turkey (78,600) (UNHCR, 2017: 3). The main countries of origin of asylum seekers in 2016 were Syria, Afghanistan, Iraq, Iran, Eritrea, Albania, Pakistan, and Nigeria.

Figure 1. Monthly asylum entries, applications and decisions in Germany 2014-2017

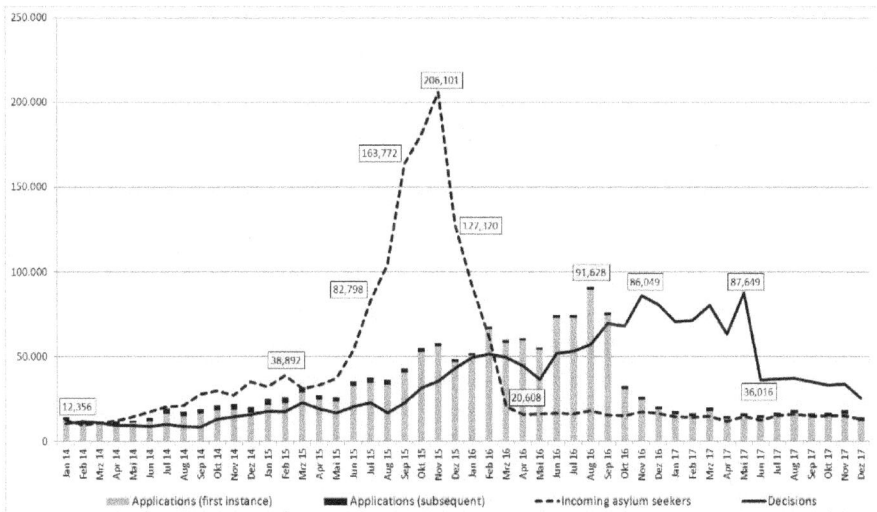

Source: Ajared from Grote, 2018: 16 (updated)

After almost one and a half years of strong discrepancy between arriving asylum seekers and those actually able to apply for asylum, in 2017, the numbers of arriving asylum seekers (just over 172,000) and asylum applications (just over 181,000) were almost fully balanced again. Nevertheless, the responsible authority, the Federal Office for Migration and Refugees (BAMF), faced major challenges. While the

Office issued 128,911 decisions in 2014, the number increased by 119.3% to 282,726 decisions in 2015. However, due to the sharp increase in applications, the number of pending cases increased in parallel. While the year 2014 had already ended with just under 170,000 pending cases, the number increased by 115.6% to just under 365,000 cases by the end of 2015. By contrast, 695,733 decisions were issued in 2016 (+ 146.1 %), but 417,000 cases were still pending, even though since October 2016 more applications could be processed per month than new ones were filed. In 2017, around 603,000 decisions were issued, which reduced the number of pending cases to 68,000 (BAMF 2018).

Behind these figures lay a large number of challenges for the actors at federal, state and local level.[2] Being responsible for asylum procedures, the BAMF first had to solve the challenge of registering the arrivals and carrying out the procedures, for which an unprecedented increase in personnel was necessary. Whereas at the beginning of 2014 the Federal Office had just over 2,000 employees, this figure had risen to around 10,000 at the end of 2016 due to new hires and the secondment of support staff from other authorities. In the course of 2015, the number of branch offices of the Federal Office increased from 22 to more than 40, and at the end of 2016, the number of branch offices peaked with over 80. In the course of the reorganisation of procedures in the Federal Office (summarised under the keyword "Integrated Refugee Management"), arrival centres were created which function as the first contact point for arriving asylum seekers. In these centres, the processes are interlinked with those of the admission authorities of the Länder and the Federal Employment Agency in order to minimise idle times and waiting times in the procedure. Furthermore, a first decision-making centre was established in Nuremberg in July 2015, in which merely asylum cases which have already been processed by the branch offices and arrival centres are to be decided in order to relieve the branch offices. Accordingly, no hearing took place in these centres. At the beginning of October 2015, three more decision centres were opened (BMI/BAMF, 2016: 17-19).

Since the accommodation and care of asylum seekers falls within the competence of the Länder and local authorities, these actors also faced considerable challenges. For example, people arriving in 2015 often had to be accommodated in emergency shelters because the number of regular facilities was insufficient. These emergency shelters were partly mobile containers and tents, partly military barracks out of use, warehouses, aircraft hangars, administration buildings, community centres, hotels, department stores, schools and gymnasiums. Welfare associations and private providers were often commissioned by the municipalities and Länder to operate the facilities. When housing was under control, challenges concerning additional support measures followed (social welfare offices, youth welfare offices, school offices etc.) which again mainly was of concern of local authorities (Meyer, 2016; Bogumil, 2017; Grote, 2018: 49).

Finally, the political and social challenges should not be forgotten, such as e.g. considerable discussions on the question of whether the opening of the border in September 2015 was a legitimate act (Di Fabio, 2016; Papier, 2016; Thym, 2016;

---

[2] For a compilation of 50 of the most important challenges see Grote 2018.

Bast/Möller, 2016). Within German society, the public mood, at least in 2015, was characterized by a great willingness to help. The pictures of volunteers receiving large numbers of asylum seekers at Munich Central Station in autumn 2015 were broadcasted worldwide. Likewise, the large number of civil society volunteers in the municipalities was extremely important, as without these helping hands many municipalities would not have been able to master the challenges on local level. This "movement" came to be known as "welcome culture". In 2016, however, this positive attitude changed significantly: problems came to the fore, xenophobic crimes increased, the call for more restrictive measures in order to decrease the inflow of asylum seekers and to ease forced return (especially for delinquent asylum seekers) grew louder and the issue of asylum immigration became a central topic of election campaigns (Hamann/Karakayali, 2016; Conrad/Aðalsteinsdóttir, 2017; Vollmer/Karakayali, 2018).

The Expectable: Restriction

In the course of the "refugee crisis" very extensive legislative action took place in order to meet the challenges emerging at all levels. The following list contains 19 legislative measures focusing, inter alia, on easing the construction of new reception facilities, improving the efficiency of the registration and the asylum procedure as well as implementing more restrictive measures for asylum seekers from specific countries of origin or extending voluntary and forced return measures, leaving aside further ordinances and regulations (compilation by Grote, 2018: 31f.).

Figure 2. Asylum related legislative changes in Germany 2014 to 2017

2014

Act on the Classification of Further Countries as Safe Countries of Origin and to Facilitate Labour Market Access for Asylum Seekers and Foreigners Whose Deportation Has Been Suspended (entered into force on 6 November 2014; Federal Law Gazette 2014, I No. 49: 1649)

Act on Measures in Construction Planning Law to Facilitate the Accommodation of Refugees (entered into force on 26 November 2014; Federal Law Gazette 2014, I No. 53: 1748)

Act Amending the Act on Benefits for Asylum Seekers and the Social Court Act (important parts entered into force on 1 March 2015; individual parts entered into force on 19 December 2014 and 1 January 2016; Federal Law Gazette 2014, I No. 59: 2187)

Act to Improve the Legal Status of Asylum Seekers and Foreigners Whose Deportation Has Been (important parts entered into force on 1 January 2015; individual parts entered into force on 1 March 2015; Federal Law Gazette 2014, I No. 64: 2439)

2015

Act on the Promotion of Investment in Financially Weak Municipalities and to Ease the Burden on Länder and Municipalities Receiving and Accommodating Asylum Seekers (entered into force on 30 June 2015; Federal Law Gazette 2015, I No. 24: 974)

Act Redefining the Right to Remain and the Termination of Residence (important parts entered into force on 1 August 2015; individual parts entered into force on 1 January 2016; Federal Law Gazette 2015, I No. 32: 1386)

Asylum Procedures Acceleration Act (important parts entered into force on 24 October 2015; individual parts entered into force on 1 November 2015, 1 January 2016 and 1 November 2016; Federal Law Gazette 2015, I No. 40: 1722)

Act on the Improvement of Care Arrangements for Foreign-Born Children and Adolescents (important parts entered into force on 1 November 2015; individual parts entered into force on 1 July 2017; Federal Law Gazette 2015, I No. 42: 1802)

Act Strengthening the Victims of Crime in Criminal Proceedings (3rd Victims' Rights Reform Act) (important parts entered into force on 31 December 2015; individual parts entered into force on 1 January 2017; Federal Law Gazette 2015, I No. 55: 2525)

2016

Act to Improve the Registration and Sharing of Data for Purposes of Residence and Asylum Law (Data Sharing Improvement Act) (important parts entered into force on 5 February 2016; individual parts entered into force on 1 May 2016 and 1 November 2016; Federal Law Gazette 2016, I No. 5: 130)

Act on the Introduction of Accelerated Asylum Procedures (Asylum Package II) (which entered into force on 17 March 2016; Federal Law Gazette 2016, I No. 12: 390)

Act on the Facilitation of Expulsions of Criminal Foreigners and Extended Reasons for Refusing Refugee Recognition to Criminal Asylum (which entered into force on 17 March 2016; Federal Law Gazette 2016, I No. 12: 394)

Integration Act (major parts entered into force on 6 August 2016; individual parts entered into force on 1 January 2017; Federal Law Gazette 2016, I No. 39: 1939)

50th Act Amending the Criminal Code – Enhancing Protection of the Right to Sexual Self-Determination (which entered into force on 10 November 2016; Federal Law Gazette 2016, I No. 52: 2460)

Act on Federal Contribution to the Costs of Integration and on Further Relief for the Länder and Municipalities (which entered into force on 7 December 2016; Federal Law Gazette 2016, I No. 57: 2755)

2017

Act on the Reform of Criminal Asset Recovery (which entered into force 1 July 2017; Federal Law Gazette 2017, I No. 22: 872)

Act Prohibiting Child Marriages (which entered into force on 22 July; Federal Law Gazette 2017, I No. 48: 2429)

Act Amending the Federal Act on Compensation for Victims of Violent Crime and Other Provisions (parts entered into force on 25 July 2017; forthcoming entry into force of amendments relating to the Asylum Act and the Act on the Central Register of Foreigners by virtue of Articles 4, 5, 6 and 29 of the Amending Act; Federal Law Gazette 2017 Part I No. 49: 2541)

Act to Improve the Enforcement of the Obligation to Leave the Country (which entered into force on 29 July 2017; Federal Law Gazette 2017 Part I No. 52: 2780.

In various cases, these laws contained measures that can be described as restrictive. The rationale behind this was the expectation of making asylum applications less attractive for those not covered by the protection provisions of the Geneva Convention (e.g. those who are referred to in public discussions as "bogus asylum seekers" or economic migrants). In a sense, the restrictive regulations represented a change from the years before, which had been characterised by a more liberal view of migration overall. The discussions revolved to a considerable degree around the immigration of qualified migrant workers (Gathmann et al., 2014; Bertoli, 2013) so that even in the situation of increasing asylum migration in 2015 the possible potential of skilled workers among asylum seekers was discussed (Hinte et al., 2015).

Many of the new laws and legal amendments were introduced with the intention, amongst other things, to intensify control mechanisms and to improve the efficiency of the asylum procedure.

With the Asylum Procedure Acceleration Act, the list of safe countries of origin was extended to include the Western Balkan states of Albania, Kosovo and Montenegro. Bosnia and Herzegovina, Serbia and Macedonia had already been declared safe countries of origin in 2014. The aim of this classification is to speed up the processing of futile asylum applications from applicants from these countries of origin. In the same line, decisions on their applications now have to be taken within one week. Subsequently, rejected asylum seekers from safe countries of origin can appeal against a negative decision only within one week. The administrative court is then also to decide on the application within one week, so that the proceedings, including the decision of the administrative court, should not take longer than three weeks in the event of an action against the negative decision. This serves to enable the authorities to end the stay in Germany more quickly in cases where there is no need for protection. Applicants from safe countries of origin may also be placed in special reception facilities and are subject to an employment ban during their procedure (provided they submitted their asylum application after 31 August 2015) (Grote, 2018: 49-51).

The extension of accommodation of asylum seekers in an initial reception centre for up to six months instead of three months intends to accelerate asylum procedures as these asylum seekers are accessible for all competent authorities within the given timeframe, in comparison to asylum seekers distributed to municipalities of whom the most recent contact address needs to be available and with whom appointments and travel arrangements need to be made. Asylum seekers from safe countries of origin must even be placed in initial reception facilities until their asylum procedure is completed which again served as a discouraging and restrictive measure. Furthermore, if their application for asylum is rejected, the persons concerned must remain in the initial reception centre until the termination of their stay, followed by diverse return measures. This should lead to a pooling of procedures and a fast and effective implementation of the respective results (right of residence or return). As long as asylum seekers are accommodated in an initial reception facility, they are prohibited from working.

Further restriction concerned family reunification. The Act on the Redetermination of the Right to Stay and Termination of Residence of August 2015 initially provided that beneficiaries of subsidiary protection were entitled to family reunification under the same privileged conditions as beneficiaries of international protection. In the case of reunification with children or spouses, neither the securing of livelihood nor the existence of sufficient housing had to be proven, if the application for family reunification was submitted within three months after the unappealable recognition as a person entitled to asylum, or the unappealable granting of refugee status or subsidiary protection. However, the Act on the Introduction of Accelerated Asylum Procedures, which came into force on 17 March 2016, temporarily suspended family reunification for beneficiaries of subsidiary protection. Family reunification for persons who were granted a residence permit as beneficiaries of subsidiary protection after 17 March 2016 was suspended until 16 March 2018 and recently extended until July 30th. The restriction applied in principle to any family reunification. In case of hardship, however, humanitarian admission may take place for urgent humanitarian reasons (§ 22 Residence Act), but this has happened in only very few exceptional cases (Grote, 2018: 57f.). This suspension of family reunification for beneficiaries of subsidiary protection is particularly relevant for persons from Syria, as they were increasingly granted subsidiary protection instead of a full refugee status since 2016. The debate on how to proceed with this regulation after its expiration dragged itself into the 2017 federal election campaign as a contested topic and also played a role during the coalition negotiations at the beginning of 2018. Ultimately, this regulation was prolonged in Parliament until end of July 2018 which again was followed by a proposed legislative amendment allowing for 1,000 family reunifications to beneficiaries of subsidiary protection per month from August 2018 on (BMI, 2018: 2).

The receipt of social benefits was strongly linked to cooperation with the authorities. The starting point is the necessary registration (which was not always done in the partially "chaotic" days at the end of 2015/beginning of 2016). With the registration in the core data system of the Central Register of Foreigners, a new proof of arrival was issued. This is a paper-based document with forgery-proof elements that can be issued by the reception facilities and the responsible branch offices of the Federal Office for Migration and Refugees. The submission of this proof of arrival to the reception facility ultimately assigned to the applicant is in principle the prerequisite for receiving full support measures (accommodation, allowances, health care) under the Asylum Seeker Benefits Act (Tangermann, 2017: 16). Furthermore, full payment of social benefits depends on asylum seekers taking up their accommodation in the district of the foreigners authority to which they have been assigned. If a right of residence already existed in another EU state or the duties to cooperate with the authorities are not fulfilled, applicants only receive benefits to cover the need for food and accommodation - including heating and utensils for personal hygiene and health care, which is less than the basic benefits otherwise to be granted in accordance with § 3 of the Asylum Seeker Benefits Act.

If they were granted a protection status and are obliged to take integration measures, the inadequate fulfilment of these obligations may also lead to reductions in benefits. Church and civil society organisations criticised that the possibilities of sanctions often imply a general lack of 'willingness to integrate' and are questionable with regard to the constitutionally guaranteed minimum subsistence level (EMN/BAMF, 2017: 41).

A further restrictive approach is the regulation for a quicker termination of residence and deportation in order to be able to deport persons without a long-term perspective to stay back to their countries of origin more quickly. In the case of convicted offenders, the level of the sentence, which justified for a deportation, was reduced. For achieving a suspension in cases of deportation for health reasons, only life-threatening and serious illnesses, which would worsen considerably due to the deportation, are sufficient from now on. In addition, additional criteria have been included in the legal text, which must be included in a medical certificate in order to prove that the foreigner is ill. It was also stipulated that deportations of persons obliged to leave the country are generally carried out without prior notice (EMN/BAMF, 2017: 61f.). Further tightening of the aliens law was introduced with the 2017 Act to Improve the Enforcement of the Obligation to Leave the Country. These include the extension of detention pending deportation for persons who are obliged to leave the country, the extension of the permitted period of detention, increased reporting obligations in the event of an interest in deportation and the possibility of monitoring mobile devices (e.g. smartphones) of asylum seekers to establish their identity even without their consent.

These and other measures (cf. Grote, 2018: 37-61) represent political and legal attempts to limit asylum immigration through restrictions. In doing so, they are part of a long tradition of corresponding measures and were, therefore, to a certain extent expectable.

The Unexpectable: Pragmatic liberalisations

What distinguishes the political handling of the "refugee crisis" 2015/2016 from other crisis management is the fact that, in addition to the restrictive measures, for the first time measures have been adopted that took asylum seekers into consideration from the perspective of integration (language and labour market). Since keeping people away from the labour market to make it clear that asylum could not be an alternative immigration channel for migration for economic reasons had been an essential part of the "deterrence policy" for decades and applied more or less to all European countries, this new approach in Germany was an innovation.

There were several reasons for this new approach: On the one hand, it was certainly a consequence of the discussion about skilled labour migration, which had been at the centre of attention when it came to migration policy in the years before the rise of asylum migration. In addition to the question of facilitating the migration of skilled workers, much space had also been devoted to the potential of migration and migrants. Therefore, in 2015 the discussion focused on potentially skilled workers among refugees and to which extent gaps in the German labour market could be closed (e.g. Hinte et al., 2015).

On the other hand, the liberal measures were influenced by the realisation of the prevailing conditions of the situation in 2015/2016. Asylum procedures took a very long time because the structures were temporarily overburdened. It was clear that the recognition rate was and would remain very high, i.e. that most asylum seekers from Syria, Eritrea or Iraq, for example, would receive protection. Accordingly, it was clear that a large proportion of those who were still in the procedure or were waiting for it would remain in the country in the long term. However, they were only eligible to participate in language courses and did only gain access to the labour market once they had been granted protection. At the same time, research showed that many of the asylum seekers had a very high motivation to work, which could however decrease considerably due to long phases of inactivity (Bakker et al., 2014; Hainmüller et al., 2016). This insight was certainly supported by the fact that since autumn 2015 the Chairman of the Board of the Federal Employment Agency, Frank-Jürgen Weise, had also been in charge of BAMF (following the resignation of the former President of BAMF) until the end of 2016. Moreover, Weise initiated a closer cooperation between the Federal Employment Agency and the BAMF (see arriving centres above) or repeatedly advertised a more liberal access to the labour market for persons whose removal has been suspended (Aretz 2017). So there was the chance to coordinate the asylum and labour market integration processes more closely. In this respect, this process can be described as "pragmatic liberalisation".

However, these "liberal" measures did not apply to all asylum seekers, but first and foremost to those who had good prospects to remain, a new category of asylum seekers introduced in 2015, which is defined in the law as asylum applicants *"who are expected to be permitted to remain lawfully and permanently"* (§ 44 (4) sentence 2 Residence Act). This was specified further as additionally requiring an overall protection rate of over 50 % over a longer period for the respective nationality (Grote, 2018: 20f.). Eritrea, Iraq, Iran and Syria met these conditions at the end of 2015 and in 2016, and since 1 August 2016 also Somalia.

The German integration system is strongly oriented towards acquiring the German language. The integration courses for new immigrants for which BAMF is responsible consist of 600 to 900 hours of German and 100 hours of orientation courses (e.g. legal system, history, culture, rights, duties, forms of living together, values). Initially, access for asylum seekers to this system, which has existed since 2005, was not envisaged. However, the Asylum Procedure Acceleration Act created various possibilities: On the one hand, the legal basis was created that the Federal Employment Agency was able to provide so-called introductory courses to impart basic knowledge of the German language, though only short-term and as a bridging measure. The funding was limited in time to admissions in the period from 24 October to 31 December 2015, with a total of over 222,000 people taking part in an introductory course - significantly more than originally expected (EMN/BAMF, 2016: 29; BA, 2016). At the same time, the aforementioned act also made it possible for asylum seekers with a good prospect to remain (as well as a number of other narrowly defined groups, e.g. certain tolerated persons[3]) to get access to BAMF integration courses even during their asylum procedure (if free places in the courses were available).[4] In addition, the acquisition of the German language shall be linked at an early stage with vocational training, employment or with measures of the "active labour market policy" in order to achieve the fastest possible integration of asylum seekers and refugees into the labour market.

Accordingly, access to the labour market for asylum seekers and persons whose removal has been suspended (tolerated stay status) has also been liberalised. If they are skilled workers, they may take up employment as temporary workers after three months of residence in Germany. In mid-2016, in 133 of the 156 agency districts of the Federal Employment Agency, priority checks on the employment of asylum seekers and persons with a tolerated stay were generally suspended for a period of three years. This shall make it easier for them to enter the labour market as early as after three months of residence in Germany. If they are not skilled workers, access to the labour market is only granted after 15 months of residence in Germany (EMN/BAMF, 2017: 39f.).

In addition, various accompanying measures were adopted. As early as 2015, the Federal Government decided to facilitate access to certain vocational and study-related internships as well as internships with no minimum wage for asylum seekers. The regulation applies to a) compulsory internships, b) internships of up to three months duration designed to provide orientation for the commencement of vocational training or studies, c) internships during training or studies of up to three months duration and d) initial qualifications or measures to prepare for vocational training. The amendments allow asylum seekers (after they have received a permission to remain pending the asylum decision from the Federal Office) to start such an internship after three months of residence in Germany. With the Integration Act, the Social Code III further opened the instruments of vocational training promotion until the end of 2018 in order to make it easier for asylum seekers with a good prospect to remain and persons whose removal has been suspended to take up and complete in-company vocational training. This way, this group can receive certain benefits of the vocational training promotion. In addition, after 15 months there is a right to a vocational training allowance and training allowance if the person seeking protection no longer lives in a reception accommodation (EMN/BAMF, 2016: 29f.).

Furthermore, the Integration Act created the basis for the Federal Temporary Labour Market Programme "Refugee Integration Measures". With this programme, 100,000 additional work opportunities for beneficiaries under the Asylum Seeker Benefits Act (with the exception of asylum seekers from safe

---

[3] A tolerated stay is a "temporary suspension of removal of a third-country national who has received a return decision but whose removal is not possible either for humanitarian reasons (as their removal would violate the principle of non-refoulement or due to the third-country national's physical state or mental capacity) or for technical reasons (such as lack of transport capacity or failure of the removal due to lack of identification or the country of origin's refusal to accept the person) and for as long as a suspensory effect is granted." See https://ec.europa.eu/home-affairs/content/postponement-removal_en.

[4] http://www.bamf.de/EN/Willkommen/DeutschLernen/IntegrationskurseAsylbewerber/integration skurseasylbewerber-node.html. Accessed: 28/5/2018.

countries of origin and persons who are obliged to leave the country, including persons whose removal has been suspended) were to be created annually from federal funds. The objectives are a low-threshold approach to the German labour market and to create a meaningful employment during the asylum procedure in and outside reception facilities. However, later on, the target of 100,000 work opportunities per year was abandoned as the anticipated demand failed to materialise (EMN/BAMF, 2017: 40f.; Grote, 2018: 56-57).

In addition to the opportunities for asylum seekers already staying in the country to enter the labour market, a further route was opened up for nationals from Western Balkan states. This was the largest group of asylum seekers in Germany in the years before 2015, however, they were almost without exception not granted a protection status. Therefore, an alternative immigration channel has been created in order to decouple asylum and labour migration. From 1 January 2016 until the end of 2020, citizens from Albania, Bosnia and Herzegovina, Kosovo, Macedonia, Montenegro and Serbia can thus obtain a residence permit for remunerated activities more easily (§ 26 (2) of the Employment Regulation). Provided that a concrete job offer already exists in Germany, any employment can now be taken up with the approval of the Federal Employment Agency, even without prior vocational training or proof of German language skills (Burkert/Haase, 2017: 2). Another important prerequisite, however, is that the application is submitted to the responsible German diplomatic mission in the country of origin and that applicants have not received any benefits under the Asylum Seeker Benefits Act in Germany in the 24 months prior to the application.[5] From November 2015 to September 2017, more than 100,000 permits were issued by the Federal Employment Agency and the diplomatic missions issued around 38,000 visas for employment to citizens from the Western Balkans (Brücker/Burkert, 2017). This Western Balkan regulation is currently being evaluated.[6]

In view of these measures, the question arises as to what predominates in practice: Restriction or integration? This question is still being discussed. For example, the authorities have been repeatedly criticised for procedures taking too long. This affects not only BAMF, which has significantly reduced the duration of its procedures, but also and above all the local implementation of policies in the foreigners authorities. The results vary depending on how the regulations are interpreted and implemented on site. Such differences were already analysed before the refugee crisis (Eule, 2014) and can be explained according to the hypothesis regarding street-level bureaucracy (Lipsky, 2010). However, they generate criticism in the discussion from employers, trade unions and other civil society actors (Kaiser, 2017).

Despite the integration opportunities created for asylum seekers and recognised refugees, no quick miracles are to be expected in terms of integration. In order to have a steering effect, the measures of language acquisition and labour market

---

[5] Exceptions to this rule apply through a transitional arrangement for persons who filed an asylum application between 1 January 2015 and 24 October 2015 and left Germany immediately after 24 October 2015.

[6]   http://www.iab.de/en/forschung-und-beratung/projektdetails.aspx/Projektdetails/k180109310. Accessed: 28/5/2018.

integration must always remain under review. To this end, both the statistical possibilities for collecting relevant data were improved and long-term research studies were launched as early as 2015, such as the "Refugee Survey", which is jointly conducted by the Institute for Employment Research (IAB) of the Federal Employment Agency, the Research Centre at the Federal Office for Migration and Refugees and the Socio-Economic Panel (SOEP) at the German Institute for Economic Research (DIW) (Brücker et al., 2016; 2017).[7] In addition, the Federal Government has commissioned two comprehensive evaluations to be completed by 2021 (accompanying evaluation of labour market integration measures for refugees, evaluation of integration courses with special consideration of refugees).

The Accompanying: Modernisation of administration

The German asylum administration experienced modernisation spurts during earlier "refugee crises" (Kreienbrink, 2013: 403-404, 406). This phenomenon is neither limited to asylum administration in Germany (Alink et al., 2011) nor to asylum (Balch/Geddes, 2011). Rather, modernising reforms in other areas of administration or the economy are often the consequences of institutional crises (Bom/t'Hart, 2000; Clark, 1998; Kiel, 1994; Archibugi et al., 2013).

Relating to the German asylum administration in 1981 in the aftermath of the first "asylum crisis" of 1980, for example, business statistics were established in the then Federal Office for the Recognition of Foreign Refugees[8], after individual data had previously only been collected manually. In the following year, the use of information technology began, both in statistics and in other administrative areas (Hölting/Schöll, 1997: 106). With the renewed increase in the number of asylum seekers at the end of the 1980s, the first online asylum system for registration, file creation and file management (ASYLON) was created. A comprehensive library and information system (ASYLIS) was set up in 1986 for the collection and administration of country information (including expert opinions, statements and case law). Both systems were developed considerably in the following years (Schmid/Gräfin Praschma, 2001). In 2001 ASYLON was replaced by an electronic file MARiS, a workflow-controlled document management system.

In the course of the events of 2015 and 2016, numerous innovations have also emerged among various administrative actors, only a few of which can be mentioned here.

A key point was the improvement of cooperation between the actors involved, i.e. the Federal Police and the police forces of the Länder, the Federal Office for Migration and Refugees, the Federal Employment Agency, the admissions authorities of the Länder and the local foreigners authorities. The aim was to accelerate the processes of initial registration, redistribution within the Federal Republic of Germany, accommodation, care, asylum application, asylum procedure and the initiation of subsequent processes - i.e. either integration or return. At the same time, many processes within the authorities were also modernised.

---

[7] http://www.bamf.de/SharedDocs/Projekte/EN/DasBAMF/Forschung/Integration/iab-bamf-soep-befragung-gefluechtete.html. Accessed: 28/5/2018.

[8] The authority was renamed the Federal Office for Migration and Refugees in 2005.

The procedures at the Federal Office were reorganised and summarised under the heading "Integrated Refugee Management" (BAMF, 2017b). Amongst other things, arrival centres have been created to act as the first point of contact for asylum seekers. In these centres, the processes are interlinked with those of the admissions authorities of the Länder and the Federal Employment Agency in order to minimise idle times and waiting times in the procedure. Two arrival centres went into operation at the end of 2015 and by mid-2017 the number had risen to 24; the entire asylum procedure - from the medical examination, the recording of personal data and the identity check, the application and hearing to the decision on the asylum application - takes place in the arrival centres. For this purpose, the applications were divided into different clusters depending on the country of origin. Applications from people from countries of origin with a low protection rate (e.g. safe countries of origin) and those with a high protection rate (e.g. Syria, Eritrea, Iraq) should be decided within 48 hours in the arrival centres, while the other applicants with more complex procedures are forwarded to the branch offices (the so-called Außenstellen).[9] Furthermore, from July 2015 a total of four decision-making centres were set up in which asylum cases ready for decision-making which have already been processed by the branch offices and arrival centres are to be decided in order to relieve the branch offices. In addition, a delivery centre was set up in Bonn at the beginning of November 2015, which is responsible for the central delivery of the notices issued in the decision centres (EMN/BAMF, 2017: 42).

Another important reason for the closer cooperation was the improvement of the data situation and the data exchange between the authorities. Until then, the respective authorities had collected the data necessary for their procedures from the asylum seekers every time they came into contact with them. The Data Exchange Improvement Act of 2016 created the conditions both for rapid registration of persons entering Germany (establishing their identity) and for improved data exchange between all authorities involved in the procedure. All data collected during registration are now recorded in a so-called core data system in the Central Register for Foreigners on first official contact. To this end, the Act on the Central Register of Foreigners was supplemented by new storage content (fingerprints, country of origin, contact data for quick access such as address, telephone numbers and e-mail addresses, information on distribution, as well as information on health examinations and vaccinations). For rapid integration and job placement, data on school education, vocational training and other qualifications shall continue to be stored in the core data system. The Central Register for Foreigners is filled by the authorities responsible for controlling cross-border traffic, the police forces of the Länder, the reception facilities, the Federal Office for Migration and Refugees as well as the foreigners' authorities. These processes are to be continued. The coalition agreement negotiated by the parties to the new federal government in February 2018 provides for a further strengthening of the Central Register for Foreigners (Grote, 2018: 52; EMN/BAMF, 2017: 42-44).

Newly introduced at the end of May 2016, the "Integrated Identity

---

[9] With the decline in the number of applicants, the clustering was discontinued in early 2017.

Management" is based on the data stored in the core data system. Asylum seekers receive a proof of arrival (on paper), which is provided with forgery-proof elements and is issued by the reception facilities and the responsible branch offices of the Federal Office for Migration and Refugees. The fact that the core data system can be accessed by several authorities makes it possible to clearly identify asylum seekers from the first contact with government agencies. The administration during the admission procedure has considerably improved; multiple registration and abuse (e.g. multiple receipt of support benefits) are prevented. With the proof of arrival, the authorities involved (e.g. immigration and registration authorities, Federal Employment Agency) have quick access to the data relevant to them (personal data, language skills, etc.). This enables, for example, better planning of asylum seekers' accommodation in the Länder, asylum procedures and measures for labour market integration (Tangermann, 2017: 14ff.).

However, integrated identity management is not limited to the proof of arrival. Instead, it was further expanded as part of a comprehensive digitalisation offensive at BAMF (BAMF 2017c). The aim is to verify information provided by applicants in the asylum process by means of "Intelligent Hearing Support" in order to increase security and quality in the asylum procedure and on that basis further increase efficiency and transparency across authorities. Amongst other things, so-called assistance systems were developed to process biometric data. Thus, the asylum procedure in Germany is also in line with the trend that has been progressing for years, to use biometric data for the management and administration of migration (see e.g. Amoore, 2006; Farraj, 2011; Ajana, 2013; Lodinová, 2016).

The Federal Office uses voice biometrics. New software shall improve the verification of the applicant's origin by biometric recognition of the spoken (grand) dialect and its known geographical distribution. In this way, at least a rough geographical plausibility check of the region of origin can be carried out (individual countries can only be identified or excluded to a limited extent so far). Within the registration process, image biometrics is also used, in which an image comparison increases data quality, for example by detecting possible duplicates in the database. It serves as a supplement to the existing use of fingerprints and can complement these.

A transliteration assistant was developed as a further tool to achieve standardisation in the transliteration of (Arabic) names. In this way, different spellings are to be prevented, which can arise, for example, from regionally different phonetic forms, the origin of the interpreter or the experience of the registration staff. The aim is to improve the cross-agency possibilities for the identification of persons through increased data quality. Finally, the analysis of mobile data carriers was also made possible, which is intended to support the identification and origin of applicants in cases of doubt. This should be based on data or metadata (e.g. stored geodata) stored on the smartphone and is as a supplement to the existing instruments for establishing identity and origin, e.g. physical-technical document examination and speech and text analysis. Since this is a sensitive intrusion into the private sphere, this data readout should only be used as ultima ratio in individual cases within strict legal regulations. With respect to all assistance systems it is emphasized that they should not serve as a substitute for the individual decision of the case worker and should not lead to automatic decisions. They should only validate the information provided and the data collected. The results of the assistance applications should always be assessed on a case-by-case basis and discussed with the asylum applicants. Nevertheless, these systems are very controversial. Critics fear interference in civil rights and see problems with data protection and constitutional law. In addition, there are doubts about the accuracy of the new procedures, since they have not yet been carried out across the board (Tangermann, 2017: 49-51). Concerning new technical equipment such as language biometrics software, against public criticism, the BAMF "regards the software to be only an assistant system, which is to "help employees to establish the identity of asylum applicants" by providing indications that make it easier to determine their origin" (Tangermann 2017: 50).

But modernisation through digitalisation goes beyond the asylum hearing. The BAMF's Digitalisation Agenda 2020 (BAMF, 2017d) also includes the digitalisation of legal transactions with administrative courts to enable the electronic transmission of files or the establishment of a central scanning office, to initially support the branch offices in the digitalisation of documents for (digital) asylum files. In the medium term, the entire mail flow at BAMF will be digitalised. Since spring 2016, video interpreters have also been used to meet the growing demand for interpreters. A central IT-supported database for recording ID documents was also created to facilitate document tracking.

Furthermore, the possibilities of digital communication with the applicants were further developed. Together with the Federal Employment Agency, Bavarian Radio and the Goethe Institute, BAMF has developed the "Arrival App"[10], which has been available free of charge since the beginning of January 2016. The aim of the app is to accompany refugees in the first weeks in Germany and contains chapters on asylum procedures and labour market access, on living in Germany as well as an online language course. The app is available in Arabic, English, Farsi, French and German. It was downloaded over 230,000 times in its first year and won numerous prizes (Goethe Institute, 2017; Grote, 2018: 39).

Conclusion

As a general summary of the above mentioned measures and reforms initiated, it can be said that on the whole Germany has mastered the so-called "refugee crisis" well. Receiving such a large number of migrants in such a short time in Europe is probably only comparable to the strong immigration of several million people in Spain at the beginning of the century until the outbreak of the economic crisis (Kreienbrink, 2007). Critics who spoke of "state failure" and of the authorities being completely overburdened were ultimately wrong. Nevertheless, it must be acknowledged that the authorities, at the beginning of the influx, were not prepared for the extent of migration. However, a diverse range of actors from federal, Länder and local level initiated a vast amount of measures, laws and innovative approaches to cope with the challenges. In this regard the state has, contrary to expectations, reacted not only with restrictions, but also with new liberal approaches to the

---

[10] http://ankommenapp.de/APP/DE/Startseite/startseite-node.html. Accessed: 28/5/2018.

integration of asylum seekers, who are expected to remain in Germany, already during the asylum procedures. The new categorisation of asylum seekers in those with good and those with little prospects to remain allowed for a differentiated approach, by easing conditions (e.g. access to the labour market) for the former while implementing more restrictive measures for the latter ones. This approach could also be supported by those political actors who traditionally have been in favour of a more restrictive policy.

Nevertheless, it remains to be seen how the large number of restrictive and liberalising regulations presented in this article will ultimately prove their worth in practice. The public discourse in the media is currently determined by the aspect of restrictions. Concerning the governmental approach, this is done in an effort to prove that the situation is under control and that the consequences of high immigration are manageable. In this way, the concerns of part of the population, which have been successfully addressed by populist opposition parties, are to be countered. Accordingly, many measures (e.g. in the area of return and repatriation) have the goal of having an immediate impact. On the one hand, it remains to be seen, however, whether substantial and rapid changes are possible, particularly in the area of return, which has received great attention from many governments before. The payoff of meaningful integration measures, on the other hand, will only become apparent in the long term and is therefore not sufficiently taken into account in some of the discussions at present. These are in part considerable extensions of the integration policy in Germany to date. Against the background of the experience of past decades, these measures are the right approach for creating the basis for the participation of new immigrants in the coming years.

The modernisation of the asylum administration described serves above all to improve and streamline procedures, which ultimately pursues the same objective as the restrictions - the control of the consequences of strong immigration. Many measures were necessary to lead the authority technically and technologically into the 21st century. The near future will show whether all modernisation measures will last, because at least some will be critically questioned with regard to their benefits (e.g. the reading of mobile phone data). However, this will not stop the trend towards further digitalisation of asylum administrations.

References

Ajana, B. (2013). "Asylum, identity management and biometric control". *Journal of Refugee Studies,* 26(4): 576-595.

Alink, F., Boin, A. and T'Hart, P. (2011). "Institutional crises and reforms in policy sectors: the case of asylum policy in Europe". *Journal of European Public Policy,* 8(2): 286-306.

Amoore, L. (2006). "Biometric borders: Governing mobilities in the war on terror". *Political Geography,* 25: 336-351.

Archibugi, D., Filippetti, A. and Frenz, M. (2013). "The impact of the economic crisis on innovation: Evidence from Europe". *Technological Forecasting and Social Change,* 80(7): 1247-1260.

Aretz, T. (2017). "Frank-Jürgen Weise will nicht Chuck Norris sein. „Teilhabe ist besser als Integration"". *Ntv.* https://www.n-tv.de/politik/Teilhabe-ist-besser-als-Integration-article 19678504.html. Accessed: 23/5/2018 (in German).

BA – Bundesagentur für Arbeit (2016). "Erfolgreiche Bilanz: BA finanziert Deutsch-

Einstiegskurse für 220.000 Flüchtlinge" [Successful balance: BA finances entry courses for German for 220,000 refugees]. Press release, 15/1/2016. https://www.arbeitsagentur.de/web/content/DE/Presse/Presseinformationen/Sonstiges/Detail/index.htm?dfContentId =L6019022DSTBAI806319. Accessed: 11/4/2018 (in German).

Bakker, L., Dagevos, J. and Engbersen, G. (2014). "The Importance of Resources and Security in the Socio-Economic Integration of Refugees. A Study on the Impact of Length of Stay in Asylum Accommodation and Residence Status on Socio-Economic Integration for the Four Largest Refugee Groups in the Netherlands". *International Migration and Integration*, 15: 431-448.

Balch, A. and Geddes, A. (2011). "Opportunity from Crisis? Organisational Responses to Human Trafficking in the UK". *The British Journal of Politics and International Relations*, 13(1): 26-41.

BAMF – Bundesamt für Migration und Flüchtlinge (2017a). *Das Bundesamt in Zahlen 2016. Asyl, Migration und Integration* [The Federal Office in figures 2016: Asylum, migration and integration]. Nürnberg: BAMF (in German).

BAMF - Bundesamt für Migration und Flüchtlinge (2017b). "Integrated Refugee Management". Nürnberg: BAMF. https://www.bamf.de/SharedDocs/Anlagen/EN/Publikationen/Broschueren/broschuere-integriertes-fluechtlingsmanagement.pdf?__blob=publicationFile. Accessed: 11/04/2018.

BAMF - Bundesamt für Migration und Flüchtlinge (2017c). "Integriertes Identitätsmanagement – Assistenzsysteme" [Integrated Identity Management - Assistance Systems], Press release 25/7/2017. Retrieved: http://www.bamf.de/SharedDocs/Anlagen/DE/Downloads/Infothek/ Presse/20160725-presseinfo-integriertes-identitaetsmgnt.pdf?__blob= publicationFile. Accessed: 11/4/2018 (in German).

BAMF - Bundesamt für Migration und Flüchtlinge (2017d). "Digitisation Agenda 2020. Success stories and future digital projects at the Federal Office for Migration and Refugees" (BAMF), Nürnberg. Retrieved: http://www.bamf.de/SharedDocs/Anlagen/EN/Publikationen/Broschueren /broschuere-digitalisierungsagenda-2020-en.pdf?__blob=publicationFile. Accessed: 11/4/2018.

BAMF - Bundesamt für Migration und Flüchtlinge (2018). *Das Bundesamt in Zahlen 2017 – Modul Asyl* [The Federal Office in figures 2017 - Asylum module]. Nürnberg: BAMF (in German).

Bast, J. and Möllers, C. (2016). "Dem Freistaat zum Gefallen: über Udo Di Fabios Gutachten zur staatsrechtlichen Beurteilung der Flüchtlingskrise" [A favour for the Free State: Udo Di Fabio's report on the state law assessment of the refugee crisis], VerfBlog, 2016/1/16. https://verfassungsblog.de/dem-freistaat-zum-gefallen-ueber-udo-di-fabios-gutachten-zur-staatsrechtlichen-beurteilung-der-fluechtlingskrise/. DOI: http://dx.doi.org/10.17176/20160902-165743. Accessed: 11/4/2018 (in German).

Bertoli, S., Brücker, H. and Fernández-Huertas Moraga, J. (2013). *The European crisis and migration to Germany. Expectations and the diversion of migration flows.* (IZA discussion paper, 7170). Bonn: IZA.

BMI – Bundesministerium des Innern, für Bau und Heimat (2018): "Gesetzentwurf der Bundesregierung. Entwurf eines Gesetzes zur Neuregelung des Familiennachzugs zu subsidiär Schutzberechtigten (Familiennachzugsneuregelungsgesetz)". https://www.bmi.bund.de/SharedDocs/downloads/DE/gesetztestexte/gesetztesentwuerfe/entwurf-familiennachzug.pdf?__blob=publicationFile&v=3. Accessed: 24/5/2018 (in German).

BMI/BAMF – Bundesministerium des Innern/Bundesamt für Migration und Flüchtlinge (2016). *Migrationsbericht des Bundesamtes für Migration und Flüchtlinge im Auftrag der Bundesregierung - Migrationsbericht 2015* [Migration Report of the Federal Office for Migration and Refugees on behalf of the Federal Government - Migration Report 2015]. Berlin/Nürnberg: BMI/BAMF (in German).

Bogumil, J., Hafner, J. and Kastilan, A. (2017). "Verwaltungshandeln in der Flüchtlingspolitik. Vollzugsprobleme und Optimierungsvorschläge für den Bereich der kommunalen Integration" [Administrative action in refugee policy. Implementation problems and optimisation proposals for the area of municipal integration]. *Verwaltungsarchiv*, 108(4): 467–488 (in German).

Bom, R.A. and T'Hart, P. (2000). "Institutional crises and reforms in policy sectors". In: Wagenaar, H. (Ed.) *Government Institutions: Effects, Changes and Normative Foundations,* Boston: Kluwer Academic Publishers.

Bosswick, W. (2000). "Development of Asylum Policy in Germany". *Journal of Refugee Studies,* 13(1): 43-60.

Brücker, H., Rother, N. and Schupp, J. (Eds.) (2016). *IAB-BAMF-SOEP-Befragung von Geflüchteten: Überblick und erste Ergebnisse* [IAB-BAMF-SOEP survey of refugees: Overview and first results]. Nürnberg: BAMF (in German).

Brücker, H., Rother, N. and Schupp, J. (Eds.) (2017). *IAB-BAMF-SOEP-Befragung von Geflüchteten 2016: Studiendesign, Feldergebnisse sowie Analysen zu schulischer wie beruflicher Qualifikation, Sprachkenntnissen sowie kognitiven Potenzialen* [IAB-BAMF-SOEP Survey of refugees 2016: Study design, field results and analyses of school and vocational qualifications, language skills and cognitive potential]. Nürnberg: BAMF (in German).

Burkert, C. and Haase, M. (2017). *Westbalkanregelung: Ein neues Modell für die Migrationssteuerung?* [Western Balkans Regulation: A new model for migration management?](WISO direkt, 2017,02). Bonn: FES (in German).

Clark, D. (1998). "The Modernization of the French Civil Service: Crisis, Change and Continuity". *Public Administration,* 76(1): 97-115.

Conrad, M. and Aðalsteinsdóttir, H. (2017). "Understanding Germany's short-lived "culture of welcome". Images of refugees in three leading German quality newspapers". *German Politics and Society,* 35(4): 1-21.

Di Fabio, U. (2016). "Migrationskrise als föderales Verfassungsproblem. Gutachten im Auftrag des Freistaates Bayern" [Migration crisis as a federal constitutional problem. Expert opinion on behalf of the Free State of Bavaria]. http://www.bayern.de/wp-content/uploads/2016/01/Gutachten_Bay_DiFabio_formatiert.pdf. Accessed: 11/4/2018 (in German).

EMN - European Migration Network (2016). *Integration of beneficiaries of international/humanitarian protection into the labour market: policies and good practices. Synthesis Report for the EMN Focussed Study 2015.* Brussels: European Commission.

EMN/BAMF – European Migration Network/Federal Office for Migration and Refugees (2016). Migration, Integration, Asylum. Political Developments in Germany 2015. Annual Policy Report by the German National Contact Point for the European Migration Network (EMN). Nuremberg: BAMF.

EMN/BAMF – European Migration Network/Federal Office for Migration and Refugees (2017). Migration, Integration, Asylum. Political Developments in Germany 2016. Annual Policy Report by the German National Contact Point for the European Migration Network (EMN). Nuremberg: BAMF.

Eule, T. G. (2014). Inside Immigration Law. Migration Management and Policy Application in Germany. Farnham: Ahsgate.

Farraj, A. (2011). "Refugees and the biometric future: the impact of biometrics on refugees and asylum seekers". Columbia Human Rights Law Review, 42(3): 891-941.

Fijalkowski. J. (1993). "Aggressive Nationalism, Immigration Pressure and Asylum Policy Disputes in Contemporary Germany". International Migration Review, 27(4): 850-869.

Frontex (2016a). Western Balkans Quarterly, Quarter 4 (October–December 2015). Warsaw: Frontex.

Frontex (2016b). Western Balkans Annual Risk Analysis 2016. Warsaw: Frontex.

Fullerton, M. (1989). "Restricting the Flow of Asylum-Seekers in Belgium, Denmark, the Federal Republic of Germany, and the Netherlands: New Challenges to the Geneva Convention Relating to the Status of Refugees and the European Convention on Human Rights". Virginia Journal of International Law, 29: 33-114.

Gathmann, C., Keller, N., Monscheuer, O., Straubhaar, T., Schäfer, H., Zimmermann, K. F. and Brücker, H. (2014). "Zuwanderung nach Deutschland. Problem und Chance für den Arbeitsmarkt" [Immigration to Germany. Problem and opportunity for the labour market]. Wirtschaftsdienst, 94(3): 159-179 (in German).

Goethe-Institut (2017). "Auszeichnung durch globale Plattform: World Government Summit in Dubai zeichnet ‚Ankommen'-App für Geflüchtete aus" [Global Platform Award: World Government Summit in Dubai honours 'Arrival' app for refugees]. 13/2/2017. https://www.goethe.de/de/uun/prs/prm/20925050.html. Accessed: 11/4/2018 (in German).

Grote, J. (2018). The Changing Influx of Asylum Seekers in 2014-2016: Responses in Germany. 2nd revised edition, Nuremberg: BAMF.

Hailbronner, K. (1994). "Asylum Law Reform in the German Constitution". American University International Law Review 9(4), 159-179

Hainmueller, J., Hangartner, D. and Lawrence, D. (2016). "When lives are put on hold: Lengthy asylum processes decrease employment among refugees". Science Advances, 2(8), e1600432. http://advances.sciencemag.org/content/2/8/e1600432. Accessed: 11/4/2018.

Hamann, U. and Karakayali, S. (2016). "Practicing Willkommenskultur: Migration and Solidarity in Germany". *Intersections. East European Journal of Society and Politics,* 2(4): 69-86.

Herbert B. and Burkert, C. (2017). "Westbalkanregelung: Arbeit statt Asyl? " [Western Balkans regulation: work instead of asylum?]. https://www.iab-forum.de/westbalkanregelung-arbeit-statt-asyl/. Accessed: 11/4/2018 (in German).

Hinte, H., Rinne, U. and Zimmermann, K. F. (2015). "Flüchtlinge in Deutschland: Herausforderung und Chancen" [Refugees in Germany: Challenge and Opportunities]. *Wirtschaftsdienst,* 95(11): 744-751 (in German).

Hölting, V. and Schöll, G. (1997). "Statistische Daten über Asylverfahren im Bundesamt" [Statistical data on asylum procedures at the Federal Office]. *Asylpraxis – Schriftenreihe des Bundesamtes für die Anerkennung ausländischer Flüchtlinge,* 2: 105-120 (in German).

Kaiser. T. (2017, October 01). "Wenn Behörden Flüchtlinge bei der Jobsuche ausbremsen" [When authorities slow down refugees in their search for a job]. *Die Welt.* https://www.welt.de/wirtschaft/article169196093/Wenn-Behoerden-Fluechtlinge-bei-der-Jobsuche-ausbremsen.html. Accessed: 11/4/2018 (in German).

Kiel, L. D. (1994). *Managing Chaos and Complexity in Government: A New Paradigm for Managing Change, Innovation, and Organizational Renewal,* New York: John Wiley & Sons.

Kimminich, O. (1982). "Die Entwicklung des Asylrechts in der Bundesrepublik Deutschland" [The development of asylum law in the Federal Republic of Germany]. *Zeitschrift für Ausländerrecht und Ausländerpolitik,* 2(1): 16-25 (in German).

Konar, Ö., Kreienbrink, A. and Stichs, A. (2015). "Zuwanderung und Integration. Aktuelle Zahlen, Entwicklungen, Maßnahmen" [Immigration and integration. Current figures, developments, measures]. *Aus Politik und Zeitgeschichte (APuZ),* 27-29/2017, 13-20 (in German).

Kreienbrink, A. (2007). "Inmigración e integración social de los inmigrantes en España entre consenso y enfrentamiento politico" [Immigration and social integration of immigrants in Spain between consensus and political confrontation]. In: Bernecker, W. L. and Maihold, G. (Eds.). *España: del consenso a la polarización. Cambios en la democracia española,* Madrid/Frankfurt am Main: Vervuert (in Spanish).

Kreienbrink, A. (2013). "60 Jahre Bundesamt für Migration und Flüchtlinge im Kontext der deutschen Migrationspolitik" [60 years Federal Office for Migration and Refugees in the context of German migration policy]. Zeitschrift für Ausländerrecht und Ausländerpolitik, 33(11-12): 397-410 (in German).

Lipsky, M. (2010). Street Level Bureaucracy: Dilemmas of the Individual in Public Services. 30th Anniversary Expanded Edition. New York, NY: The Russell Sage Foundation.

Lodinová, A. (2016). "Application of biometrics as a means of refugee registration: focusing on UNHCR's strategy". Development, Environment and Foresight, 2(2): 91-100.

Meyer, H. (2016). "Migration, Asyl und Integration als organisatorische Herausforderung für Land und Kommunen" (Migration, asylum and integration as an organisational challenge for the Land and municipalities). Verwaltung und Management, 22(3): 144-156 (in German).

Münch, U. (1993). Asylpolitik in der Bundesrepublik Deutschland: Entwicklung und Alternativen [Asylum policy in the Federal Republic of Germany: development and alternatives], 2nd rev.

and exp. edition. Opladen: Leske & Budrich (in German).

Papier, H.-J. (2016). *"Asyl und Migration – Recht und Wirklichkeit" [Asylum and migration - law and reality]*, *VerfBlog*, 2016/1/18. https://verfassungsblog.de/asyl-und-migration-recht-und-wirklichkeit. DOI: http://dx.doi.org/10.17176/20160902-165530. Accessed: 11/4/2018 (in German).

Poutrus, P. (2009). "Zuflucht im Nachkriegsdeutschland. Politik und Praxis der Flüchtlingsaufnahme in Bundesrepublik und DDR von den späten 1940er Jahren bis zu den 1970er Jahren" [Refuge in post-war Germany. Policy and practice of refugee reception in the Federal Republic and the GDR from the late 1940s to the 1970s]. Geschichte und Gesellschaft, 35: 135-175 (in German).

Schmid, A. and Gräfin Praschma, U. (2001). "Informationszentrum Asyl im Bundesamt für die Anerkennung ausländischer Flüchtlinge" [Asylum Information Centre at the Federal Office for the Recognition of Foreign Refugees]. Zeitschrift für Ausländerrecht und Ausländerpolitik, 21(2): 59-65 (in German).

Schönwälder, K. (1999). „„Ist nur Liberalisierung Fortschritt?" Zur Entstehung des ersten Ausländergesetzes der Bundesrepublik" ["Is only liberalization progress?" On the Origin of the First Aliens Act of the Federal Republic]. In: Motte, J., Ohliger, R. and von Oswald, A. (Eds.) *50 Jahre Bundesrepublik – 50 Jahre Einwanderung. Nachkriegsgeschichte als Migrationsgeschichte*. Frankfurt am Main: Campus(in German).

Tangermann, J. (2017). *Documenting and establishing identity in the migration process. Challenges and practices in the German context*. Nuremberg: BAMF.

Thym, D. (2016). *"Der Rechtsstaat und die deutsche Staatsgrenze" [The rule of law and the German border]*, *VerfBlog*, 2016/1/22. https://verfassungsblog.de/der-rechtsstaat-und-die-deutsche-staatsgrenze. DOI: http://dx.doi.org/10.17176/20160902-114339. Accessed: 11/4/2018 (in German).

UNHCR (2017). *Global Trends – Forced displacement in 2016*, Geneva: UNHCR.

Vollmer, B. and Karakayali, S. (2018). "The Volatility of the Discourse on Refugees in Germany ". *Journal of Immigrant and Refugee Studies*, 16(1-2): 118-139.

Weber, B. (2017). *The EU-Turkey Refugee Deal and the Not Quite Closed Balkan Route*. Sarajewo: Friedrich-Ebert-Stiftung Dialogue Southeast Europe. http://library.fes.de/pdf-files/bueros/sarajevo/13436.pdf. Accessed: 11/4/2018.

COMMUNICATING REFUGEES AND HUMAN RIGHTS: THE GERMAN GOVERNMENT'S ASSESSMENT OF THE ROLE OF THE EUROPEAN COURT OF HUMAN RIGHTS

Johanna C. Günther [1]

Introduction

The European Union's asylum and refugee policies have evoked as much vehement criticism from human rights activists as from media outlets – most expressly in 2015 and 2016, when the numbers of refugees crossing the EU's external borders either in Greece and Italy or in Bulgari, and Hungary, reached their peak. There are various accounts of human rights violations at the EU's external borders, and within national asylum systems[2]. The same holds true for analyses addressing the EU's asylum and refugee policies, the acts of its agencies, and decisions made by individual member states in terms of their compatibility with the European human rights regime[3].

Germany is one of several countries which have been most affected by the comparatively high influx of asylum-seekers occurring since 2013. With 441,899 first applications for asylum in 2015 and 722,370 in 2016 (BAMF, 2017), the country has faced a considerable number of asylum-seekers. By comparison, the total of first asylum applications in 2013 (109,580) and 2014 (173,072) never even approached 200,000. Consequently, Germany has expressly pushed for the commitment among EU member states to form a joint European approach to mass migration. As yet however, human rights concerns remain audible when it comes to several recent political decisions, and legislative acts in Germany.[4]

In view of legislative proposals and reforms initiated since the peak of the so-called migration crisis, it is pertinent to ask what role case-law of the European Court of Human Rights (ECtHR; Court) has played in the decision-making processes. How relevant does the German government consider the judgments of the European Court of Human Rights – in general, and more specifically –

---

[1] Johanna C. Günther is a PhD candidate in Political Science at the Center for Area Studies, Friedrich-Alexander-University Erlangen-Nuremberg, Germany. E-Mail: johanna.c.guenther@fau.de

[2] For instance, see Human Rights Watch, 2018; ECRE, 2017; Belgrade Center for Human Rights, Macedonian Young Lawyers Association & Oxfam, 2017 or Amnesty International, 2015

[3] For instance, see Bendel, 2017; Nasser, 2016; Stevens, 2017; Trauner, 2016

[4] For instance, the German Institute for Human Rights criticised the new integration law due to its inherent constraints to the right to asylum (German Institute for Human Rights, 2016). Amnesty International complained that the integration law also creates disproportionate constraints to the mobility of asylum-seekers (Amnesty International, 2016).

concerning its asylum policy? This is not a question of superficial compliance with ECtHR case-law versus in-depth implementation of the Court's judgments. Rather, the question dives deep into the practical relevance the German government attributes to norms[5] promoted by the ECtHR. A second question focuses on the different groups of actors within the government: Do these actors speak about the role of the ECtHR differently, depending on the specific situation, and on the wider context?

Why do these questions matter? A viable European human rights regime essentially depends on the integration and application of human rights norms in the domestic context (Acharya, 2004; Cortell & Davis, 2000; Risse, 1999; Sikkink, 1998; Zwingel, 2012). There are many ways to measure human rights compliance at the international and domestic levels (Dai, 2013; Hafner-Burton & Ron, 2009). However, if the goal is to determine the strength of a specific norm or set of norms within a given national context, it is useful to examine their resonance with different groups of society in order to understand how embedded the norm is within that particular culture (Checkel, 1997; Cortell & Davis, 2000). This study will focus on the perspective of the German government on this subject, to learn about the role the ECtHR plays in its communications in general, and specifically concerning matters of asylum policy. It is argued that a thorough analysis of government communications is crucial to understand the norms at stake in the current political agenda. Limiting the analysis to one group of actors allows us to continue along the qualitative path much further than with a comparative approach.

A viable human rights regime also requires the protection of third country nationals. In an ever more integrated European Union, this protection is not solely the responsibility of domestic courts and institutions. On the contrary, in attempting to find European responses to mass migration, the EU increasingly relies on cooperation agreements with third states. However, this approach also includes states that have problematic human rights records, such as Libya, Morocco, Tunisia and Turkey.

The institutional veto points are multifold when it comes to the abuse of human rights across the European continent. Yet, with its mandate to review cases based on the European Convention on Human Rights and Fundamental Freedoms (ECHR), the European Court of Human Rights has a lighthouse function. While the European Court of Justice (ECJ) also has a human rights instrument at hand – the Charter of Fundamental Rights of the European Union – the jurisdiction of the ECtHR reaches farther. Beyond geographical scope, the ECtHR does not encounter the dilemma of having to balance the protection of human rights with the interests of the common market. Also, in the specific case of enhanced cooperation with Turkey, the ECtHR is virtually the only Court that can address human rights issues that concern practices of both EU member states and Turkey.

In the last few decades however, the European Court of Human Rights has had to deal with a number of criticisms regarding its difficulties in handling its caseload, in its effectiveness, in its activism (perceived to undermine states' sovereignty) and

---

[5] In line with Finnemore and Sikkink's definition, norms are understood as "standard(s) of appropriate behaviour for actors with a given identity" (Finnemore & Sikkink, 1998, p. 891).

in its lack of pragmatism.[6] On the other hand, there have been judgments – particularly in the area of asylum and refugee policy – which have triggered considerable public and political response.[7] It is therefore most meaningful to understand the influence of ECtHR decisions as well as the impact of the norms promoted through these decisions. This study aims to add one piece to the puzzle: capturing the German government's perception of the ECtHR as one expression of the normative struggles underlying the attempt to build a common European strategy for asylum and migration.

These considerations touch upon a number of theoretical considerations that travel beyond disciplinal borders. While political science and communication studies have a lot to offer when it comes to the way governments communicate their policy choices, international relations and sociology scholars add a valuable complementary perspective on norm diffusion and norm salience.

In answering these questions, this study focuses on publicly available documents issued by the German government and investigates their content as to its statements about the relevance of the European Court of Human Rights, and its role within the realm of domestic asylum and refugee policy. I then suggest interpretations based on my inter-disciplinary approach, and as part of the discussion of findings.

Methodological Approach

This study pursues a methodological approach based on what Kuckartz calls *Thematic Qualitative Content Analysis* (Kuckartz, 2014, pp. 69-88), and Mayring describes as *Structuring Qualitative Content Analysis* (Mayring, 2015, pp. 97-103).

Qualitative Content Analysis (QCA) is a method that allows systematic analysis of textual meanings. Assigning categories, which are inductively determined or theory-guided, to parts of a text enables the user to systematically describe the meaning of its content (Schreier, 2013, p. 170). QCA pairs the rules-based, reproducible proceedings of quantitative content analysis with the more open, and flexible trajectory of capturing the meaning of text. While this process is mainly qualitative in nature, it also allows for quantitative statements, for instance about the frequency of categories (Mayring, 2010, p. 602). "In fact, qualitative content analysis claims to synthesize two contradictory methodological principles: openness and theory-guided investigation" (Kohlbacher, 2006, p. 8).

Every Qualitative Content Analysis is built around its system of categories. Categories – like codes in Grounded Theory – represent the key concepts of the analysis. Categories must be defined in detail to allow the researcher to assign them without ambiguity to a certain text segment in a later step. This process may occur based on theoretical concepts (deductive application of categories) or because inductively established categories are grouped together as main categories (inductive application of categories) (Mayring, 2010, p. 605). The assignment of categories to text segments is guided by strict analytic rules that ensure transparency

---

[6] For instance, see European Law Institute, 2012; Judd, 2013; Madsen, 2016; Oomen, 2015; Popelier or Lemmens & Lambrecht, 2016

[7] For instance, see Bowcott, 2014; Chan, 2017; McDonald, 2015 or Sims, 2015

and traceability throughout the entire analysis, and even allow for mixed-methods approaches at a later point (Mayring, 2012, p. 29). Thus, QCA enables a researcher to extract and organise the data in a way that is both different from the original text, and most conducive to answering the research question. Whether the approach is primarily deductive or inductive, QCA is well suited to address variables and assumptions about causal relationships in a theory-guided manner because categories can be formulated, assessed and organised based on theoretical considerations (Gläser & Laudel 2009, pp. 200-204).

A crucial step of the analytical process is the decision for a level of abstraction, i.e. the "analytical sensitivity" of the identified categories. In other words, if categories are formulated and divided very closely along the wording of the original text, one can speak of a low level of abstraction; contrastingly, the more analytical the categories, the higher the level of abstraction. In the latter case, it is likely that one text segment can be assigned several sub-categories during the analysis (Mayring, 2012, pp. 31-33).

In order to best approach the research question and capture the characteristics of the material at hand, I have pursued a deductive-inductive approach. In other words, while starting out with consulting theory and related scholarship, I subsequently built the categories for analysis along the empirical data from the documents. Prior to this process, I had to go through several steps of data collation and selection. I identified three main concepts which together served as the criterion for defining and collating the research sample; and which I then applied in a simple search to the websites of the German government[8]: 'Europäischer Gerichtshof für Menschenrechte' (European Court of Human Rights) in combination with either 'Asyl' (asylum) or 'Flüchtling' (refugee)". Only entries published between January 1st, 2013 and March 5th, 2018 were taken into account as this time frame sufficiently covers the pre-migration crisis and post-migration crisis phases, as well as the peak of the culmination of the political and legal crises. As Kohlbacher puts it, "the main idea of this procedure is to formulate a criterion of definition, derived from the theoretical background and the research question, which determines the aspects of the textual material taken into account" (2006, p. 12).

After eliminating duplicate entries, and publications that did not explicitly contain the German government's perspective, such as research reports provided by other institutions or judgments of European Court of Human Rights, 84 texts remained. These documents included information leaflets, interviews, speeches, legislative drafts, and opinions. Aiming to produce a differentiated analysis, the material was grouped into six sorts of texts: A) Press conferences, B) Interviews and op-eds, C) Legislative drafts, D) Speeches, E) Reports, F) Information material, and G) Other.

Qualitative Content Analysis requires precise definition of the units of analysis before starting to explore the data. This procedure allows for a systematic, verifiable

---

[8] Specifically, the websites of the Federal Government, the Ministry of Justice and Consumer Protection, the Ministry of the Interior, and the Federal Foreign Office were searched as these ministry – respectively, their websites – contain most information on the European Court of Human Rights and its role within German asylum and refugee policies.

examination of the material. While the recording unit determines the scope of text which is to be analysed, the coding unit specifies the minimum amount of words that can be coded, i.e. assigned to one category. The context unit defines what kind of material may be used to adequately interpret the meaning of the text segments, which are to be coded (Mayring, 2015, p. 61).

For the purpose of this study, the following units of analysis were defined:

Coding unit: clear semantic elements (*whole sentences*) in the text

Context unit: individual text groups (*A – G*)

Recording unit: individual documents

In a next step, three deductively determined main categories were applied to the texts for each text group[9] in order to identify relevant sections in the documents: A) the ECtHR's role in general, B) the role of ECtHR judgments, and C) the ECtHR's role in the area of asylum and refugee policies. As a consequence, almost two thirds of the material could be eliminated, as they did not provide information on the role of the ECtHR in general, the Court's judgments, or the Court's relevance in the context of asylum and refugee policy.

Table 1. Document groups examined in the analysis

Text sort		Number
A)	Press conferences	9
B)	Interviews & op-eds	3
C)	Legislative drafts	3
D)	Speeches	5
E)	Reports	6
F)	Information material	2
G)	Other	2
Total		30

The definition of the three main categories was based on two reference points: the research question, and multiple insights from scholarship on political communication[10] and norm diffusion[11]. After identifying the relevant text segments dictated by the three main categories, a second analysis of the remaining sample was conducted. The aim was to inductively define sub-categories in the texts and subsume recurring assessments of the ECtHR's activities for all text groups under the respective main categories. I undertook this process twice, in order to ensure that all relevant text segments were taken into account.[12]

The categories found were adjusted to the research question and revised according to the structure of the material. Since the material available had not been composed based on the research question, most of the text remained uncoded as

---

[9] For a detailed description of the steps proposed for different kinds of and approaches to QCA, see for instance Kuckartz, 2014, pp. 65-103; Mayring, 2015, pp. 50-106 or Schreier, 2012, pp. 58-219.

[10] For instance, see Chaffee, 1975; Stuckey, 2016

[11] For instance, see Finnemore & Sikkink, 1998; Risse, 1999; Sikkink, 1998

[12] For a more detailed description of the different steps of the analysis, see Kuckartz, 2014, pp.69-88.

only very few segments contained relevant information in relation to the question at hand. As suggested by Mayring (2015, p.72), I also paraphrased the identified text segments to be able to extract and summarise relevant pieces of information and assessments. Hereafter, I summarised all sub-categories, and main categories, and systemised them. The analysis of texts across all six groups revealed the categories presented below.

Table 2. Main and sub-categories with definitions and examples

Main Category	Category Definition	Sub-Categories	Category Definition	Example	
				German	English
ECtHR's role in general	All references to the ECtHR, the ECtHR's activities or history – excluding all mentions in the context of asylum/refugee policy	"Dialogue" of ECtHR and other courts	All references to interaction, cooperation, common judicial approaches & activities of ECtHR and other courts	„Die Verfassungsgerichte in Europa sind nicht hierarchisch geordnet. Sie arbeiten miteinander am selben Ziel: einem starken Schutz der Menschenrechte."	"The constitutional courts in Europe aren't organised hierarchically. They work together towards a common goal: a strong protection of human rights."

Table 2. Continued.

Main Category	Category Definition	Sub-Categories	Category Definition	Example	
				German	English
		ECtHR as "norm setter" / "normative power" [norm setter]	All assessments of the relevance of the ECtHR in relation to establishing or promoting (new) norms; references to ECtHR jurisdiction as an expression of values	„Die Bundesrepublik Deutschland hat nicht nur umfangreiche Verpflichtungen zum Schutz der Menschenrechte übernommen, sondern auch internationalen Kontrollorganen Befugnisse eingeräumt. Besondere Bedeutung erlangt dabei der Europäische Gerichtshof für Menschenrechte, der die Einhaltung der Europäischen Konvention zum Schutz der Menschenrechte und Grundfreiheiten überwacht."	"The Federal Republic of Germany has not only assumed extensive responsibilities regarding the protection of human rights. The state has also accepted the supervision of various international bodies. Among these, the European Court of Human Rights which monitors compliance with the ECHR plays an especially important role."
		ECtHR's influence in/ on third states	References to the ECtHR's influence in states other than Germany	„Bezogen auf die Bevölkerungszahl gehört Serbien zu den Vertragsstaaten mit den höchsten Fallzahlen vor dem EGMR. Neben der langen Verfahrensdauer sind dafür im Wesentlichen die vielen gleichgelagerten Fälle verantwortlich."	"In relation to the size of its population, Serbia is among the states with the most cases pending before the ECtHR. In addition to the long duration of trials, the large number of similar cases is to blame."

Table 2. Continued.

Main Category	Category Definition	Sub-Categories	Category Definition	Example	
				German	English
		Case overload	References to the high number of pending cases before the Court, its effectiveness, needs to reform	„Die Zahl der Verfahren dort nimmt ständig zu. Wir müssen gemeinsam dafür sorgen, dass der Europäische Menschenrechtsgerichts-hof reformiert wird, damit er nicht einfach durch die schiere Masse von Verfahren an seinem eigenen Erfolg erstickt. Er muss arbeitsfähig bleiben."	"The number of proceedings is steadily growing. We must jointly ensure that the ECtHR undergoes reform, so that the court's success won't be suffocated by the sheer amount of cases. The court must keep functioning."
		Judicial powers of ECtHR	Descriptions of the ECtHR's legal competences	„Hierin liegt ein fundamentaler Unterschied gegenüber Urteilen des Europäischen Gerichtshofs für Menschenrechte, die für denjenigen Vertragsstaat, gegen den sie ergehen, verbindlich sind (vgl. Art. 46 EMRK)."	"This is a fundamental difference compared to judgments of the ECtHR which are binding for the involved signatory state (see Art. 46 ECHR)."
Role of ECtHR judgments	All references to ECtHR cases & judgments – excluding all mentions of judgments concerning asylum/refugee policy	Prohibition of Dublin transfers, push-backs & refoulement	References to judgments/ cases of the ECtHR concerning Dublin transfers, collective expulsion or refoulement, and the impact of those judgments	„Außerdem haben der Europäische Gerichtshof für Menschenrechte und der Gerichtshof der Europäischen Union Rückführungen nach Griechenland wegen der humanitären Lage dort verboten. Auch diese Urteile sind Bestandteil unserer Rechtsordnung."	"Moreover, the ECtHR and the ECJ have prohibited returns to Greece because of the humanitarian situations there. These judgments are a part of our legal order, too."

Table 2. Continued.

Main Category	Category Definition	Sub-Categories	Category Definition	Example	
				German	**English**
Role of ECtHR judgments	All references to ECtHR cases & judgments – excluding all mentions of judgments concerning asylum/refugee policy	ECtHR's influence on receptions conditions & asylum procedures	References to judgments/ cases of the ECtHR concerning receptions conditions & asylum procedures	„Immer mehr Menschen kommen nach Europa, um Krieg und Verfolgung in ihrer Heimat zu entkommen. Wie sie hier aufgenommen werden, darüber hatten der Europäische Gerichtshof für Menschenrechte und der Europäische Gerichtshof zuletzt mehrmals entschieden.“	"More and more people come to Europe to escape war and persecution in their home country. The way they are treated here, the ECtHR and the ECJ have repeatedly dealt with."
ECtHR's role in asylum and refugee policies	All references to ECtHR judgments in the context of asylum and refugee policies	Judgments against Germany	References to all judgments delivered and cases pending against Germany	„Die Zahl der Verurteilungen der Bundesrepublik Deutschland durch den Europäischen Gerichtshof für Menschenrechte ist – sowohl in absoluten Zahlen (2015: 6) als auch bezogen auf die Einwohnerzahl – niedrig.“	"The number of condemnatory sentences of the Federal Republic of Germany by the ECtHR is small – looking at absolute numbers as well as in view of the population size."

Table 2. Continued.

Main Category	Category Definition	Sub-Categories	Category Definition	Example German	English
ECtHR's role in asylum and refugee policies	All references to ECtHR judgments in the context of asylum and refugee policies	Need to comply with/ implement ECtHR judgments [compliance]	All references to the (need to) comply with ECtHR decisions	„Die Urteile des EGMR werden anerkannt, ohne dass zu Verurteilungen führende strukturelle Defizite im Justizwesen wie die lange Verfahrensdauer bisher beseitigt werden konnten. Die Umsetzung der EGMR-Urteile ist nicht gänzlich zufriedenstellend, bewegt sich aber auf dem Niveau, wie es viele EU-Mitgliedstaaten praktizieren."	"The judgments of the ECtHR are generally accepted without eliminating the structural deficits within the justice system such as the long duration of trials. The implementation of ECtHR judgments is not entirely satisfying, yet remains on the same level as many other EU member states."
		ECtHR's role in the Yücel case	All references to the ECtHR's role for the case of the imprisoned journalist Deniz Yücel	„Wir werden in Deniz Yücels Fall eine Stellungnahme vor dem Europäischen Gerichtshof für Menschenrechte abgeben, weil wir der Meinung sind, dass seine Haft ungerechtfertigt ist."	"We will make a statement before the ECtHR in the case of Deniz Yücel because it is our opinion that his detention is not justified."

Hereafter, a third round of coding was performed along the definitions of the finalised category system. In a concluding step, coded text segments for the categories "norm setter" and "compliance" were weighted based on the assessment of the ECtHR's role. Negative assessments are marked 0, neutral evaluations equal 2, and positive assessments are valued 3. This weighting of statements in the two categories allows for an interpretation of findings beyond the mere representation of quantitative features.

While this section aimed at leading the reader through the different methodological steps of the data analysis, the following section presents the main findings stemming from the examination of texts.

Findings

Findings from the analysis are divided into three sections to facilitate their discussion at a later point: 1) Findings related to document groups, 2) Findings related to categories, and 3) Assessments of the ECtHR's relevance.

Findings Related to Document Groups

While transcripts of press conferences of the German government indicate that almost all identified categories occur at least once, legislative drafts and information leaflets mention only three categories each. Speeches include a slightly wider portfolio of categories than reports (see table 3).

The amount of codes assigned per document group does not correspond to the number of documents included in that group. While the document group "press conferences" encompasses nine documents, seventeen text segments could be coded within that group. Contrastingly, the group "speeches" consists of only five documents but amounts to twenty-one coded sections with a comparatively large variety of categories identified.

Table 3. Distribution of code frequencies across document groups. Large squares indicate high frequencies.

Code System	Press conferences	Interviews and op eds	Legislative drafts	Speeches	Reports	Information	Other
ECtHR in general					5	2	1
"Dialogue" of ECHR and other courts	1			3	1		
ECtHR as "norm-setter"/"normative power"	2	2	1	7	4		
ECtHR's influence on/in third states	2	4		2			
Case overload	1			2			
Judicial powers of the ECtHR						2	1
ECtHR's role in asylum and refugee policy	1	1					
Prohibition of Dublin transfers, push-backs and refoulement	3	2		1			
ECtHR's influence on reception conditions and asylum procedures	1			2			
ECtHR Judgments	1		1		2	1	1
Judgements against GER				1	3		
Need to comply with/implement ECtHR judgements	2	5	2	3	4		
ECtHR's role in the Yucel Case	3						

Findings Related to Categories

The distribution of assigned textual references varies starkly across document groups and across categories. While ten sub-categories appear at least once but no more than three times in the group "press conferences", only six are mentioned as

63

part of the "reports" group. Yet, "reports" feature a good amount of general information about the ECtHR. Remarkably, "speeches" address, in particular, the role of the ECtHR as a norm setter or normative power while they pick up all other categories comparatively little. The category featured the most is the "Need to comply with/ implement ECtHR judgments", followed by the ECtHR as a 'norm setter'/ 'normative power'".

Table 4. Frequencies of categories within document groups

Code System	Press conferences	Interviews and op eds	Legislative drafts	Speeches	Reports	Information	Other
ECtHR in general					5	2	1
"Dialogue" of ECHR and other courts	1			3	1		
ECtHR as "norm-setter"/"normative power"	2	2	1	7	4		
ECtHR's influence on/in third states	2	4		2			
Case overload	1			2			
Judicial powers of the ECtHR						2	1
ECtHR's role in asylum and refugee policy	1	1					
Prohibition of Dublin transfers, push-backs and refoulement	3	2		1			
ECtHR's influence on reception conditions and asylum procedures	1			2			
ECtHR Judgments	1		1		2	1	1
Judgements against GER				1	3		
Need to comply with/implement ECtHR judgements	2	5	2	3	4		
ECtHR's role in the Yucel Case	3						
#N (Documents)	9 (30%)	4 (13%)	2 (6%)	5 (16%)	6 (20%)	2 (6%)	2 (6%)

Only three of the six document groups contain information assigned to the categories involving asylum and refugee policy: "Press conferences", "Interviews & op-eds", and "Speeches" (Table 4).

The categories which most often appear together across all document groups are, firstly, the "ECtHR's influence on/ in third states" combined with the "Need to comply with/ implement ECtHR judgments"; and secondly, the "ECtHR as a 'norm setter'/ 'normative power'" in conjunction with the "Need to comply with/ implement ECtHR judgments".

Table 5. Co-occurrences of two categories within a coded segment across all document groups

Code System	ECtHR as "norm-setter"/"normative power"	ECtHR's influence on/in third states	Prohibition of Dublin transfers, push-backs & refoulement	Judgments against GER	Need to comply with/implement ECtHR judgments	SUM
ECtHR in general	0	0	0	0	0	0
ECtHR as "norm-setter"/"normative power"	0	2	1	1	3	9
ECtHR's influence on/in third states	2	0	1	0	5	8
ECtHR's role in asylum & refugee policy	0	0	1	0	1	2
Prohibition of Dublin transfers, push-backs & refoulement	1	1	0	0	2	5
ECtHR's influence on reception conditions & asylum procedures	1	0	0	0	0	1
ECtHR Judgments	1	0	0	0	0	1
Judgments against GER	1	0	0	0	0	1
Need to comply with/implement ECtHR judgments	3	5	2	0	0	11
SUM	9	8	5	1	11	38

Assessments of the ECtHR's Relevance

Two sub-categories were weighted to examine statements of actors of the German government in detail. On the one hand, references to the "ECtHR's role as a 'norm setter'/'normative power'" were assigned ranks spanning 0, 2, and 3. On the other hand, the "Need to implement/ comply with judgments of the ECtHR" was weighted either 0, 2 or 3 to better understand the diversity of statements delivered in this category.

With respect to the ECtHR's role as a norm setter, statements marked 0 include all references to cases or events where the ECtHR was not regarded or even challenged as a norm setter. Text segments ranked 2 encompass neutral descriptions of the normative respectively legal, and judicial powers of the ECtHR, while a weight of 3 was given to statements which involve appeals to the ECtHR's role as an important norm setter or normative power. Similarly, those references to the "Need to implement/ comply with judgments of the ECtHR" which involved accounts of non-compliance or partial compliance with decisions of the Court were ranked 0. Neutral descriptions of implementation processes were marked 2, while appeals to the importance of complying with ECtHR jurisdiction were assigned 3.

Interestingly, the document group "speeches" contains the most statements marked 3 with respect to both weighted sub-categories, while descriptions of the ECtHR's role as a norm setter in respect to the assessment of its judgments occurs in a more neutral fashion in "press conferences".

Table 6. Weighted categories concerning the ECtHR's role, and its judgments

Code	Document group	Color	Weight score	Document name
ECtHR in general\ECtHR as "norm-setter"/ "normative power"	Interviews & op eds	●	3	180308_BR_wortlaut_Interview_130117
ECtHR in general\ECtHR as "norm-setter"/ "normative power"	Speeches	●	3	180308_BR_wortlaut_Rede_BP_161013
ECtHR in general\ECtHR as "norm-setter"/ "normative power"	Speeches	●	3	180308_BR_wortlaut_Rede_BP_130422
ECtHR in general\ECtHR as "norm-setter"/ "normative power"	Speeches	●	3	180308_BR_wortlaut_Rede_BP_130422
ECtHR in general\ECtHR as "norm-setter"/ "normative power"	Speeches	●	3	180305_BMJV_Rede_150530
ECtHR in general\ECtHR as "norm-setter"/ "normative power"	Speeches	●	3	180305_BMJV_Rede_150530
ECtHR in general\ECtHR as "norm-setter"/ "normative power"	Speeches	●	3	180305_BMJV_Rede_150530
ECtHR in general\ECtHR as "norm-setter"/ "normative power"	Reports	●	3	180305_BMJV_Kernbericht_2016_DE
ECtHR in general\ECtHR as "norm-setter"/ "normative power"	Press conferences	●	2	180308_BR_wortlaut_RPK_170722
ECtHR in general\ECtHR as "norm-setter"/ "normative power"	Press conferences	●	2	180304_BR_wortlaut_RPK_150504
ECtHR in general\ECtHR as "norm-setter"/ "normative power"	Legislative drafts	●	2	180305_BMJV_RegE_Gesetz_ueber_den_Umfang_der_Personensorge_bei_
ECtHR in general\ECtHR as "norm-setter"/ "normative power"	Reports	●	2	180304_BR_fb-445
ECtHR in general\ECtHR as "norm-setter"/ "normative power"	Reports	●	2	180304_BR_Sozialbericht-2013
ECtHR in general\ECtHR as "norm-setter"/ "normative power"	Reports	●	2	180305_BMJV_CAT_QPR6_Beantwortung_Fragenkatalog
ECtHR in general\ECtHR as "norm-setter"/ "normative power"	Interviews & op eds	●	0	1_gesetzentwurf_sichere herkunftsstaaten
ECtHR in general\ECtHR as "norm-setter"/ "normative power"	Speeches	●	0	180308_BR_wortlaut_Rede_BP_161007
ECtHR Judgments\Need to comply with/ implement ECtHR judgments	Press conferences	●	3	180304_BR_wortlaut_RPK_170607
ECtHR Judgments\Need to comply with/ implement ECtHR judgments	Interviews & op eds	●	3	180305_BMJV_Anstoesse_und_Einwuerfe_BR
ECtHR Judgments\Need to comply with/ implement ECtHR judgments	Interviews & op eds	●	3	180305_BMJV_Gastbeitrag_160225
ECtHR Judgments\Need to comply with/ implement ECtHR judgments	Speeches	●	3	180308_BR_wortlaut_Rede_BP_130422
ECtHR Judgments\Need to comply with/ implement ECtHR judgments	Speeches	●	3	180305_BMJV_Rede_150530
ECtHR Judgments\Need to comply with/ implement ECtHR judgments	Press conferences	●	2	180304_BR_wortlaut_RPK_160115
ECtHR Judgments\Need to comply with/ implement ECtHR judgments	Legislative drafts	●	2	180305_BMJV_RegE_SchutzSexualleSelbstestimmung
ECtHR Judgments\Need to comply with/ implement ECtHR judgments	Legislative drafts	●	2	180305_BMJV_RegE_SchutzSexualleSelbstestimmung

Table 6. continued.

Code	Document group	Color	Weight score	Document name
ECtHR Judgments\Need to comply with/ implement ECtHR judgments	Reports	●	2	180304_BR_fb-445
ECtHR Judgments\Need to comply with/ implement ECtHR judgments	Reports	●	2	180304_BR_Sozialbericht-2013
ECtHR Judgments\Need to comply with/ implement ECtHR judgments	Reports	●	2	180305_BMJV_CAT_QPR6_Beantwortung_Fragenkatalog
ECtHR Judgments\Need to comply with/ implement ECtHR judgments	Reports	●	2	180305_BMJV_CAT_QPR6_Beantwortung_Fragenkatalog
ECtHR Judgments\Need to comply with/ implement ECtHR judgments	Interviews & op eds	●	0	1_gesetzentwurf_sichere herkunftsstaaten
ECtHR Judgments\Need to comply with/ implement ECtHR judgments	Interviews & op eds	●	0	1_gesetzentwurf_sichere herkunftsstaaten
ECtHR Judgments\Need to comply with/ implement ECtHR judgments	Interviews & op eds	●	0	1_gesetzentwurf_sichere herkunftsstaaten
ECtHR Judgments\Need to comply with/ implement ECtHR judgments	Speeches	●	0	180308_BR_wortlaut_Rede_BP_161007

The following examples illustrate the category weights. All three text segments are translations from the German originals.

"ECtHR's role as a 'norm setter'/'normative power'" – 0

"However, there are tendencies of denial with regard to proceedings of the European Court of Human Rights, where states – when found guilty – refuse to ensure a better protection of fundamental rights and freedoms. Even in those signatory states that are proud of their legal and judicial traditions, some people do not always want to remember their duty to accept the supranational supervision of the Court." (Speeches\180308_BR_wortlaut_Rede_BP_161007: 7: 697 - 7: 1157)

"ECtHR's role as a 'norm setter'/'normative power'" – 2

"There is no suspension [of Dublin transfers] in the case of Bulgaria. Also, in terms of rulings of the highest courts – the topic has not yet reached the ECtHR and the ECJ, according to my knowledge – there are shortcomings, but not in such a systematic and structural way that per se excludes the transfer [of asylum-seekers] to Bulgaria." (Press conferences\180304_BR_wortlaut_RPK_150504: 2: 19|387 - 2: 523|443)

"Need to implement/ comply with judgments of the ECtHR" – 3

"That refugees who entered the EU via Greece are not sent back there, is also a result of the decisions of the European Court of Human Rights and the European Court of Justice. Both courts prohibited this due to the problematic humanitarian situation in Greece. We must comply with these judgments. Whoever propagates the opposite, would breach the law." (Interviews & op eds\180305_BMJV_Gastbeitrag_160225: 1: 25|351 - 1: 529|416)

Discussion

Two angles of analysis present themselves when investigating the German government's statements on the role of the European Court of Human Rights and its judgments. When attempting to understand why the government stresses the Court's relevance in some instances while it does not mention its rulings in others, insights from scholarship on political communication are particularly enlightening. Research on political communication deals with a plethora of topics; yet, it has much to offer when it comes to strategic communication and government rhetoric. On the other hand, when aiming to explain the effects of judgments of the ECtHR – or more generally, the normative power of the Court – norm diffusion theory, scholarship on norm salience, and human rights literature provide valuable insights. While the former is especially useful for capturing the motives behind the government's communications, the latter touches upon the wider normative context within which the German government operates. Therefore, both fields open up valuable windows for understanding the statements extracted within the analysis in their respective contexts.

Research on political communication goes back to the first half of the 19th century when Harold Lasswell published his well-known model of communication (Lasswell, 1948). While the field has attracted interest from various disciplines, political science and communication studies are the predominating disciplines from which scholarship on political communication has emerged (Dahlgren, 2004, p. 15). Due to its openness and flexibility, research on political communication is often criticised for its lack of rigorous methodology and profound theory; yet the field is such a complex, multi-faceted one that approaching it from a variety of disciplinal backgrounds can only be conducive to understanding the diverse aspects of political communication.

For the purpose of this study, particularly normative approaches to investigating political communication are fruitful: they overlap naturally with key concepts from scholarship on the diffusion and adaptation of (international) norms. In fact, Blumler emphasises that "there is a need for diverse normatively minded scholars, who appreciate that values are ever at stake in how political communication is organized, practiced, and received" (2016, p. 435). Adding another layer to this statement – much in line with norm diffusion or norm salience scholars: Political actors reveal norms in their communication every day; communication can disclose which norms are at stake in politics. That is, if we listen and read carefully.

Findings based on the modest sample of this study strongly suggest that context matters in at least two ways. While the kind of text is telling with regard to the way statements are worded, the broader context appears to decide whether there are any references made to the ECtHR at all.

Speeches feature the majority of references to the ECtHR as a norm setter in Europe. Unsurprisingly, reports are much more likely to rely on neutral statements about the competences of the Court. Similarly, in view of the weighting of text segments, speeches, interviews, and Op-Eds contain almost all normative appeals to the importance of the ECtHR, and its normative power. Statements delivered in press conferences address the Court's norm-setting functions in a more tempered, neutral fashion. This observation speaks to the nature and purpose of press conferences as opportunities for the government to set an agenda, amplify media coverage and attempt to position its policies in a positive light (McNair, 2011, 131). Thus, the references to the Court imply a different normative quality. The subsequent segments from a speech of the German Federal President and a government press conference shall illustrate the argument:

> *"Sometimes, one needs an impulse from the outside to reconsider longstanding habits. In this case [the reform of preventive custody], the impulse came from Strasbourg. The European Court of Human Rights detected a gap in the protection of human rights. And then, the German Constitutional Court filled this void." (Gauck | Speeches\180305_BMJV_Rede_150530: 2: 32|484 - 2: 524|522)*

> *"Perhaps, an additional comment on the European Convention on Human Rights: I think, it's important to know that a deviation from it is only acceptable if the situation absolutely requires it. This means that the measures undertaken in Turkey must be proportionate and cannot be in contradiction to other standards of international law. (…). All this can be reviewed by the European Court of Human Rights." (Fischer | Press conferences\180308_BR_wortlaut_RPK_170722: 6: 25|740 - 6: 513|814)*

The sample of texts covered a period of just over five years. Statements about the ECtHR's ruling related to Dublin transfers or other aspects of the Common European Asylum System mostly stem from the years 2015 and 2016 – when the European crisis concerning asylum policy reached its peak. Additionally, the *welcome culture* of German society pushed government actors to make faster, sometimes riskier, decisions. Hence, the wider context is crucial when it comes to a) the presence of references to the ECtHR in general, and b) the concrete topics and judgments addressed. Another example from an Op-Ed written by former Minister of Justice, Heiko Maas, in January 2016 is characteristic for this observation:

> *"The European Court of Human Rights and the European Court of Justice prohibited returns to Greece because of the humanitarian situation. These judgments are too part of our legal system. So, nobody can say that Germany has breached the law when accepting all these people." (Maas | Interviews & op eds\180305_BMJV_Anstoesse_und_Einwuerfe_BR: 90: 434 - 90: 774)*

Maas responds in this statement to accusations by Eastern European leaders that the German government breached European law by allowing a high number of asylum-seekers to enter the country. Interestingly, the norms he implicitly addresses – the non-refoulement principle as established in Article 33 of the Convention Relating to the Status of Refugees, and the prohibition of inhumane and degrading treatment as determined in Article 3 ECHR – trace back to a judgment of the ECtHR in January 2011[13]. Yet, that judgment did not involve Germany but Greece and Belgium. The minister however stresses that the prohibition of returns to Greece are related to a norm which is also part of the German legal system.

It follows that two questions can be posed in addition to the initially introduced research question: 1) Why does the German government assess and communicate the relevance of the ECtHR the way it does? 2) What possible explanations for the

---

[13] The Grand Chamber judgment in the case of *MSS v Belgium and Greece*, 21 January 2011

specific function of the ECtHR do government documents offer? Attempting to suggest some answers to both questions, it is useful to combine insights from scholarship on political communication and rhetoric (Gronbeck, 2004; Lorenzo, 1996) with concepts of norm localisation or acculturation (Acharya, 2004; Cortell & Davis, 2000; Goodman & Jinks, 2009).

In his article about the significance of human rights for media, Rai rightly stresses that "governments themselves adopt a selective focus drawing on human rights principles and rhetoric time and again (...) as a strategic tool of foreign policy" (Rai, 2015, p. 485). However, governments do not only use human rights rhetoric in the realm of foreign policy but also to defend domestic policy choices, directed at their domestic audiences. As Risse points out, rhetoric communication especially – in contrast to argumentative behaviour – serves the purpose of justifying one's choices, preferences or definitions of a situation. "Rhetorical action means giving reasons for one's actions and defending the validity claims inherent in one's preferences and worldviews" (Risse, 1999, p. 532).

If Heiko Maas, then Minister of Justice, emphasises that Germany must comply with the ECtHR judgment prohibiting returns to Greece due to the inhumane conditions for asylum-seekers there, he actually justifies the government's decision to allow more asylum-seekers to enter Germany. When he adds the sentence "Whoever propagates the opposite, would breach the law" he simultaneously condemns his opponents' respectively critical political discourse, which was in 2016 steadily growing stronger.

As argued previously, a thorough analysis of government communications is crucial to learn about the norms at stake in the current political agenda. Cortell and Davis claim that "the first sign of an international norm's domestic impact is its appearance in the domestic political discourse" (Cortell & Davis, 2000, p. 69). A powerful actor within that discourse is the government. Beyond the question of which norms are being raised and debated it is meaningful to inquire into the context in which these norms are brought up.

Federal President, Joachim Gauck, speaking in front of a large, high level international audience at the International Tribunal for the Law of the Sea during a ceremonial act, expresses his concerns about the lack of compliance with ECtHR jurisdiction. In this case, it appears safe to assume that he attempts to seize an opportunity for the public shaming of other allegedly less compliant signatory states of the ECHR. He then reminds the black sheep firstly, of their own longstanding legal traditions, and secondly, of their duty to respect and implement the Court's decisions:

> *"Even in those signatory states that are proud of their legal and judicial traditions, some people do not always want to remember their duty to accept the supranational supervision of the Court."*

The repetitiveness of statements on the need to comply with ECtHR rulings or the fact that those judgments are part of the German legal order may be categorised as mere rhetoric communication. Yet, Cortell and Davis point out that the normative pronouncements of authoritative officials "become part of the society's legitimating discourse, establish intersubjective understandings and expectations at both the domestic and international levels, and constrain policy options" (Cortell & Davis, 2000, p. 76). Hence, the (verbal) commitment to certain norms and values – in other words, the process of putting these norms on the societal agenda – is an important step towards weaving them into the political and cultural fabric of a society until they become what Risse and Ropp call "habitualized practice" (1999, p. 237). On the other hand, there are numerous examples of studies which show that the prevalence of habitualised human rights practices within a region and the availability of information hereof create a social environment that affects the practices and preferences of other states (Goodman & Jinks, 2013; Simmons, 2009).

This observation does not only lead back to Sikkink's argument that "states may make changes in their behaviour not only because of the economic costs of sanctions, but because leaders of countries care about what leaders of other countries think of them" (Sikkink, 1998, p. 520); it also refers back to the statements of the German Federal President – the promotion of human rights is somewhat inscribed in his role. The social environment in which all member states of the European Union operate offers ample opportunity to admonish a government due to its insufficient human rights performance while expressly distinguishing oneself through compliance with ECtHR jurisdiction.

Conclusion

This article has investigated the German government's assessment of the role of the European Court of Human Rights – in general, and more specifically, concerning matters of asylum and refugee policy. It is based on a Qualitative Content Analysis of 30 texts issued by the German government and encompasses transcripts of press conferences, interviews and op-eds, speeches, legislative drafts, reports, and information material. Within, I have presented and discussed some of the characteristics and contexts of the extracted statements about the ECtHR and its judgments. Linking selected statements from the documents to underlying normative dynamics, I aimed to stress the importance of a thorough reading of government communications through the lens of norm diffusion and habitualisation.

The analysis of text groups revealed that even though "press conferences" contained the most documents only 17 text segments could be coded; contrastingly, the group "speeches" consisted of only five documents but amounted to 21 coded sections with a comparatively large variety of categories identified. Categories identified the most often were the "Need to comply with/ implement ECtHR judgments", followed by the ECtHR as a 'norm setter'/ 'normative power'". In terms of the weight of statements, the document group "speeches" contained the most statements marked 3 with respect to both weighted sub-categories. Most neutral descriptions of the ECtHR's role as a norm setter as well as of the relevance of its judgments occurred in the group "press conferences".

The analysis has furthermore shown that context matters in at least two ways. While the text sort is telling with regard to the way statements are framed, the broader context appears to decide whether there are any references made to the ECtHR at all. This becomes most apparent when taking into account both the context of "speeches" vi-a-vis "press conferences", as well as the different wording and objectives of various statements. Furthermore, the overall frequency of references to the ECtHR is higher within these groups in 2015 and 2016, indicating that the peak of the migration flows and the crisis of European asylum policy has affected the perceived relevance of the ECtHR among government actors.

Statements of government actors stressing the need to comply with ECtHR judgments or the fact that ECtHR case-law is an integral part of the German legal order can be read as mere rhetoric. Nevertheless, they also constitute a legitimising discourse within society that promotes human rights norms as opposed to for instance security-related norms. This (verbal) commitment to certain norms and values is an important step towards weaving them into the political and cultural fabric of a society until they become habitualised practice.

To complement the research presented here and to build a more comprehensive sample mirroring the complexity of societal structures, I propose to integrate texts from civil society and media into the analysis. On the one hand, this will allow us to draw a more holistic picture of the discourses and assessments of the European Court of Human Rights in Germany. On the other hand, adjoining the role of non-state actors to the analysis promises great additional value in order to understand the normative dynamics underlying the ECtHR's influence in Germany, and in the field of asylum.

References

Acharya, A. (2004). How Ideas Spread: Whose Norms Matter? Norm Localization and Institutional Change in Asian Regionalism. *International Organization*(58), pp. 239–275.

Amnesty International. (2016, July 6). *Stellungnahme zum Integrationsgesetz.* Retrieved from Amnesty International: https://www.amnesty.de/2016/7/6/stellungnahme-zum-integrationsgesetz

Arora, S. K., & Lasswell, H. D. (1969). *Political communication: the public language of political elites in India and the United States.* New York: Holt, Rinehart and Winston.

Belgrade Center for Human Rights; Macedonian Young Lawyers Association; Oxfam. (2017, April). *A Dangerous 'Game'. The pushback of migrants, including refugees, at Europe's borders.* Oxford: Oxfam GB for Oxfam International. Retrieved from https://www.oxfam.org/sites/www.oxfam.org/files/file_attachments/bp-dangerous-game-pushback-migrants-refugees-060417-en_0.pdf

Bendel, P. (2017). *EU Refugee Policy in Crisis. Blockades, Decisions, Solutions.* Bonn: Friedrich-Ebert-Stiftung. Retrieved from http://library.fes.de/pdf-files/wiso/13536.pdf

Blumler, J. G. (2015). Core Theories of Political Communication: Foundational and Freshly Minted. *Communication Theory*(25), pp. 426–438.

Bowcott, O. (2014, October 3). *The European court of human rights' judgments that transformed British law. From curbing the British army's use of torture in Ireland to ending bans on homosexuality, the court has shaped UK law.* Retrieved from The Guardian: https://www.theguardian.com/law/2014/oct/03/landmarks-human-rights-echr-judgments-transformed-british-law

Bundesamt für Migration und Flüchtlinge. (2017, August). *Das Bundesamt in Zahlen 2016. Asyl, Migration und Integration.* Retrieved from BAMF: https://www.bamf.de/SharedDocs/Anlagen/DE/Publikationen/Broschueren/bundesamt-in-zahlen-2016.pdf?__blob=publicationFile

Carbonara, E., Parisi, F., & Wangenheim, G. v. (2008, December 31). Lawmakers as Norm Entrepreneurs. *Review of Law & Economics, 4*(3), pp. 779–799. Retrieved from https://www.degruyter.com/view/j/rle.2008.4.3/rle.2008.4.3.1320/rle.2008.4.3.1320.xml

Chaffee, S. H. (1975). *Political Communication: Issues and Strategies for Research.* Thousand Oaks, CA: SAGE Publications.

Chan, S. (2017, July 25). *Sex for Women After 50 Is Important After All, European Court Rules.* Retrieved from The New York Times: https://www.nytimes.com/2017/07/25/world/europe/sex-after-50-portugal-european-court.html

Checkel, J. (1997). International Norms and Domestic Politics: Bridging the Rationalist-Constructivist Divide. *European Journal of International Relations, 3*(4), pp. 473-495.

Cortell, A. P., & Davis, J. W. (2000). Understanding the Domestic Impact of International Norms: A Research Agenda. *International Studies Association*, pp. 65-87.

Dahlgren, P. (2004). Theory, Boundaries and Political Communication. The Uses of Disparity. *European Journal of Communication, 19*(1), pp. 7–18.

Dai, X. (2013). The 'compliance gap' and the efficacy of international human rights institutions. In T. Risse, S. C. Ropp, & K. Sikkink, *The Persistent Power of Human Rights: From Commitment to Compliance* (pp. 85-102). Cambridge: Cambridge University Press.

European Council on Refugees and Exiles. (2017, April 14). *New report documents wide-spread abuse of migrants along the West Balkan route.* Retrieved from ECRE: https://www.ecre.org/new-report-documents-wide-spread-abuse-of-migrants-along-the-west-balkan-route/

European Law Institute. (2012). *Statement on Case-Overload at the European Court of Human Rights.* Vienna: European Law Institute.

Finnemore, M. (2000). Are Legal Norms Distinctive? *N.Y.U. Journal of International Law & Politics*(591), pp. 699-705. Retrieved from http://heinonline.org/HOL/LandingPage?handle=hein.journals/nyuilp32&div=22&id=&page=

Finnemore, M., & Sikkink, K. (1998). International Norm Dynamics and Political Change. *International Organization, 52*(4), pp. 887-917. Retrieved from https://www.cambridge.org/core/journals/international-organization/article/international-norm-dynamics-and-political-change/0A55ECBCC9E87EA49586E776EED8DB57

Finnemore, M., & Sikkink, K. (1998). International Norm Dynamics and Political Change. *International Organization, 52*(4), pp. 887-917.

Florini, A. (1996, September 1). The Evolution of International Norms. *International Studies Quarterly, 40*(3), pp. 363–389. Retrieved from https://academic.oup.com/isq/article-abstract/40/3/363/1812717

Forsythe, D. P. (2014). *Human Rights in International Relations* (4 ed.). Cambridge: CUP.

Frantziou, E., Staiger, U., & Chaytor, S. (2014, May). *Refugee Protection, Migration and Human Rights in Europe.* Retrieved from University College London: https://www.ucl.ac.uk/european-institute/ei-publications/europe-briefing-refugee.pdf

German Institute for Human Rights. (2016, June 1). *Versteckte Einschränkung des Asylrechts im Entwurf des Integrationsgesetzes grund- und menschenrechtswidrig.* Retrieved from institut-fuer-menschenrechte: www.institut-fuer-menschenrechte.de/aktuell/news/meldung/ article/ pressemitteilung-versteckte-einschraenkung-des-asylrechts-im-entwurf-des-integrationsgesetzes-grund/

Gläser, J., & Laudel, G. (2009). *Experteninterviews und qualitative Inhaltsanalyse: als Instrumente rekonstruierender Untersuchungen.* Heidelberg: Springer.

Goodman, R., & Jinks, D. (2013). Social mechanisms to promote international human rights: complementary or contradictory? In T. Risse, S. C. Ropp, & K. Sikkink, *The Persistent Power of Human Rights: From Commitment to Compliance* (pp. 103-124). Cambridge: CUP.

Gronbeck, B. E. (2004). Rhetoric and Politics. In L. L. Kaid, *Handbook of Political Communication Research* (pp. 135-154). Mahwah, NJ: Lawrence Erlbaum Associates.

Guiraudon, V. (2000). European Courts and Foreigners' Rights: A Comparative Study of Norms Diffusion. *International Migration Review, 34*(4), pp. 1088-1125.

Hafner-Burton, E., & Ron, J. (2009, April). Seeing Double: Human Rights Impact through Qualitative and Quantitative Eyes. *World Politics, 61*(2), pp. 360–401.

Human Rights Watch. (2017). *European Union. Events of 2016.* Retrieved from HRW: https://www.hrw.org/world-report/2017/country-chapters/european-union

Judd, T. (2013, January 14). *What has the European Court of Human Rights ever done for us?* Retrieved from Independent: http://www.independent.co.uk/news/uk/home-news/what-has-the-european-court-of-human-rights-ever-done-for-us-8451406.html

Kaid, L. L. (2004). *Handbook of Political Communication Research*. Mahwah, NJ: Lawrence Erlbaum Associates, Publishers .

Kohlbacher, F. (2006, January 21). The Use of Qualitative Content Analysis in Case Study Research. *Forum: Qualitative Social, 7*, p. Art. 21. Retrieved from http://www.qualitative-research.net/index.php/fqs/rt/printerFriendly/75/153

Kratochwil, F. V. (1995). *Rules, Norms, and Decisions: On the Conditions of Practical and Legal Reasoning in International Relations and Domestic Affairs*. Cambridge, NY: Cambridge University Press.

Krippendorff, K. (2004). *Content Analysis: An Introduction to Its Methodology* (2. ed.). Thousand Oaks, CA: Sage Publications.

Kuckartz, U. (2014). *Qualitative Text Analysis*. London: Sage Publications.

Lasswell, H. (1948). *The Structure and Function of Communication in Society. The Communication of Ideas.* New York: Institute for Religious and Social Studies.

Lorenzo, D. (1996). Political Communication and the Study of Rhetoric: Persuasion from the Standpoint of Literary Theory and Anthropology. In M. E. Stuckey, *The Theory and Practice of Political Communication Research* (pp. 2-27). Albany: State University of New York Press.

Madsen, M. R. (2016). The Challenging Authority of the European Court of Human Rights. From Cold War Legal Diplomacy to the Brighton Declaration and Backlash. *Law and Contemporary Problems, 79*, pp. 141-178.

Mayring, P. (2010). Qualitative Inhaltsanalyse. In G. Mey, & K. Mruck, *Handbuch Qualitative Forschung in der Psychologie* (pp. 601-613). Wiesbaden: VS Verlag für Sozialwissenschaften.

Mayring, P. (2012). Qualitative Inhaltsanalyse - ein Beispiel für Mixed Methods. In M. Gläser-Zikuda, T. Seidel, C. Rohlfs, A. Gröschner, & S. Ziegelbauer, *Mixed Methods in der empirischen Bildungsforschung* (pp. 27-36). Münster: Waxmann.

Mayring, P. (2015). *Qualitative Inhaltsanalyse. Grundlagen und Techniken* (12 ed.). Weinheim; Basel: Beltz.

Mazzoleni, G., Barnhurst, K. G., Ikeda, K., Wessler, H., & Maia, R. C. (2015). *The International Encyclopedia of Political Communication* (Vol. I). Hoboken, NJ: John Wiley & Sons.

McDonald, H. (2015, November 13). *Northern Ireland law on abortion ruled 'incompatible with human rights'*. Retrieved from The Guardian: https://www.theguardian.com/uk-news/2015/nov/30/northern-ireland-law-on-abortion-ruled-as-incompatible-with-human-rights

McNair, B. (2011). *An Introduction to Political Communication* (4 ed.). Oxon: Routledge.

Milanovic, M. (2009). Norm Conflict in International Law: Whither Human Rights. *Duke Journal of Comparative & International Law*, pp. 69-132. https://scholarship.law.duke.edu/djcil/vol20/iss1/2

Muller, H., & Wunderlich, C. (2013). *Norm Dynamics in Multilateral Arms Control: Interests, Conflicts, and Justice*. Athens, Georgia: The University of Georgia Press.

Nasser, S. (2016, May 23). Refugees Between EU policies and Human Rights Law. The case of Syrian Refugees on Hungarian Borders. School of Global Studies, University of Gothenburg; School of Business and Social Sciences, Roehampton University; Department of Archaeology and Social Anthropology, University of Tromsø. Retrieved from https://munin.uit.no/bitstream/handle/10037/9767/thesis.pdf?sequence=2

Oomen, B. M. (2016). A serious case of Strasbourg-bashing? An evaluation of the debates on the legitimacy of the European Court of Human Rights in the Netherlands. *The International Journal of Human Rights, 20*(3), pp. 407-425.

Popelier, P., Lemmens, K., & Lambrecht, . S. (2016). *Criticism of the European Court of Human Rights: Shifting the Convention System: Counter-Dynamics at the National and EU Level*. Cambridge: Intersentia Ltd.

Posner, E. A. (1998, June). Symbols, Signals, and Social Norms in Politics and the Law. *The Journal of Legal Studies*.

Puschkarsky, T. (2009, September 28). Norm Entrepreneurs in International Politics - A Case Study of Global Footprint Network and the Norm of Sustainability. Ruprecht-Karls-Universität Heidelberg. https://conservation-development.net/Projekte/ Nachhaltigkeit/ DVD_ 10_Footprint/Material/pdf/Puschkarsky_2009_GFN_Norm_of_Sustainability.pdf

Rai, M. (2015). Human Rights. In G. Mazzoleni, K. G. Barnhurst, K. Ikeda, H. Wessler, & R. C.

Maia, *The International Encyclopedia of Political Communication* (pp. 483-487). Hoboken, NJ: John Wiley & Sons.

Risse, T. (1999, December). International Norms and Domestic Change: Arguing and Communicative Behavior in the Human Rights Area. *Politics & Society, 27*(4), pp. 529-559.

Risse, T., & Ropp, S. C. (1999). International human rights norms and domestic change: conclusions. In T. Risse, S. C. Ropp, & K. Sikkink, *The Power of Human Rights: International Norms and Domestic Change* (pp. 234-278). Cambridge: Cambridge University Press.

Risse, T., Ropp, S. C., & Sikkink, K. (2013). *The Persistent Power of Human Rights: From Commitment to Compliance.* Cambridge: Cambridge University Press.

Savarimuthu, B. T., & Cranefield, S. (2011, May 5). Norm creation, spreading and emergence: A survey of simulation models of norms in multi-agent systems. *Multiagent and Grid Systems, 7*(1), pp. 21-54.

Schreier, M. (2012). *Qualitative Content Analysis.* London: Sage Publications.

Schreier, M. (2013). Qualitative Content Analysis. In U. Flick, *The SAGE Handbook of Qualitative Data Analysis* (pp. 170-183). Thousand Oaks, CA, USA: SAGE Publishing.

Shany, Y. (2012, April). Assessing the Effectiveness of International Courts: A Goal-Based Approach. *American Journal of International Law, 106*(2), pp. 225-270. Retrieved from https://www.cambridge.org/core/journals/american-journal-of-international-law/article/div-classtitleassessing-the-effectiveness-of-international-courts-a-goal-based-approachdiv/B40D7051563AF2D8BD5BFAD500FB14A5

Sikkink, K. (1998, September). Transnational Politics, International Relations Theory, and Human Rights. *Political Science and Politics, 31*(3), pp. 516-523.

Simmons, B. (2009). *Mobilizing Human Rights: International Law in Domestic Politics.* New York: Cambridge University Press.

Sims, A. (2015, December 15). *Vladimir Putin signs law allowing Russia to ignore international human rights rulings. Russia's Constitutional Court said the country's constitution would take priority over international law.* Retrieved from Independent: http://www.independent.co.uk/news/world/europe/vladimir-putin-signs-law-allowing-russian-court-to-overthrow-international-human-rights-rulings-a6773581.html

Stevens, D. (2017, July 1). Asylum, Refugee Protection and the European Response to Syrian Migration. *Journal of Human Rights Practice, 9:2*, pp. 184–189. Retrieved from https://academic.oup.com/jhrp/article/9/2/184/4084303

Stuckey, M. E. (1996). *The Theory and Practice of Political Communication Research.* Albany, NY: State University of New York Press.

Trauner, F. (2016). Asylum policy: the EU's 'crises' and the looming policy regime failure. *Journal of European Integration*(38: 3), pp. 311-325. Retrieved from https://www.tandfonline.com/doi/pdf/10.1080/07036337.2016.1140756

Zwingel, S. (2012). How Do Norms Travel? Theorizing International Women's Rights in Transnational Perspective. *International Studies Quarterly*(56), pp. 115–129.

SOLIDARITY VS. SOVEREIGNTY: PERSPECTIVE ON THE SLOVAK FOREIGN POLICY REACTIONS TO THE MIGRATION CRISIS

Barbora Olejárová *

Introduction

Migration crisis that hit the European Union in 2015 did not influence the Slovak Republic in terms of numbers of irregular migrants and asylum seekers. Yet, it has become one of the central issues of the Slovak domestic and foreign policy following very negative attitude of the Slovak general public and domestic political elites towards acceptance of asylum seekers and third-countries migrants on the state's territory. The definite stance of the country was expressed when the state filled an action for annulment to the Court of Justice of the EU (case C-643/15), challenging legality of the Asylum-Seekers Relocation Decision from 22 September 2015. The basic matter of argument was rejection of obligatory quotas as determined by the Council Decision (EU) 2015/1601. Radical position of the Slovak government was – among other factors – influenced by the upcoming parliamentary election that was supposed to take place on 5 March 2016 and by striving of all political parties to gain public votes by promoting general public will of refusing asylum seekers and settlement of the third-countries migrants in the Slovak Republic. However, the domestic opposition towards the common European solution to the crisis based on the quota system got into contradiction with the upcoming role of Slovakia as the country presiding over the Council of the European Union in the second half of 2016. As the presiding country, Slovakia was expected to take over the role of a mediator among the other EU Member States in all areas, including migration. The accrued dichotomy was sharpened by adoption of the EU-Turkey migration deal that assumed allocation of the Syrian refugees into the EU Member States based on the free places created according to the aforementioned Council Decision (EU) 2015/1601. Over the course of its Presidency, Slovakia acknowledged effectiveness of the deal with Turkey, but the country was still refusing allocation of refugees to the state's territory. The Slovak representatives strived to solve the migration crisis, which eventually turned out to be also the crisis of solidarity in the EU, by introducing the concept of effective solidarity in the European Union. However, this was sharply criticised by the EU

* Barbora Olejárová is a PhD Candidate at the Department of International Relations and Diplomacy, Faculty of Political Science and International Relations, Matej Bel University, Kuzmányho 1, 974 01, Banská Bystrica, Slovak Republic. E-mail: olejarovab@imafex.sk.

Member states located at the external borders, as well as by the countries accepting largest numbers of migrants and asylum seekers. These states were reasoning by the fact, that the concept of effective solidarity is insufficient in the situation which arose in the aftermath of the Syrian civil war and that the stance of Slovakia is misinterpreting the concept of solidarity as anchored in the EU *acquis communautaire*.

The main aim of the paper is to evaluate legal and political implications of the Slovak government's policy reactions to the migration crisis – namely rejection of the mandatory quota and relocation system as proposed by the EU; as well as introduction of the "effective solidarity concept". Besides, the paper aims to provide evidence of how intensively can migration waves affect even those countries that are neither source countries nor transit or final destination countries for the migrants. The research questions of the presented study are as follows: 1. Was the political rejection of the mandatory quota by the Slovak government and the consequent action for annulment at the Court of Justice of the EU a breach of the country's legal obligations under the law of the EU? 2. Was Slovakia's stance in accordance with the principle of solidarity as one of the basic values of the EU? 3. In which ways did the migration crisis and subsequent foreign policy reactions of Slovakia impact the country's position in the EU? The first chapter deals with the concept of solidarity in the law of the EU. By means of a content analysis of the primary law of the EU and further relevant EU directives and resolutions, the text explores aspects of external and internal solidarity with regard to the issues of migration and asylum in the Union and its practical application in terms of already existing particular policies of the EU that were put into practice. After that, the second part of the paper summarizes Slovak domestic and foreign policy reactions to the migration crisis; evaluates adopted measures on the domestic and European level and explains its causes taking into account political development in the country and historical experiences of the Slovak Republic with the third-countries migration. Finally, by means of the SWOT analysis, last chapter confronts different perspectives on political accuracy and legality of the Slovak government's policy reactions to the migration crisis. The text concludes by answering the research questions raised in the introductory part of this paper.

Migration and the Principle of Solidarity in the EU Law

Solidarity is the fundamental principle of the European Union's law. Already Robert Schuman, one of the founders of the EU, delivered in his declaration of 9 May 1950 that: *„Europe will not be made all at once, or according to a single plan. It will be built through concrete achievements which first create a de facto solidarity. "* (Foundation Robert Schuman, 2011, p. 1)   The Court of Justice of the European Union refers to solidarity for the first time in the Rediscount Rate Case (6/69 and 11/69) from 1969. Solidarity is directly mentioned in several primary sources of the EU law, and many other sources of law refer to solidarity indirectly. The sixth clause of the consolidated version of the Treaty on European Union states that the Member States desire to *„...to deepen the solidarity between their peoples while respecting their history, their culture and their traditions."* (Consolidated version of the Treaty on European Union, 2016, p. 13) Solidarity is further mentioned in Article 2 and 3(3)(5) TEU as the basic value of the EU, as well as in Article 21(1), 24(2)(3), 31(1), 32 TEU; Article

67(2), 80, 122(1), 194(1) and 222(1)(3) TFEU and in Chapter IV of the Charter of Fundamental Rights of the European Union. As noted by Hilpold (2015), we can distinguish three dimensions of solidarity:

(i) solidarity between the EU Member States;

(ii) solidarity between the state and the citizens;

(iii) solidarity between generations.

Regarding the migration crisis, there is an additional categorization of solidarity, namely:

Financial solidarity – in terms of financial support to the most burdened states, in the period 2014-2020 materialized by means of The Asylum, Migration and Integration Fund (AMIF) with a total of EUR 3,137 mld. for the seven years and The Internal Security Fund – Borders and Visa (ISF) with a total of EUR 3,8 mld. for the seven years (European Commission, 2018a; European Commission, 2018b);

Physical solidarity – in terms of transfer of the asylum seekers, refugees and people with other form of granted international protection from the most burdened EU Member States or the third countries (non-members of the EU) to the other EU Member States (relocations and resettlement).

The other typology of solidarity concerning migration issues is based upon classification of solidarity according to the recipients of solidarity. In this regard, we can speak of external and internal solidarity.

External solidarity

In the external dimension, the EU approached with solidarity third countries burdened by unbearable inflow of migrants and people seeking any form of international protection, as well as the third country citizens, who are entitled to international protection or the status of a refugee according to the Convention Relating to the Status of Refugees (the Geneva Convention) from 1951 and the 1967 Protocol Relating to the Status of Refugees, according to which the term refugee shall apply – with an exception of the provisions of the Article 1 D, E and F – to any person, who

> *"...owing to well-founded fear of being persecuted for reasons of race, religion, nationality, membership of a particular social group or political opinion, is outside the country of his nationality and is unable or, owing to such fear, is unwilling to avail himself of the protection of that country; or who, not having a nationality and being outside the country of his former habitual residence as a result of such events, is unable or, owing to such fear, is unwilling to return to it."* (UNHCR, 1951, p. 14)

The external solidarity can be expressed as follows:

Resettlement – transfer of the person from the first country of asylum outside of the EU to one of the EU Member States. Resettlement as an expression of solidarity is put to use especially in the situations, when the person cannon return to his/hers home country, but at the same time, he/she cannot gain effective protection in the current host country, usually due to instability of particular host country. (Perrin, McNamara, 2013; European Parliament, 2015) The law of the EU specifies resettlement in Article 2 of the Regulation (EU) No 516/2014 of the

European Parliament and of the Council establishing the Asylum, Migration and Integration Fund, as a process, whereby, on a request from the United Nations High Commissioner for Refugees based on a person's need for international protection, third-country nationals are transferred from a third country and established in a Member State where they are permitted to reside with one of the following statuses:

i) refugee status within the meaning of Directive 2011/95/EU;

ii) subsidiary protection status within the meaning of Directive 2011/95/EU; or

iii) any other status which offers similar rights and benefits under the national and Union law as those referred to in points (i) and (ii)

Other humanitarian admission programs – which are defined as an

> "...ad hoc process whereby a Member State admits a number of third-country nationals to stay on its territory for a temporary period of time in order to protect them from urgent humanitarian crises due to events such as political developments or conflicts." (Regulation (EU) No 516/2014 ..., 2017, p. 175)

Search and rescue operations (SAR) – most of irregular migrants arrive to the EU by the sea. Therefore, the EU Member States respect Article 98 of the United Nations Convention on the Law of the Sea, which is ratified by all Member States and by the Union itself and requires assistance to be given to any person in distress at sea. (European Parliament, 2015)

Internal Solidarity

The internal dimension of solidarity relates mostly to the EU Member States located at the external borders of the Union in the Mediterranean, which are burdened by the inflow of migrants more widely than the other EU state members. Article 80 TFEU states that the policies on border checks, asylum and immigration (Articles 77-79 TFEU) shall be governed *"...by the principle of solidarity and fair sharing of responsibility, including its financial implications, between the Member States."* (Consolidated version of the Treaty on Functioning of the European Union, 2016, p. 78) Similarly, Article 67(2) states that the EU *"...shall frame a common policy on asylum, immigration and external border control, based on solidarity between Member States, which is fair towards third-country nationals."* (Consolidated version of the Treaty on Functioning of the European Union, 2016, p. 73) The internal solidarity can be expressed by following means:

Relocations – transfer of an applicant for international protection or a person with granted international protection from one EU Member State to another state member of the Union. According to Article 7(2) of the Regulation (EU) No 516/2014, relocation is in both cases conditioned by the agreement of the relocated person. (European Parliament, 2015)

Temporary protection - Council Directive 2001/55/EC of 20 July 2001 on minimum standards for giving temporary protection in the event of a mass influx of displaced persons and on measures promoting a balance of efforts between Member States in receiving such persons and bearing the consequences thereof

(Temporary Protection Directive)[1]. It is a tool of the EU drafted for the situations of mass influx of displaced persons from particular third country or a region seeking international protection, where the review of individual asylum applications would be time-consuming or too demanding in terms of capacities and the mass granting of protection for the specifically defined period of time is considered to be a more effective solution. The fixed period of granted temporary protection relieves the EU Member States in two ways: ad1) it gives the EU more time to review applications of those beneficiaries of temporary protection, who decide to apply for asylum in the EU; ad2) before the duration of temporary protection ends up, the reasons for influx of displaced persons might cease to exist and the migrants can return to their home countries. However, according to the Article 25, implementation of the Directive is conditioned by the principle of solidarity, as the people in need shall be granted temporary protection according to the state's capacities to accept those people, and it is solely up to the Member States to indicate whether they are able and willing to accept such people. (Council Directive 2001/55/EC, 2001) In other words, there is no mechanism creating obligation for states to offer temporary protection to the third country nationals unless they give their voluntary consent to do so. The paradox is, that since its adoption, the Directive has never been put to use until nowadays. It is questionable, why Greece or Italy did not activate the Directive, as it was designed specifically for situations such as the current crisis of mass influx of Syrian migrants coming to the EU. The possible answer is the general doubts on the Member State's willingness to accept these people on their territories, as it is required by the Temporary Protection Directive. We suppose that Greece, Italy and other EU Members expected lack of solidarity and the goodwill in the EU, and therefore they gave priority to the mandatory quota system over activation of the Temporary Protection Directive.

In the context of internal solidarity, the Dublin system is quite often stated as a set of measures inconsistent with the principle of solidarity as determined by the European acquis. The Dublin Convention (Dublin I, signed 1990, came into force in 1997) determines state responsible for review of the asylum application submitted in one of the EU Member States. The Dublin Regulation (Dublin II – Council Regulation (EC) No 343/2003), has almost the same content as the Dublin Convention. The difference is the legal character of both documents – whereas Dublin I is an international treaty; Dublin II is a secondary legislation of the EU itself. Dublin II determines that the country responsible for the review of an asylum application is the country of first arrival of the person and if the migrant applies for asylum in the other EU state, it can be transferred to the country of first arrival based on the Dublin criteria. However, this principle caused unequal distribution

---

[1] The Directive was adopted in response to the 1999 Kosovo refugee crisis, when the local population approached the EU searching for international protection in the aftermath of the local conflict. Directive provides temporary protection for the period of one year, which can be extended by the decision of the Council of the EU by up to one more year. The person under temporary protection can apply for asylum, however, according to Article 19; the Member States "...*may provide that temporary protection may not be enjoyed concurrently with the status of asylum seeker while applications are under consideration.*"(Council Directive 2001/55/EC, 2001, p. 17) The temporary protection ends after the period of one year or by the decision of the Council, which shall be "...*based on the establishment of the fact that the situation in the country of origin is such as to permit the safe and durable return of those granted temporary protection.*" (Council Directive 2001/55/EC, 2001, p. 15)

of asylum applicants in the EU and created pressure on the Member States at the EU external borders. An example is the situation in Greece – one of the countries with highest numbers of new migrants from North Africa and the Middle East, who were paradoxically arriving at the time when the country faced recession caused by the financial crisis. Unfairness of the Dublin II towards the EU Mediterranean countries was reflected in drafting of the Regulation (EU) No 604/2013 - Dublin III, which entered into force on 19 July 2013 and applies for review of asylum applications submitted after 1 January 2014. Dublin III includes adapted rules and criteria for determining the Member State responsible for examining an application for international protection lodged in one of the Member States by a third-country national or a stateless person. The state responsible for the review of asylum application is not the country of first entry anymore. Competence is determined according to the set of criteria which shall be applied in the order of which they are set out in Chapter III of the Regulation. The hierarchy begins with unaccompanied minors; presence of family members who are beneficiaries of international protection; presence of family members who are applicants for international protection; issue of residence documents or visa by the receiving country; entry and/or stay and finally the state of the first arrival to the EU territory.

Migration Crisis in Slovakia – Numbers and Policy Reactions

The Slovak Republic is located in the Central Europe surrounded by five other countries – Austria (106,7 km), the Czech Republic (251,8 km), Poland (541,1 km), Ukraine (97,8 km) and Hungary (654,8 km). Out of these, only Ukraine is not a member of the European Union neither of the Schengen area. The geographic location restrains migratory flows passing through the state's territory. Unlike the migratory routes from the countries of origin to the fringes of Europe (Eastern Africa Route, Western and Central Africa Route, Asian Route) and the routes crossing the EU external borders (including the Eastern Mediterranean Route, Central Mediterranean Route, Western Balkan Route, Western Mediterranean Route, Circular Route, Eastern Borders Route, Western Africa Route and the Black Sea Route), the continuation of these routes on the territory of the EU is not particularly classified and named. However, the practical analysis suggests that most migrants continue from the EU borders to the Western and Northern Europe by using transfer via the Balkan states and later passage from Hungary to Austria and thus, avoiding the Slovak territory. The only direct route crossing the Slovak Republic is the Eastern Borders Route, which connects Belarus, Moldova, Ukraine, the Russian Federation and the eastern EU Member States - Estonia, Finland, Hungary, Latvia, Lithuania, Norway, Poland, Slovakia, Bulgaria and Romania. However, the number of illegal border crossings on this route (1,349 in 2016 and 1,920 in 2015) is minor compared to the numbers on the Eastern Mediterranean Route, for example (182,534 in 2015 and 885,386 in 2016) (Frontex, 2017; Kuschminder, de Bresser, Siegel, 2015).

With regard to the geographic location of the country, migration crisis did not hit Slovakia significantly in the sense of numbers. When comparing the amount of granted asylums on the Slovak territory (Table 1), we can conclude that the numbers are relatively constant and do not exceed several dozens of granted asylums per year. Quantitative difference is obvious only regarding number of asylum seekers. Yet, paradoxically, the peaks of submitted asylum applications in Slovakia were not reached over the course of the migration crisis between 2014-2017, as one might assume, but in the period between 2001-2007, i.e. in the years shortly before and after Slovakia joined the EU.

Table 1. Asylum applications, refugees and subsidiary protection in Slovakia

Year	Number of asylum applications	Granted asylum	Refused asylum	Subsidiary protection granted/re fused	Suspended procedure
2000	1,556	11	123		1,366
2001	8,151	18	130		6,154
2002	9,743	20	309		8,053
2003	10,358	11	531		10,656
2004	11,395	15	1,592		11,782
2005	3,549	25	827		2,930
2006	2,849	8	861		1,940
2007	2,642	14	1,177	82/646	1,693
2008	909	22	416	66/273	455
2009	822	14	330	98/165	460
2010	541	15	180	57/104	361
2011	491	12	186	91/48	270
2012	732	32	334	104/153	383
2013	441	15	123	34/49	351
2014	331	14	197	99/41	163
2015	330	8	124	41/24	148
2016	146	167	82	12/13	35
2017	59	10	31	11/7	20
Total	58,526	830	8,021	695/1,519	49,493

Source: MVSR (2017)

Domestic Policy Reactions to the Migration Crisis

Despite almost none quantitative impact of migration crisis in the Slovak Republic, migration has become the central issue of the Slovak domestic policy discourse in 2015 - the year preceding the election to the National Council of the Slovak Republic, which was held on 5 March 2016. Resulting from our previous analysis, it is possible to conclude that the issue of migration has become subject of securitization in the country. (Bolečeková, Olejárová, 2016) General public fears from the third-countries migrants showed up in the 2015 November Eurobarometer 84 survey, where over 19 % of Slovakia's population declared that immigration is the biggest threat to the country at the moment, compared to 4% of the people in Eurobarometer 83 from May 2015 (having in mind that the number of foreign population legally present at the Slovak territory at the time was only of

1,56 %) (European Commission, 2017a). Negative attitude towards third-countries migrants can be explained by the historical experience with migration on one hand, and the rising tendency to connect migration with religious terrorism, on the other hand. Before 1989, Slovakia had only limited experience with migrants from non-European countries. Due to the political regime and the influence of the USSR, immigration to Slovakia after the Second World War consisted for the most part from students and foreign workers from the "friendly countries", mostly from the Balkan states, Vietnam and Cuba. The country did not register any significant quantitative increase of the third countries migrants after Slovakia gained independence in 1993, neither. Total number of the valid residence permits at the end of 2014 (the year regarded as the beginning of the migration crisis in Europe) was 76,715; out of which 29,171 were the third country nationals and 47,544 the EU nationals. Top 10 groups of the third country nationals with valid residence permits in Slovakia in 2014 included migrants from Ukraine, Serbia, the Russian Federation, Vietnam, China, the Republic of Korea, the USA, the Former Yugoslav Republic of Macedonia, Turkey and Israel – i. e. mostly European and non-Muslim countries. (MVSR, 2014) As correctly stated by Miroslav Lajčák, Minister of Foreign Affaires of the Slovak Republic (2012-2016) (2016-nowadays) and since May 2017 also President of the United Nations General Assembly: "*Our people have not been exposed to Muslims and they are frightened. It's a new phenomenon for them (…). Hundreds of Muslims mean nothing in Belgium or London but it does mean something in Slovakia.*" (DW, 2016, p. 1) This lack of experience explains fears of the Slovak citizens from the Middle Eastern migrants, which was eventually used as a mobilization tool in the pre-election campaign before the Slovakia general election in 2016.

In an effort to increase the political gain, a rare political unity occurred and all of the political parties generally agreed on the same set of measures aimed to solve the migration crisis. Following the analysis of the parties' pre-election programs, these measures included: protection of the EU external borders; refusing of the EU mandatory quotas on migrants; creation of detention facilities outside of the EU territory which should concentrate migrants heading to the EU in order to review their asylum requests; stabilization of the situation in the home countries of migrants, especially in Syria, Libya and Iraq; precise selection of asylum seekers and economic migrants, who are not eligible for the refugee status, subsidiary protection, temporary protection or any other form of protection in the EU. Another significant measure adopted by the Slovak government included purchase of a transportable barrier that might be used for redirection of migration flows at the Slovak-Hungarian or Slovak-Austrian border in case the migration flows would have changed their direction to the Slovak territory. Yet, one year after the purchase, this measure turned up to be more a pre-election gesture than a real possibility.

Foreign Policy Responses to the Migration Crisis

Slovak foreign policy responses to the crisis were influenced by the generally negative stance of the Slovak public and domestic political elites towards mandatory relocation of migrants to the Slovak territory, which resulted into the Slovak action for annulment to the Court of Justice (case C-643/15). The action for annulment to the Court of Justice (case C-643/15) was targeted against introduction of the quota system for relocation of migrants from Italy and Greece passed by the Council of the European Union on 22 September 2015 - Council Decision (EU) 2015/1601. The scheme proposed relocation of 120,000 people to the EU Member States with Slovakia required taking 802 refugees – 190 from Italy and 612 from Greece. Relocations based on mandatory quotas are an essential part of the EU-Turkey Statement from 20 March 2016, which proved to be the most effective solution implemented by the EU to curb the inflow of the Middle Eastern and African migrants to the territory of the EU's Member States. Recent statistics show that the amount of irregular border crossings between the border crossing points declined from 1,822,177 in 2015 to 511,371 in 2016, which proves effectiveness of the deal that is generally supported also by the Slovak representatives on the EU level. Resettlement from Turkey to the EU Member States is based on the principle 'one-for-one'.

> *"For each Syrian returned from Greece to Turkey, another Syrian will be resettled in an EU Member State. The idea is for a total of 72,000 Syrians to be relocated from Turkey to EU Member States. This number is calculated "within the framework of existing commitments" consisting of 18,000 from the European Resettlement Scheme ... and 54,000 unallocated places under the temporary relocation scheme (places originally allocated for relocation from Hungary but remained unallocated due to Hungary's refusal to participate)." (Provera, 2016, p. 21)*

The action for annulment was submitted by Slovakia on 2 December 2015 (C-643/15) and Hungary submitted very similar action one day later, on 3 December 2015 (C-647/15), with the Polish support. However, on 6 September 2017, the CJEU dismissed the actions, stating that the EU Council decision from September 2015 that imposed the quota system was valid. The Slovak action was based on the legal and political arguments and relied on six pleas in law. The first group of arguments included several claims regarding the procedure of adopting the contested legislation, whereas the other one objected the provisional character of the Decision, as well as its effectiveness and suitability for the emerged situation. Slovakia is alleging (Court of Justice of the European Union, 2017):

1. Infringement of Article 68 TFEU and Article 13(2) TEU, and breach of the principle of institutional balance. The decision of the Council of European Union (made up of national ministers) was adopted in contradiction to the guidelines set by the European Council (made up of heads of states and governments), that stated on 23 April 2015, that there was a need to "*consider options for organizing emergency relocation between all Member States on a voluntary basis*" and to "*set up a first voluntary pilot project on resettlement across the EU.*" (Vikarská, 2015, p. 1) – even though conclusions of the European Council are not legally binding (Article 15(1) TEU).

2. Infringement of Article 10(1) and (2) TEU, Article 13(2) TEU, Article 78(3) TFEU, Articles 3 and 4 of Protocol (No 1) on the role of the national parliaments in the European Union, annexed to the EU and FEU Treaties ('Protocol (No 1)'), and Articles 6 and 7 of Protocol (No 2) on the application

of the principles of subsidiarity and proportionality, annexed to the EU and FEU Treaties ('Protocol (No 2)'), and breach of the principles of legal certainty, representative democracy and institutional balance. This point is based on the complaint of interfering to the rights of national parliaments and the EP, as the EP was not properly consulted after Hungary refused to participate in the process of relocations of migrants from its territory.

3. Breach of essential procedural requirements relating to the legislative process and infringement of Article 10(1) and (2) TEU and Article 13(2) TEU, and breach of the principles of representative democracy, institutional balance and sound administration (in the alternative).

4. Breach of essential procedural requirements and infringement of Article 10(1) and (2) TEU and Article 13(2) TEU, and breach of the principles of representative democracy, institutional balance and sound administration (partly in the alternative).

5. Failure to meet the conditions under which Article 78(3) TFEU is applicable (in the alternative) – concerns the provisional character and the emergency character/sudden inflow.

6. Breach of the principle of proportionality. As stated in the official statement of the Slovak Ministry of Justice, "*The contested decision is manifestly incompatible with the principle of proportionality, as it is manifestly neither suitable nor necessary to achieve the desired end.*" (MSSR, 2015, p. 1) Moreover, the contested measure is

> "*...not suitable to reach the desired aim (i.e. to relieve the burden borne by the external border states and to show solidarity and fair sharing of responsibility between the Member States as outlined in the decision's preamble), since relocating people is too difficult and their further movement is too unpredictable*". (MSSR, 2015, p. 1)

However, refusal of the mandatory quotas on migration was not the only foreign policy reaction of Slovakia to the migration crisis. The country decided to help according to its own possibilities – by sending police units to the borders of the most burdened Member States and the third countries; by temporary relocating asylum seekers from Austria to the newly re-opened asylum facility in Gabčíkovo; by granting asylum to 149 Assyrian Christians from Iraq; by allocating 500,000 € from the sources of the national lottery company TIPOS for humanitarian projects of non-governmental organizations rendering assistance in the refugee crisis; or by committing to create 550 governmental scholarships for refugees until 2021. (Úrad vlády SR, 2015) This concept is called effective solidarity and became one of the most important and debated tools introduced by the Slovak Council Presidency.

SWOT Perspective on the Slovak Foreign Policy Reactions towards Migration Crisis

In order to confront different perspectives on political accuracy and legality of the Slovak government's policy reactions to the migration crisis, simple SWOT analysis is offered in the following chapter of this paper. Its results show legality of the Slovak attitude in respect of the EU acquis and the soundness of arguments regarding ineffectiveness of the mandatory quota system. Yet, at the same time, relatively large amount of threats and weaknesses emerged. These relate mostly with the political perception of the Slovak activities by the EU institutions and the "old"

Member States.

Strengths

Legality of the Slovak reactions/respect for the EU law

Despite the unsuccessful action on the CJEU and international criticism for non-compliance with the principle of solidarity, the Slovak reaction was fully in accord with the law of the EU. Slovakia contested Decision (EU) 2015/1601, however, at the same time, it made very clear that until the final decision of the CJEU will be made, Slovakia adheres to its commitment according to the EU law and takes part in the process of relocations from Italy and Greece despite rejection of the system on the political level. Until 16 February 2018, Slovakia relocated 16 people from Greece, unlike some other EU countries, such as Poland or Hungary, who refuse to participate at the relocation scheme at all. The Czech Republic relocated 12 migrants from Greece, but stated that it will not perform any other relocations based on mandatory quotas. (European Commission, 2017b) Resulting from this fact, the European Commission has on 7 December 2017 decided to refer the Czech Republic, Hungary and Poland to the Court of Justice of the EU for non-compliance with their legal obligations on relocation. This step was preceded by launch of an infringement procedure against the Czech Republic, Hungary and Poland on 15 June 2017. As stated in the press release of the European Commission,

> *"...the three countries have given no indication that they will contribute to the implementation of the relocation decision....The Council Decisions require Member States to pledge available places for relocation every three months to ensure a swift and orderly relocation procedure. Whereas all other Member States have relocated and pledged in the past months, Hungary has not taken any action at all since the relocation scheme started, Poland has not relocated anyone and not pledged since December 2015. The Czech Republic has not relocated anyone since August 2016 and not made any new pledges for over a year." (European Commission, 2017b, p. 1)*

The reason why Slovakia avoided the infringement procedure was the wise diplomacy and manifestation of the political will to abide to the country's obligations resulting from the EU law. Based on the domestic political opposition towards the quota, the country used all legal means to avoid mandatory relocations, yet after these legal means failed, it acknowledged the decision of the Court and behaved as a responsible member of the EU in accord with the EU treaties and other secondary legislation.

Demonstration of the mandatory quota shortfalls

Despite the failure of the Slovak action at the CJEU, one political argument of the Slovak action proved to be correct – the system of mandatory quota is not functioning in a way it was designed. Out of the total number of 120,000 relocated migrants according to the Decision (EU) 2015/1601, only 34,689 have been relocated so far (situation from 15 May 2018). When it comes to the EU-Turkey Statement, which was also undermined by the EU relocation mechanism, the statistical data show, that the number of irregular border crossings on the Eastern

Mediterranean Route declined from 885,386 in 2015 to 182,534 in 2016. This comparison indicates that the migration deal with Turkey works by deterring people from using the route between Turkey and Greece to get irregularly to the European territory.

However, the other part of the deal related to the exchange of one irregular asylum seeker from Greece for one Syrian refugee from Turkey and the further relocation of Syrian refugees from Greece to the other Member States according to the quotas within the framework of the existing commitments consisting of 18,000 places from the European Resettlement Scheme and 54,000 unallocated places under the temporary relocation scheme originally allocated for relocation from Hungary seems to be clumsy. According to the Communication from the European Commission from March 2018, only 12,476 people were resettled from Turkey to the EU under the 1:1 mechanism since the activation of the system. The scheme aims to replace irregular flows of migrants travelling across the Aegean Sea by an orderly legal resettlement process; however, it seems that the relocation based on mandatory quotas is not functioning properly (European Commission, 2018d). Thus, despite certain overwhelming caused by the securitization and upcoming parliamentary election, the Slovak Republic was not completely wrong when claiming (see Ministry of Justice's statement on CJEU stated above) that the system of mandatory relocations will not bring desired outcomes.

Weaknesses

Image of a migrant-hostile country

Discriminatory rhetoric of some Slovak politicians; decision to grant asylum to 149 Christian migrants or refusal of the Muslim asylum seekers in the political proclamations creates the image of Slovakia as an illiberal homogenous country hostile towards migrants and discriminating people with other ethnicity, race or religion. This rhetoric includes statements of the Slovak top-ranking representatives, but also quotes introduced in several political parties' pre-election programs. The People's Party Our Slovakia stated in the 10-points election program that they *"...will not accept any single migrant"* to the Slovak territory or that they *"...will not let aggressive immigrants harass our women in a way they did it to the German women in Cologne."* (10 bodov za..., 2015, p. 2) Similarly, the party SME Rodina (We are the Family) compared the current migration waves to the migration period of the Barbarian nations leading to the fall of the Roman Empire, claiming that the migrants want to destroy our society completely. (Volebný program Hnutia..., 2015) Several of these quotes and statements have been misinterpreted and most of them have been used only as part of the anti-immigration propaganda with no impact on the functioning of the asylum system in the country. However, the abovementioned statements together with rejection of the mandatory quota have enough power to form an unfavorable image of Slovakia abroad.

Opportunities

Reinforcement of Slovakia as an independent actor on the EU level

On the level of the Council of the EU, all of the EU Member States are treated as equal entities regardless of their size, economic power, population or date of entry to the integration block. Yet, the younger democracies and the smaller or

Table 2. Member States' Support to Emergency Relocation Mechanism (15 May 2018)

Member States	Relocations from Italy	Relocations from Greece
Austria	43	x
Belgium	471	700
Bulgaria	10	50
Croatia	22	60
Cyprus	47	96
Czech Republic	x	12
Denmark	x	x
Estonia	6	141
Finland	778	1,202
France	635	4,394
Germany	5,434	5,391
Greece	x	x
Hungary	x	x
Ireland	x	1,022
Italy	x	x
Latvia	34	294
Lithuania	29	355
Luxembourg	249	300
Malta	67	101
Netherlands	1,020	1,755
Poland	x	x
Portugal	356	1,192
Romania	45	683
Slovakia	x	16
Slovenia	81	172
Spain	235	1,124
Sweden	1,392	1,656
United Kingdom	x	x
Norway	816	693
Switzerland	920	580
Liechtenstein	x	10
Iceland	x	x
Total	12,690	21,999

Source: European Commission (2018c).

economically weaker countries historically always tended to adapt their foreign policies to the bigger and stronger states. The migration crisis and subsequent reaction of the Slovak Republic, as well as the entire V4 - which had quite similar attitude towards the obligatory quotas, created an opportunity to show impact of Slovakia when solving problems in the EU. A different approach of Slovakia to the solutions on the EU level compared to the other states was an opportunity for the country to start to be perceived more seriously - as an independent and relevant actor and fully-fledged member of the EU that must be taken into account in the process of formation of the EU policies, and not only as an object of other state's interests.

Threats

Doubts on the Slovak ability to manage state's Presidency in the Council of the EU

Beginning on 1 July 2016, Slovakia took over the Presidency in the Council of the EU with all of the responsibilities connected with this position. The presiding country

> *"... is responsible for driving forward the Council's work on EU legislation, ensuring the continuity of the EU agenda, orderly legislative processes and cooperation among Member States. To do this, the presidency must act as an honest and neutral broker."(Council of the EU, 2017, p. 1)*

Consequently, concerns have been made about how the state that is rejecting common European solutions (based on mandatory quotas) would be able to act as a neutral mediator among the other Member States and the EU institutions. Moreover, migration has never been a priority of the Slovak Presidency. In 2012, Slovakia drafted the first conceptual document dealing with the program priorities of the Slovak Presidency called *Preparing the Slovak Presidency of the Council of the EU 2016 – Basic Data and Current Priorities*. The report proposed; that the priorities of the Presidency should reflect the Slovak strategic interests, especially cooperation with the states in the Eastern Europe and in the Balkans; the EU enlargement; or the management of water resources of the EU – topics which might have emphasized the particularities of Slovakia as the presiding country. The issue of migration was completely absent in this document, although sustainable migration and asylum policies finally turned into one of the four main priorities of the Slovak Presidency in 2016, together with economically strong Europe; modern single market; and globally engaged Europe.

Few months after the end of the Slovak Presidency in the Council of the EU, it is possible to conclude that the country accomplished its role of the neutral mediator and the intrastate negative opinion on the quota system did not influence the Trio Presidency priorities. Slovakia fulfilled the statement made by the then Slovak Prime Minister in July 2016, stating that:

> *"We are well aware of the presidency country's role, and we want to be an honest broker. It doesn't necessarily mean that we will change our national positions; we will just refrain from putting them on the table." (Szalai, 2016, p. 1)*

Although Slovakia's Presidency did not manage to move the Union closer to a wider agreement on how to handle migration, there are other specific successes such as finalization of the legislative process for the proposals regarding the Smart Borders Package from April 2015; Creation of the European Border and Coast Guard or approval of Regulation changing the Schengen Border Code in December 2016.

Conclusion

Migration crisis significantly affected the Slovak Republic despite the fact that the State is not located on the main migratory routes. Moreover, Slovakia is not the final destination or even transit country of migrants from the Middle East and sub-Saharan Africa and the number of refugees and asylum seekers in Slovakia did not exceed several dozens of people pro year since the outbreak of the crisis. Nevertheless, domestic political leaders reacted by securitization of the topic and strictly rejected mandatory quotas on migration, which provoked discussion on legality and lawfulness of the Slovak foreign policy reactions to the crisis.

Regarding the research questions raised in the introductory part of the presented study, one can conclude by the following statements:

Was the political rejection of mandatory quota by the Slovak government and consequent action for annulment at the Court of Justice of the EU a breach of the country's legal obligations under the law of the EU?

No, the Slovak reactions were in accordance with the EU acquis. Political statement of the Slovak government claiming that the country will never admit any migrants on the mandatory basis harmed the image of the country as a modern western democracy. However, Slovakia had the right to question the Decision (EU) 2015/1601 at the CJEU and after the court dismissed country's action, Slovakia pledged available places for relocation based on the contested Decision (EU) 2015/1601. The lawfulness of the Slovak policy was indirectly confirmed also by the decision of the European Commission from 7 December 2017, which decided to refer the Czech Republic, Hungary and Poland – not Slovakia – to the Court of Justice of the EU for non-compliance with their legal obligations on relocation.

Was Slovakia's stance in accordance with the principle of solidarity as one of the basic values of the EU?

Slovakia expressed solidarity towards third-countries migrants by granting asylum to 149 Assyrian Christians from Iraq or by offering 550 governmental scholarships for refugees until 2021; as well as towards the EU Member States by temporary relocating asylum seekers from Austria to the newly re-opened asylum facility in Gabčíkovo, or by sending police units to the EU external borders. This was considered to be insufficient by some EU Member States which accepted more asylum seekers than Slovakia and considered the situation to be unfair. The Slovak government therefore had to find a compromise between its obligation under the EU law to manifest solidarity on one hand and to respect the will of the Slovak citizens (whose interests it shall represent following basic principles of a representative democracy). Yet, the main problem of applying the principle of solidarity as a solution to the migration crisis (but also in any other situation in general) is the issue of its (non)enforceability. According to the current EU acquis, solidarity remains only a generally respected value and its binding force is based only upon the other secondary legislation adopted by the EU institutions. The other – rather philosophical than legal – issue is that no piece of legislation of the EU does explicitly define how solidarity shall be expressed and how much of solidarity is enough and how much it is not. Lack of solidarity cannot be quantitatively expressed. Therefore, unless codified by other legal documents, solidarity in the field of migration always has to be the result of a political agreement between the EU Member States.

In which ways did the migration crisis and subsequent foreign policy reactions of Slovakia impact the country's position in the EU?

Whereas the legal aspects of the Slovak position towards the migration crisis did not breach any international obligations of the country; the political impacts of the Slovak decision to stick to the concept of effective solidarity instead of physical relocations did negatively affect position of the country on the European level. Firstly, the Slovak attitude created worries over how would the country fulfil its task of a neutral broker stemming from Slovakia's Council Presidency. Secondly, Slovakia gained image of a reluctant state contravening the common decisions of the EU as a whole. The third point is that the statements of the Slovak politicians – especially in the period preceding the 2016 parliamentary election – regarding non-acceptance of Muslim refugees intertwined with the general public refusal towards third-countries migrants produced an impression of Slovakia as an illiberal state, which does not tolerate people with other cultures and religion. Especially this last point is very unfortunate, as it has more to do with the securitization and overwhelming of the entire migration issue in the country than with the real perception of migrants by the Slovak people.

References

10 bodov za naše Slovensko. (2015). Received from http://www.naseslovensko.net/wp-content/uploads/2015/01/Volebn%C3%BD-program-2016.pdf Accessed: 25.07.2016.

Bolečeková, M. and Olejárová, B. (2016). Medzinárodná migrácia: faktor ovplyvňujúci podobu a vnímanie zahraničnej politiky Slovenskej republiky. In: Koziak, T. and Ušiak, J. (eds.) *Zahraničná politika Slovenskej republiky v rámci vybraných oblastí vonkajšej činnosti Európskej únie.* Banská Bystrica: Belianum. pp. 141-175.

Consolidated Version of the Treaty on European Union. (2016). Received from http://eur-lex.europa.eu/legal-content/EN/TXT/PDF/?uri=CELEX:12016M/TXT&from=EN Accessed: 23.02.2018.

Consolidated Version of the Treaty on Functioning of the European Union. (2016). Received from http://eur-lex.europa.eu/legal-content/EN/TXT/PDF/?uri=CELEX:12016E/TXT&from=EN Accessed: 23.02.2018.

Council Directive 2001/55/EC. (2001). Received from http://eur-lex.europa.eu/LexUriServ/LexUriServ.do?uri=OJ:L:2001:212:0012:0023:EN:PDF Accessed: 25.2.2018.

Council of the EU. (2017). The Presidency of the Council of the EU. Received from http://www.consilium.europa.eu/en/council-eu/presidency-council-eu/Accessed: 10.04.2017.

Court of Justice of the European Union. (2017). Judgment of the Court (Grand Chamber) 6 September 2017. Received from http://curia.europa.eu/juris/document/document.jsf;jsessionid=9ea7d0f130defe9334c0913649c09dbf9e64942b8269.e34KaxiLc3eQc40LaxqMb N4Pb30Oe0?text=&docid=194081&pageIndex=0&doclang=EN&mode=lst&dir=&occ=f irst&part=1&cid=260318 Accessed: 25.2.2018.

DW. (2016). Europe Slovak Foreign Minister Miroslav Lajcak: 'Our people haven't been exposed to Muslims and they're frightened'. Received from http://www.dw.com/en/slovak-foreign-minister-miroslav-lajcak-our-people-havent-been-exposed-to-muslims-and-theyre-frightened/a-19414942 Accessed: 26.02.2018.

European Commission. (2017a). Public Opinion. Received from http://ec.europa.eu/commfrontoffice/publicopinion/index.cfm/Survey/getSurveyDetail/instruments/STAND

ARD/yearFrom/2012/yearTo/2017/surveyKy/2098 Accessed: 25.03.2017.

European Commission. (2017b). Relocation: Commission Refers the Czech Republic, Hungary and Poland to the Court of Justice. Received from http://europa.eu/rapid/press-release_IP-17-5002_en.htm Accessed: 20.02.2018.

European Commission. (2018a). Asylum, Migration and Integration Fund (AMIF). Received from https://ec.europa.eu/home-affairs/financing/fundings/migration-asylum-borders/asylum-migration-integration-fund_en Accessed: 20.02.2018.

European Commission. (2018b). Internal Security Fund – Borders and Visa. Received from https://ec.europa.eu/home-affairs/financing/fundings/security-and-safeguarding-liberties/internal-security-fund-borders_en Accessed: 20.02.2018.

European Commission. (2018c). Member States' Support to Emergency Relocation Mechanism. Received from https://ec.europa.eu/home-affairs/sites/homeaffairs/files/what-we-do/policies/european-agenda-migration/press-material/docs/state_of_play_-_relocation_en.pdf Accessed: 23.05.2018.

European Commission. (2018d). Communication from the Commission to the European Parliament, the European Council and the Council. Received from https://ec.europa.eu/neighbourhood-enlargement/sites/near/files/com_2018_250_f1_communication_from_commission_to_inst_en_v10_p1_969116.pdf Accessed: 23.05.2018.

European Parliament. (2015). Working Document on Article 80 TFEU – Solidarity and Fair Sharing of Responsibility, Including Search and Rescue Obligations. Received from http://www.statewatch.org/news/2015/jul/ep-working-document-migration-solidarity.pdf Accessed: 20.02.2018.

Foundation Robert Schuman. (2011). Declaration of 9th May 1950 Delivered by Robert Schuman. Received from https://www.robert-schuman.eu/en/doc/questions-d-europe/qe-204-en.pdf Accessed: 23.02.2018.

Frontex. (2017). Migratory Routes Map. Received from http://frontex.europa.eu/trends-and-routes/migratory-routes-map/ Accessed: 16.04.2017.

Hilpold, P. (2015). Understanding Solidarity within EU Law: An Analysis of the "Islands of Solidarity" with Particular Regard to Monetary Union. *Yearbook of European Law*, 34(1), 257-285.

Kuschminder, K.; De Bresser, J. and Siegel, M. (2015). Irregular Migration Routes to Europe and Factors Influencing Migrants' Destination Choices. Received from www.merit.unu.edu/publications/uploads/1436958842.pdf Accessed: 15.04.2017.

MSSR. (2015). Summary of the Action. Received from http://www.justice.gov.sk/Stranky/aktualitadetail.aspx?announcementID=2038 Accessed: 10.02.2017.

MVSR. (2014). Statistical Overview of Legal and Illegal Migration in the Slovak Republic. Received from https://www.minv.sk/swift_data/source/policia/uhcp/rocenky/rok_2014/Annual_Statistical_Overview_of_Legal_and_Illegal_Migration_in_the_Slovak_Republic_2014.pdf Accessed: 10.02.2018.

MVSR. (2017). Štatistiky. Received from http://www.minv.sk/?statistiky-20 Accessed: 06.04.2017.

Perrin, D. and McNamara, F. (2013). Refugee Resettlement in the EU: Between Shared Standards and Diversity in Legal and Policy Frames. Received from http://www.migrationpolicycentre.eu/docs/Know-Reset-RR-2013-03.pdf Accessed: 20.02.2018.

Provera, M. (2016). The EU-Turkey Deal. Received from https://jrseurope.org/assets/Publications/File/JRS_Europe_EU_Turkey_Deal_policy_analysis_2016-04-30.pdf Accessed: 10.04.2017.

Regulation (EU) No 516/2014 of the European Parliament and of the Council of 16 April 2014. (2014). Received from http://eur-lex.europa.eu/legal-content/EN/TXT/PDF/?uri=CELEX:32014R0516&from=EN Accessed: 22.02.2018.

Szalai, P. (2016). Can Slovakia Overcome the Paradox of Euro-Sceptic Politics and Euro-Optimist Policies? Received from http://visegradrevue.eu/can-slovakia-overcome-the-paradox-of-euro-sceptic-politics-and-euro-optimist-policies/ Accessed: 05.04.2017.

UNHCR. (1951) Convention and Protocol Relating to the Status of Refugees. 1951. Received from http://www.unhcr.org/3b66c2aa10.pdf Accessed: 22.02.2018

Úrad vlády SR. (2015). Informácia o možnej podpore aktivít mimovládnych organizácií pri humanitárnej a integračnej podpore utečencom predložených iniciátormi petície „Výzva k ľudskosti". Received from http://www.rokovania.sk/File.aspx/ViewDocument Html/Mater-Dokum-192230?prefixFile=m_ Accessed: 10.04.2017.

Vikarská, Z. (2015). The Slovak Challenge to the Asylum-Seekers' Relocation Decision: A Balancing Act. Received from http://eulawanalysis.blogspot.sk/2015/12/the-slovak-challenge-to-asylum-seekers.html Accessed: 15.04.2017.

Volebný program Hnutia SME Rodina – Boris Kollár. (2015). Received from http://www.hnutiesmerodina.sk/volebny-program.php Accessed: 25.07.2016.

ASYLUM UNDER PRESSURE: INTERNATIONAL DETERRENCE AND ACCESS TO ASYLUM

Vasiliki Kakosimou[**]

Introduction

As a result of mass refugee influxes, few states have the willingness and capacity to assess each entrance individually. Faced with many challenges, receiving States have responded to the increase in the number of migrants by increasing border surveillance and reinforcing migration controls. The measures taken include visa restrictions, push-backs by building fortresses, financing third states for capacity building or bilateral agreements to patrol their borders. All these measures are aimed at preventing refugees and other migrants from entering a state's territory by controlling or managing migration flows or maintaining internal security -even though these deterrence policies imply breaching obligations of states under national and international law. The deterrence policies do not comply with the non-derogable principle of non-refoulement and violate the right to have access to protection from persecution, torture, degrading or other inhuman treatment.

Non -Refoulement

International refugee law and international human rights law are complementary and mutually reinforcing legal regimes. It follows that Article 33(1), which embodies the humanitarian essence of the 1951 Convention and safeguards fundamental rights of refugees, must be interpreted in a manner which is consistent with developments in international human rights law.

Non-refoulement is a concept which prohibits states from returning a person to any territory where there is a risk that his or her life or freedom would be threatened on account of race, religion, nationality, membership of a particular social group or political opinion. The principle of non-refoulement reflects customary international law and is most prominently reflected in the Geneva Convention relating to the Status of Refugees and its 1967 Protocol. Article 33(1) of the Convention provides that:

> *No Contracting State shall expel or return ('refouler') a refugee in any manner whatsoever to the frontiers of territories where his life or freedom would be threatened on account of his race, religion, nationality, membership of a particular social group or political opinion.*

[**] Vasiliki Kakosimou is Head of the Regional Asylum Office of the Greek Asylum Service in Piraeus, Nav. Notara 106, Piraeus, 18535, Greece. E-mail: v.kakosimou@asylo.gov.gr.

The prohibition of refoulement must be respected in any type of forcible removal, including deportation, expulsion, extradition, informal transfer or 'renditions' and return of refugees to countries of origin or unsafe third countries. The principle of non-refoulement requires not only that refugees or asylum seekers shall not be returned to a country where their life or freedom is threatened, but also implies that they cannot be prevented from requesting protection, even if they enter unlawfully, or if they are at the border. It encompasses non-admission of stowaway asylum seekers, fences, border closures and push-backs of boat arrivals or interdictions on the high seas and in general the non-rejection at the frontier, if rejection would result in an individual being forcibly returned to a country of persecution.

Application of Non-Refoulement at Borders

States have a right under international law to control the entry of non-nationals into their territory. However, states that turn asylum seekers away at their border or erect walls and fences to avoid giving asylum seekers the opportunity to have their status determined, can breach the prohibition of refoulement. In Amuur v. France (ECtHR, Amuur v. France, No 19776/92, 25 June 1996, paras. 43 and 5) the ECtHR clarified that people in international transit zones of airports are protected by the ECHR. Thus, borders should not be closed or impenetrable to prevent the entry of refugees, as this may violate the state's non-refoulement obligations.

Extra-Territorial Application of Non-Refoulement

The obligation set out in Art. 33(1) of the 1951 Convention is subject to a geographical restriction only with regard to the country where a refugee may not be sent to, not the place where he/she is sent from. The extra-territorial applicability of the non-refoulement obligation under Art. 33(1) is clear from the text of the provision itself. The principle of non-refoulement in a human rights context is a fundamental component of the prohibition of torture, cruel, inhuman or degrading treatment or punishment. UNHCR has stressed that the principle of non-refoulement applies equally on a state's territory, at a state's borders, and on the high seas. States are bound by their obligations not to return any person over whom they exercise jurisdiction to a risk of irreparable harm. In determining whether a State's human rights obligations with respect to a particular person are engaged, the decisive criterion is not whether that person is on the State's national territory, or within a territory which is de jure under the sovereign control of the State, but rather whether or not he or she is subject to that State's effective authority and control.

Under human rights law, a state's obligations are engaged as soon as the State can be said to be exercising effective control. The ECtHR in Hirsi Jamaa v. Italy (ECtHR, Hirsi Jamaa and Others v. Italy, No 27765/09, 23 February 2012) and the UN Committee Against Torture in Marine I (UN, CAT, J.H.A. v. Spain, CAT/C/41/D/323/2007, 21 November 2008) both held that states are bound by the prohibition of refoulement from the moment a person comes within the jurisdiction of a state, even if this person is outside the state's physical territory. This ruling was reinforced by the UN Special Rapporteur on Torture who explained that

the obligations enshrined in the Torture Convention also apply to state vessels patrolling or conducting border control operations on the high seas and states' pushbacks of migrants under their jurisdiction can breach the prohibition of torture and ill-treatment and non-refoulement obligations (UN General Assembly, "Interim report of the Special Rapporteur on torture and other cruel, inhuman or degrading treatment or punishment" UN Doc A/70/303, 7 August 2015, para 42).

The decisive criterion for extraterritorial human rights obligations is thus a state's acts, which must create a qualified relationship with the victim of the violation. De facto control creates de jure responsibilities. De facto control over persons requires a certain level of physical constraint (UN, Human Rights Committee (2004), para 10). In addition, an internationally wrongful act can consist of either an action or an omission; if the third country's authorities violate human rights and the EU Member State's authorities fail to fulfill their legal obligation to stop these violations, they become co-responsible.

Hirsi – a landmark case

In Hirsi Jamaa and Others v Italy the ECtHR, issued a landmark judgment regarding the interpretation of Article 4 of Protocol No 4 of the ECHR. The case concerned Italy's push back practices of Somali and Eritrean migrants travelling from Libya who had been intercepted by the Italian authorities at sea, way out of Italian territorial waters by the Italian authorities and sent back to Libya[1]. The ECtHR noted that the personnel on the military ships which returned the migrants to Libya were neither trained to conduct personal interviews nor assisted by interpreters or legal advisers. It concluded that the absence of such guarantees made it impossible to examine the individual circumstances of each person affected by the return measures. As to the question of territoriality and where the used definition mentions 'to leave the country', the ECtHR clarified that whenever state agents exercise control and authority over an individual, then that state is obliged to respect the principle of non-refoulement , even if the state is operating outside its own territory. Furthermore, the prohibition of collective expulsions also applies to measures taken at high seas, the effect of which is to prevent migrants from reaching the borders of the state or even to push them back to another state (Hirsi Jamaa and Others v Italy, Application No 27765/09, Council of Europe: European Court of Human Rights, 23 February 2012, paragraphs 74-75, 180-181 and 183-186).[2]

Deterrence Strategies

States have pursued a series of measures to prevent refugees and other migrants from entering their territory. These have included imposing restrictive visa regimes and air carrier sanctions, erecting physical barriers at borders, the summary

---

[1] Within the territorial waters of the Member States, the EU asylum acquis applies, including all substantial and procedural guarantees for applicants. In contrast, the EU asylum acquis does not extend to persons who seek asylum while they are rescued or intercepted at high seas, including within a Member States' search and rescue zone, or in the territorial sea of third countries

[2] The case is available at http://www.refworld.org/docid/4f4507942.html Access in April 2018.

rejection of asylum-seekers at borders or points of entry, creating international zones, creating buffer zones or designating safe areas as well as the maritime interception of asylum seekers and other migrants.

Pushbacks, interception on the High Seas, off-shore processing arrangements, financial assistance and other policies of extra-territorial deterrence are pursued, sometimes under the guise that a receiving country is a safe third country. These are some characteristic examples:

US Government has developed a "deterrence strategy" of migration flows along the border that stretches from California to Texas. The militarization process of the border resulted in a significant increase of human and material resources to stop and detain migrants that try to cross the border: the number of Borders Patrols (BP) were tripled, miles of metallic wall were built in the urban areas of California and Texas, new technologies are used to detect population movement, helicopters, all terrain vehicles, etc. The B.P. is equipped with significant infrastructure, including temporary vehicle barriers, unmanned aerial vehicles, night vision cameras, trucks equipped with watchtowers (see picture below), and helicopters. Also, high technology tools such as infra-red cameras and round sensors are dispersed in the desert areas. When censors indicate a presence, the closest B.P. agent is immediately sent on-site. The Immigration and Nationality Act (INA) of 1952 is the basis for the current immigration law[3], but the immigration landscape changed dramatically in 1996 with the Antiterrorism and Effective Death Penalty Act (AEDPA) & the Illegal Immigration and Immigrant Responsibility Act (IIRIRA) (1996), enacted to "deter terrorism."[4], [5]

Australia has used geographical and political strategies such as border excision and offshore detention centers to avoid responsibility for asylum seekers[6]. The Migration Amendment Bill of 2001 removed in a lawful way the Christmas islands, Ashmore reef, Cartier islands and Cocos island from Australia's migration area (Morris, 2003: 55, 58). In 2014, Australia used the same technique for the country's entire migration area. Secondly, Australia has been running extra territorial detention centers (Nauru or PNG). Asylum seekers are detained in facilities financed by the Australian government, but their asylum application is evaluated under the laws of the country of detention. Australia has also made agreements with state and non-state actors to justify their deterrence policy; detention centers in Nauru and PNG are operated by private organisations (Achiume et al., 2017:56). However, even in these cases, Australian officials still exercise power over the centers since the private companies running the facilities (such as Ferrovial and Wilson Security) have direct communication with and act on behalf of the Australian government. Therefore, the Australian government operates a de facto authority over the asylum seekers (Achiume et al., 2017:102; Gammeltoft-

---

[3] CRS Report for Congress: Immigration Legislation and Issues in the 109th Congress. Updated December 7, 2006. Congressional Research Service. Prepared for Members and Committees of Congress

[4] International Federation for Human Rights, United States - Mexico. Walls, Abuses, and Deaths at the Borders, 11 March 2008, available at: http://www.refworld.org/ docid/47e0ea16d.html

[5] United States Committee for Refugees and Immigrants, U.S. Committee for Refugees World Refugee Survey 1997 - United States, 1 January 1997, available at: http://www.refworld.org/docid/3ae6a8b930.html

[6] http://foreignpolicy.com/2016/05/02/australia-papua-new-guinea-refugee-manus-nauru/

Hansen and Hathaway, 2015:43). Another commonly used deterrence method is the transfer of asylum seekers through bilateral or multilateral arrangements such as the "safe third country" agreement (Vedsted-Hansen, 1999). PNG and Nauru have been labelled by the Australian Government as safe third countries. Additionally, Australia has made bilateral agreements with Cambodia, offering development assistance in return for Cambodian admittance of asylum seekers and refugees from Nauru (Gammeltoft-Hansen and Tan, 2017:36). Australian authorities have arranged other bilateral agreements such as the training of Sri Lankan officials to prevent human smuggling approaching Australia (Gammeltoft-Hansen and Hathaway, 2015:24).

EU- Turkey: According to the EU-Turkey statement of the 18th March 2016, asylum-seekers are being held in refugee settlement centers and then sent back to Turkey; they are not allowed to travel to any EU States to claim asylum.

Some EU Member States have similarly sought to limit the extraterritorial nature of the prohibition of torture and ill-treatment to minimize its impact on expulsion cases; the United Kingdom, No. 14038/88, 7 July 1989; ECtHR, Vilvarajah and Others v. the United Kingdom, Nos. 13163/87, 13164/87, 13165/87, 13447/87 and 13448/87, 30 October 1991, Malta, Abdul Hakim Hassan Abdulle Et v. Ministry tal-Gustizzja u Intern Et, Qorti Civili Prim'Awla (Gurisdizzjoni Kostituzzjonali), No. 56/2007, 29 November 20117. In Saadi (Saadi v. Italy (Grand Chamber), Appl no 37201/06, 28 February 2008), the Grand Chamber of the European Court of Human Rights made clear that Human rights law allows for no derogations; the absolute prohibition of torture allows for no balancing of the risk of torture against national security risks and is not subject to any exception whatsoever. Since protection against the treatment prohibited by Article 3 is absolute, that provision imposes an obligation not to extradite any person who would run the real risk of being subjected to such treatment. The conduct of the person concerned, however undesirable or dangerous, cannot be taken into account.

Push-Backs at Sea[8]: Any policy or practice that involves pushing asylum-seeker boats back at sea without a proper consideration of individual needs for protection, would raise significant issues and potentially place the State under question in breach of its obligations under the Refugee Convention and other international law obligations. Border management activities must respect the principle of non-refoulement. Operations carried out at sea not only need to respect human rights and refugee law, but must also be in line with the international law of the sea. Activities on the high seas are regulated by the UN Convention on the Law of the Sea as well as by the Safety of Life at Sea (SOLAS) and Search and Rescue (SAR) Conventions. These instruments contain a duty to render assistance and rescue persons in distress at sea. States are bound by these obligations from the moment effective power or control is exercised upon these people by State agents including

---

[7] European Union: European Agency for Fundamental Rights, Handbook on European law relating to asylum, borders and immigration, June 2014, available at: http://www.refworld. org/docid/53ad3c1a4.html
[8] European Union: European Agency for Fundamental Rights, Handbook on European law relating to asylum, borders and immigration, June 2014, available at: http://www.refworld. org/docid/53ad3c1a4.html

actions or omissions. Apart from depriving refugees from their right not to be refouled to a territory where his/her life or freedom would be at risk, these people cannot ask for international protection, get involved into the asylum procedure or enjoy the rights of the recognised beneficiaries of international protection[9].

Also, preventing people from entering a State's territory may expose them to risk of torture, inhuman or degrading treatment, another fundamental and non-derogable human right.

In Hirsi Jamaa and Others v. Italy, the migrants had been intercepted by the Italian coastguards on the high seas, they were returned to Libya and were given no opportunity to apply for asylum. The ECtHR noted that the situation in Libya was well-known and easy to verify on the basis of multiple sources. It therefore considered that the Italian authorities knew, or should have known, that the applicants, when returned to Libya as irregular migrants, would be exposed to treatment in breach of the ECHR and that they would not be given any kind of protection. They also knew, or should have known, that there were insufficient guarantees protecting the applicants from the risk of being arbitrarily returned to their countries of origin, which included Somalia and Eritrea. The Italian authorities should have had particular regard to the lack of any asylum procedure and the impossibility of making the Libyan authorities recognise the refugee status granted by UNHCR. The ECtHR reaffirmed that the Italian authorities should have ascertained how the Libyan authorities fulfilled their international obligations in relation to the protection of refugees.

Conclusion

Deterrence strategies breach the States' responsibilities under human rights law, expose refugees to persecution, torture or other inhuman treatment and violate the right to fair asylum procedure. The States' responsibilities and the migrants' right not to be refouled and also not to be exposed to risk of torture or inhuman treatment overcome the States' right to control the entry of migrants and to safeguard national security, security of the community or public order. Governments should establish procedures for the routine exchange of information concerning attacks on asylum-seekers at sea and for the apprehension of those responsible, and should cooperate between each other for the regular exchange of general information on the matter; and that no one who has been tortured or ill-treated, or faces a risk of such treatment, will have to experience any treatment akin to this while looking for safety and protection. A State is bound by its obligation under Article 33(1) of the 1951 Convention not to return refugees to a risk of persecution wherever it exercises effective jurisdiction. As with non-refoulement obligations under international human rights law, the decisive criterion is not whether such persons are on the State's territory, but rather, whether they come within the effective control and authority of that State.

---

[9] Euro-Mediterranean Human Rights Network (EMHRN), Violations of the Rights of Migrants and Refugees at Sea, June 2014, available at: http://www.refworld.org/ docid/56fccbcbd.html

References

Achiume T. E., Aleinikoff T. A., Cavallaro J., Chetail V., Cryer R., Shamas D., … Van Schaack B., (2017), 'The Situation in Nauru and Manus Island: Liability for crimes against humanity in the detention of refugees and asylum seekers', Communiqué to the Office of the Prosecutor of the International Criminal Court Under Article 15 of the Rome Statute, Available at: https://www-cdn.law.stanford.edu/wp-content/uploads/2017/02/ Communiqué-to-Office-Prosecutor-IntlCrimCt-Art15RomeStat-14Feb2017.pdf

Amnesty International, Amnesty International Report 2016/17 - Bulgaria, 22 February 2017, available at: http://www.refworld.org/docid/58b0341613.html

Amnesty International, EU-Turkey deal: Greek decision highlights fundamental flaws, 20 May 2016, available at: http://www.refworld.org/docid/5742b63b4.html

Cambridge University Press, The Scope and Content of the Principle of Non-Refoulement: Opinion, June 2003, available at: http://www.refworld.org/docid/470a33af0.html

Council of Europe: Committee of Ministers, Declaration on Territorial Asylum, 18 November 1977, available at: http://www.refworld.org/docid/3ae6b3611c.html

Council of Europe: Committee of Ministers, Resolution (67) 14 : Asylum to Persons in Danger of Persecution, 29 June 1967, 14 (1967), available at: http://www.refworld.org/docid/3ae6b38168.html

Council of Europe: Parliamentary Assembly, Monitoring the return of irregular migrants and failed asylum seekers by land, sea and air, 7 November 2013, Doc. 13351, available at: http://www.refworld.org/docid/52f49c9f4.html

European Commission, Return Handbook (annex to Commission Recommendation of 1.10.2015 establishing a common 'Return Handbook' to be used by Member States' competent authorities when carrying out return related tasks), available at http://ec.europa.eu/dgs/home-affairs/what-we-do/policies/european-agenda-migration/proposal-implementation-package/docs/return_handbook_en.pdf

European Court of Human Rights (ECtHR), case of Saadi v Italy, 2008, available at: http://hudoc.echr.coe.int/eng?i=001-85276#{"itemid":["001-85276"]}

European Court of Human Rights (ECtHR), factsheet 'Collective expulsions of aliens', September 2015, available at: http://www.echr.coe.int/Documents/ FS_Collective _expulsions_ENG.pdf

European Court of Human Rights (ECtHR), factsheet 'Dublin Cases', July 2015, available at: http://www.echr.coe.int/Documents/FS_Dublin_ENG.pdf

European Court of Human Rights (ECtHR), factsheet 'Expulsions and extraditions', July 2013, available at: http://www.echr.coe.int/Documents/FS_Expulsions_Extraditions_ENG.pdf

European Union: European Agency for Fundamental Rights, Scope of the principle of non-refoulement in contemporary border management: evolving areas of law, December 2016, available at: http://www.refworld.org/docid/5857b3bb4.html

European Union: European Agency for Fundamental Rights, Guidance on how to reduce the risk of refoulement in external border management when working in or together with third countries, December 2016, available at: http://www.refworld.org/docid/ 5857b2b94.html

European Union: European Agency for Fundamental Rights, Fundamental Rights Report 2016, May 2016, available at: http://www.refworld.org/docid/574fce384.html

European Union: European Agency for Fundamental Rights, Opinion of the European Union Agency for Fundamental Rights concerning an EU common list of safe countries of origin, 23 March 2016, available at: http://www.refworld.org/docid/576d48a94.html

Fundamental Rights Agency (FRA), Fundamental rights at Europe's southern sea borders, available at https://fra.europa.eu/sites/default/files/fundamental-rights-europes-southern-sea-borders-jul-13_en.pdf

Fundamental Rights Agency (FRA), Handbook on European law relating to asylum, borders and immigration, available at: http://fra.europa.eu/sites/default/files/handbook-law-asylum-migration-borders-2nded_en.pdf

Gammeltoft-Hansen T. and Hathaway J., (2015), 'Non-refoulement in a World of Cooperative Deterrence.', Columbia Journal of Transnational Law, Vol. 53 No. 2, pp.235- 85.

Gammeltoft-Hansen T. and Tan N. F., (2017), 'The End of the Deterrence Paradigm? Future Directions for Global Refugee Policy', Journal on Migration and Human Security 2017 by the Center for Migration Studies of New York, Vol. 5 No. 1, pp. 28-56.

Hungarian Helsinki Committee, Pushed Back at the Door: Denial of Access to Asylum in Eastern EU

Member States, 2017, available at: http://www.refworld.org/docid/5888b5234.html

International Association of Refugee Law Judges, Extraterritorial Effect of Non-Refoulement, 9 September 2011, available at: http://www.refworld.org/docid/557030f64.html

International Commission of Jurists (ICJ), Procedural rights in the proposed Dublin IV Regulation" - Comments of the International Commission of Jurists on specific procedural measures in the Recast of the Dublin Regulation, 27 September 2016, available at: http://www.refworld.org/docid/57ee6de04.html

Morris J. C., (2003), 'The Spaces In Between: American and Australian Interdiction Policies and *Their Implications for the Refugee Protection Regime*', Interdiction at the Expense of Human Rights, Refuge, Vol. 21 No. 4, pp. 51-62.

Office of the United Nations High Commissioner for Refugees (UNHCR), UNHCR Manual on Refugee Protection and the ECHR Part 4.1 Selected Case Law on Article 3, available at http://www.refworld.org/pdfid/3f4cd5c74.pdf

Office of the United Nations High Commissioner for Refugees (UNHCR), UNHCR Manual on Refugee Protection and the ECHR Part 2.1 – Fact Sheet on Article 3, available at: http://www.unhcr.org/3ead2d262.pdf

Office of the United Nations High Commissioner for Refugees (UNHCR), Rescue at Sea. A Guide to Principles and Practice as Applied to Refugees and Migrants, January 2015, available at: http://www.refworld.org/docid/54b365554.htm

Overseas Development Institute (ODI), Closing borders: the ripple effects of Australian and European refugee policy. Case studies from Indonesia, Kenya and Jordan, September 2016, available at: http://www.refworld.org/docid/57dbed964.html

Sir Elihu Lauterpacht and Daniel Bethlehem, The scope and content of the principle of non-refoulement: Opinion, available at: http://www.unhcr.org/419c75ce4.pdf

UN General Assembly, Declaration on Territorial Asylum, 14 December 1967, A/RES/2312(XXII), available at: http://www.refworld.org/docid/3b00f05a2c.html

UN High Commissioner for Refugees (UNHCR), La protection des refugies en droit international, 2008, available at: http://www.refworld.org/docid/5177ffda4.html

UN High Commissioner for Refugees (UNHCR), UNHCR Note on the Principle of Non-Refoulement, November 1997, available at: http://www.refworld.org/docid/438c6d972.html

UN High Commissioner for Refugees (UNHCR), Advisory Opinion on the Extraterritorial Application of Non-Refoulement Obligations under the 1951 Convention relating to the Status of Refugees and its 1967 Protocol, 26 January 2007, available at: http://www.refworld.org/docid/45f17a1a4.html

UN High Commissioner for Refugees (UNHCR), Note on Non-Refoulement (Submitted by the High Commissioner), 23 August 1977, EC/SCP/2, available at: http://www.refworld.org/docid/3ae68ccd10.html

UN High Commissioner for Refugees (UNHCR), Regional Refugee and Migrant Response Plan for Europe - Eastern Mediterranean and Western Balkans Route, January-December 2016, January 2016, available at: http://www.refworld.org/docid/56a9e5134.html

UN News Service, UN rights chief concerned over 'collective expulsion' of migrants after EU-Turkey deal, 24 March 2016, available at: http://www.refworld.org/docid/ 56fa200840d.html

United States Department of State, Office of the Historian, The League of Nations, 1920 https://history.state.gov/milestones/1914-1920/league

Univ.-Prof. MMag. Dr. August Reinisch, LL.M /Mag. Melanie Fink, University of Vienna, Non-Refoulement and Extraterritorial Immigration Control – The 15. Case of Immigration Liaison Officers', available at https://intlaw.univie.ac.at/fileadmin/user_upload/ int_beziehungen/ Internetpubl/Baxewanosl.pdf

Vedsted-Hansen J., (1999), '*Europe's Response to the Arrival of Asylum Seekers: Refugee Protection and Immigration Control*', New Issues in Refugee Research, No. 6, Geneva: UNHCR.

LEGAL AND CIRCULAR MIGRATION IN THE EUROPEAN UNION MOBILITY PARTNERSHIPS

Katarzyna A. Morawska[*]

Introduction

Until quite recently, the European Union did not hold competence in the field of the immigration policy. For many years, following the initiation of the process of European integration, it was a sphere within the competence of the Member States. It was the creation of the Schengen area and the common market that induced the actions leading to the gradual introduction of immigration policy regulations at the EU level. It should be emphasized that in the context of the EU, immigration policy regards the arrival and stay of third-country nationals (non-members of the EU) in the territory of a Member State, and it does not concern entirely free movement of persons within the EU.

The breakthrough moment for the development of the immigration policy at the EU level was the integration of issues related to asylum and immigration into the third pillar of Justice and Home Affairs (JHA) based on the intergovernmental cooperation, and then transferring this area to the first pillar, the so-called communitarisation. Consequently, since the adoption of the Treaty of Amsterdam, immigration policy has been covered by the EU regime (Borawska-Kędzierska, Strąk, 2011, p.10). The Treaty of Lisbon, valid since 2009, confirms the EU's commitment to matters related to population movements, recognizing immigration policy as a shared competence between the EU and Member States.

The attitude of the EU and Member States to the common immigration policy changed significantly after the immigration crisis of 2015, when it turned out that the EU is not able to effectively protect its borders against the increased influx of third-country nationals. Lots of them passed the EU boarders without having their fingerprints collected. The inefficiency of the EU mechanisms in the field of asylum policy was discernible as clearly as the lack of solidarity between the Member States in this matter. The EU countries took and still do take different stands on the migrant relocation plan. Let us take the example of the approach favoured by Central and Eastern European countries, in particular the Visegrad Group countries, which do not attract the interest of refugees and have not experienced any "threats" from immigrants from Syria, Eritrea or Afghanistan, but are the first to criticize the relocation system proposed by the European Commission.

---

* Katarzyna A. Morawska, PhD, Lecturer and research officer in the Emigration Museum in Gdynia, ul. Świętojańska 45/31, 81-368 Gdynia. E-mail: k.morawska@muzeumemigracji.pl, kata.morawska@wp.pl.

It is therefore not surprising that in such circumstances, a discussion concerning legal migration has been pushed into the background, and most Member States distanced themselves from the idea of creating at the EU level attractive conditions for the arrival and residence of third-country nationals. Nonetheless, for more than two decades, the European Commission has been stressing that demographic forecasts indicate that in the near future the EU will increasingly dependent on migrant labour, which in many Member States can be seen with the naked eye even today. Moreover, the European Commission recalls, promoted since 2000, stand emphasizing the need for effective cooperation with third countries in the field of migration in order to efficiently prevent illegal immigration to the EU (European Commission, 2001). What is important today, care must be taken to make sure that the refugee crisis and its consequences will not make the activities in the field of legal migration to the Member States limited or completely abandoned, and that the European Union will not become a closed fortress. Therefore, it is worth reminding the idea of Mobility Partnerships, which since the beginning of the 21st century have been promoted in the EU as a multidisciplinary tool facilitating cooperation in the field of broadly understood migration and mobility.

The purpose of this article is to elucidate the Mobility Partnerships under the European immigration policy as well as the analysis of their assumptions contained in the documents of the EU institutions. The partnerships are non-binding agreements concluded between the Member States of the European Union and third countries, the purpose of which is broadly understood cooperation in the field of migration management. The article is particularly concerned with mobility that is supporting the legal migration, including circular migration of third-country nationals to the EU.

The conducted research is predominantly of theoretical and qualitative nature. The first part of the paper presents the characteristics of Mobility Partnerships. The theoretical assumptions of Mobility Partnerships have been subjected to a legal and comparative analysis, which is followed by their confrontation with the actual provisions of the signed declarations. In the sections devoted to the analysis of official documents of the European Union the dogmatic method has been applied. The analysis of Eurostat and OECD statistics provides a source of information on the initial changes in the number of third-country nationals flowing to particular Member States from the countries which were the first to sign the Mobility Partnerships. The conducted research and the critical evaluation of the source materials, mainly the literature on the subject, made it possible to evaluate the adopted Mobility Partnerships and propose a few recommendations.

The concept of Mobility Partnerships

In December 2005, the European Council adopted the so-called global approach to migration, which assumes broad cooperation between the EU Member States and countries from which arrive the highest numbers of immigrants (European Council, 2005, p.2). The global approach aims to combine all political migration strategies in a more coherent way. Mobility Partnerships established between the EU and third countries are a key instrument supposed to foster implementation of the global approach to migration (European Commission,

2006). That is why Mobility Partnerships are seen as a multidimensional concept as they affect not only the EU immigration policy but also different fields of policy, e.g. external security, labour market policy, development policy, neighbourhood policy (Brocza/Paulhart, 2015, p.3). Moreover, they are intended to create "triple win" situation by offering opportunities of legal migration to third country nationals, supporting the development of countries of origin and supplying EU Member States with much needed labour migrants.

According to the communication published in 2007, Mobility Partnerships are supposed to foster effective management of migration flows (European Commission, 2007, p.9-10). The EU aims to create in this way a framework for dialogue and cooperation with countries in its immediate neighbourhood and with countries whose citizens have been entering the EU for a long time (i.e. Morocco, Tunisia, Egypt). In practice Mobility Partnership

> *is supposed to be put together and, in association with interested Member States, negotiated by the EC with third countries that have committed themselves to cooperating actively with the EU on management of migration flows, includingby fighting against illegal migration, and that are interested in securing better access to EU territory for their citizens (European Commission, 2007, p.3).*

Mobility Partnerships are a legal instrument, quite characteristic for the EU, which fall into the soft law category, i.e. their provisions are devoid of legally binding force. They can therefore be regarded as a political declaration made between a particular Member State and a third country. It entails the lack of jurisdiction of the Court of Justice of the EU, as the provisions of the partnerships do not fall within the jurisdiction of the Court. The institution responsible for the negotiation, adoption and implementation of the partnerships is the European Commission.

The accession of Member States to partnerships with individual third countries is not mandatory. Partnerships are an instrument of a complex legal nature owing to the fact that their provisions do not always fall within the scope of the EU powers. Although in accordance with the provisions of the Treaty of Amsterdam plenty of the issues related to asylum and migration were "communized", the decision on admission of migrant workers in the territory of the Member States remains a national competence (Art. 79 TFEU).

The cited Communication of the Commission contains, however, a number of elements that can be included in the content of the Mobility Partnerships. These are both obligations of third countries as well as of Member States. Among the postulates to be fulfilled by third countries one can find, among others, effective readmission of own citizens and cooperation in determining their identity and, under certain circumstances, readmission of third-country nationals and stateless persons who entered the EU through the territory of a given Member State. In addition, third countries should undertake initiatives to reduce the scale of illegal immigration, streamline border controls and prevent forging travel documents. Combat against smuggling and human trafficking is of equal importance. In order to eliminate illegal immigration, the EU partners may be also required to undertake to improve their economic and social situation. Implementation of the partnerships assumes full respect for fundamental rights of individuals and provides financial and technical assistance to third countries. On the other hand, Member States commit themselves to introduce

> *mechanisms facilitating labour migration, which should correspond to the labour market needs of the concerned Member States, in line with their assessment, with full respect of the principle of the Community preference for EU citizens (European Commission, 2007, p.5).*

Properly formulated provisions can prevent the phenomenon of brain drain, i.e. the outflow of educated citizens. The Member States should also take actions to streamline the procedure for issuing short-stay visas to third-country nationals, which should contribute to an increased interest in legal forms of migration.

Mobility Partnerships in practice

The first Mobility Partnerships were signed in 2008 with Moldova and the Republic of Cape Verde (Council of the European Union, 2008). Both documents, deemed as a model for other agreements, provide for the promotion of solutions supporting legal migration accompanied by reduction of illegal migration flows. It is worth emphasizing, however, that the latest partnerships (with Jordan, Tunisia and Belarus) no longer contain annexes detailing specific initiatives proposed by individual states or the European Commission. The history of mobility partnerships is presented in Table 1.

Table 1. The History of Mobility Partnerships in the EU

Date	Country	EU Members States
2008	Moldova	Bulgaria, Cyprus, Czech Republic, France, Germany, Greece, Hungary, Italy, Lithuania, Poland, Portugal, Romania, Slovakia, Slovenia, Sweden
2008	Cape Verde	France, Luksemburg, Portugal, Spain
2009	Georgia	Belgium, Bulgaria, Czech Republic, Denmark, Estonia, France, Germany, Great Britain, Greece, Italy, Netherlands, Latvia, Lithuania, Poland, Romania, Sweden
2011	Armenia	Belgium, Bulgaria, Czech Republic, France, Germany, Italy, Netherlands, Poland, Romania, Sweden
2013	Marocco	Belgium, France, Germany, Great Britain, Italy, Netherlands Portugal, Spain, Sweden,
2013	Azerbaijan	Bulgaria, Czech Republic, France, Lithuania, Netherlands, Poland, Slovakia, Slovenia
2014	Jordan	Cyprus, Denmark, France, Germany, Greece, Hungary, Italy, Poland, Portugal, Romania, Spain, Sweden
2014	Tunisia	Belgium, Denmark, France, Germany, Great Britain, Italy, Poland, Portugal, Spain, Sweden
2015	Belarus	Bulgaria, Finland, Hungary, Latvia, Lithuania, Poland, Romania

Source: elaborated by the author based on the European Commision's Mobility Partnerships documents

The partnerships begin with a very similar preamble referring to the existing forms of cooperation between Member States and partner countries and to the key EU documents on migration (i.e. to European Commission communications and Council conclusions). In the introduction the parties undertake to facilitate population flows and better manage migration movements, including combat against illegal immigration. The provisions of the first partnerships focus on three main themes: mobility, legal migration and integration; migration and development; border management, travel documents and fight against illegal migration and human trafficking. Partnership with Armenia has initiated cooperation in the issues of international protection and asylum (Council of the European Union, 2011). Each category contains some more detailed assumptions of the contracting parties.

In the first group of activities directly related to legal migration, we can highlight the most often repeated elements, i.e. enhancement of the institutional capacity of the partner countries in the area of migration, providing potential migrants with accurate information on the possibilities of legal work, living standards in the Member States and risks associated with illegal arrival and employment in the EU, as well as ensuring social protection for migrants.

The declarations contain also provisions on the practical implementation of the Mobility Partnerships. These agreements are considered as a long-term form of cooperation based on a political dialogue that will evolve over time. There are scheduled regular meetings (twice a year) at an appropriate level in order to review priorities of the partnerships and to evaluate them. The partnership promise the implementation of initiatives aimed at maximizing the positive impact of migration on the development of third countries through, among other things, encouraging financial transfers made by migrants and promoting circulation and returns of foreign workers to their home countries. Another significant element is also the promise of a mechanism monitoring the movement of people and assessing the impact of migration on the domestic labour market. The last part of the partnerships is an annex which contains proposals for concrete measures aimed at realization of the assumptions contained therein. Individual projects are an initiative of the parties - the Member States, the partner country, the European Commission or several specified partners.

Analysing the partnerships as a whole, it is clearly observed that the signed declarations focus mainly on two aspects – the enhanced border control and the fight against illegal immigration. What stems from the provisions of the partnerships is the observation that the Member States are more interested in the tightened control or even reduction in the flow of population, rather than in the increased legal mobility of third-country nationals (Parkes, 2009, p.2). Economic migration, migrants' rights or mutual recognition of workers' qualifications have been marginalized, and issues related to family reunification or migrant integration in the Member States have been almost completely ignored. The resignation from provisions on labour migration was probably the result of the EU's lack of competence in certain areas - the Member States did not agree to delegate to the organization the competences related to economic migration, which remains a sphere of competence attributable to the Member States. This explains why the Mobility Partnerships, on the one hand, are not focused on the regulation of labour migration and, on the other one, are not binding.

Legal and circular migration in Mobility Partnership

Analysing the Mobility Partnerships assumptions with regard to legal and circular migration, it is possible to indicate several elements which, if actually implemented, may contribute to fostering of this kind of population movements to the Member States. In the first place, it should be noted that legal migration to the EU includes not only the labour migration but also the migration of students and trainees.

One of the aspects that underlie the Mobility Partnerships is the relatedness of migration to the development of sending countries. To avoid the adverse phenomenon in the form of the brain drain, which means the departure of skilled employees, the Commission promotes circular migration schemes. The concept of circular migration itself has been gaining importance in the EU since 2007, when there was published a communication devoted entirely to the circular migration and Mobility Partnerships (European Commission, 2007). In this document, the Commission adopts a general definition of circular migration (*form of migration that is managed in a way allowing some degree of legal mobility back and forth between two countries*) and announces the creation of an effective legal basis that would support the circular form of movement. Mobility Partnerships are supposed to be one of the ways to implement circular migration. The concept of circular migration, as well as the idea of mobility partnerships, assumes the previously mentioned triple win situation. Thanks to the circular migration, the receiving countries may eliminate shortages of employees, countries of origin benefit from cash transfers from emigrants and - in the future - from the acquired knowledge and experience, while migrants are provided with a legal source of additional income and a chance for professional development without a permanent change of residence. At the same time, circulation reduces the threat associated with the brain drain in the migrants' countries of origin. What is more, the temporary and circular migration perfectly fit in the current migration trends in Europe. At the time when the growing number of immigrants is not perceived favourably by European societies, the solutions promoting temporary residence in the Member States are more likely to gain greater acceptance.

The visa facilitations, also provided for as a component of Mobility Partnerships, can trigger third-country nationals' interest in legal migration. The vehicle of the partnerships promises also an increase in the efficiency of consular services, facilitation of the access to these institutions and more staff in the most frequently visited ones. It can be assumed that a shorter visa waiting time, its lower costs or the introduction of other procedural facilitations will yield an increased scale of legal immigration resulting from the signed partnerships. Facilitation in the issuance of short-stay visas may positively affect the aforementioned threat of the brain drain and contribute to a more desired phenomenon, i.e. the brain circulation.

Here, we should put the question: to what extent the abovementioned proposals of the European Commission regarding legal migration are reflected in the adopted declarations? The analysis of the partnerships signed so far makes it possible to draw the following conclusions.

Regarding the provisions supporting legal migration to the Member States all agreements contain provisions on the need to effectively inform potential migrants on employment opportunities and living conditions in the EU countries as well as on risks of illegal migration (for example Joint declaration establishing a Mobility Partnership between the European Union and the Republic of Moldova, p.5-6 ; Joint declaration establishing a Mobility Partnership between the Hashemite Kingdom of Jordan and the European Union and its participating Member States, p.4,). For this purpose, it is proposed, among others, cooperation with the European employment portal, seminars and exchanges of information between institutions and bodies responsible for managing the population flows, and even preparation of a manual containing relevant information on residence and employment in EU countries for potential migrants. In addition, the provisions of all Mobility Partnerships stipulate support of the Member States for all institutions and their staff, including employment agencies and state bodies involved in migration management.

The Partnerships include also proposals to introduce measures that will facilitate obtaining visas for migrant workers, temporary work and migrants' circulation programmes as well as recognition of professional and academic qualifications of partner countries citizens. Particular attention has been paid to students and young professionals who have been offered various forms of mobility to the EU. Collaboration of academic centres in order to enable the exchange of students and researchers is also incorporated. In an overwhelming majority of partnerships, for instance with Armenia, Azerbaijan, Belarus, Moldova there is a promise of special courses on entry procedures and integration measures in host countries for future migrants in order to prepare them for their stay and work in the EU to be taken even before leaving a home country. The actual implementation of the abovementioned provisions in practice remains the key issue.

Evaluation of Mobility Partnership

The European Commission is convinced of the effectiveness of the Mobility Partnerships and points out that the lack of binding force of the declarations makes it less time-consuming to adopt them in comparison with legal acts with binding force (European Policy Center, 2012). In the communication, which evaluates the first Mobility Partnerships signed with Moldova and the Republic of Cape Verde, the institution emphasizes their flexibility - they can be quickly adapted to the current needs of the partners (European Commission, 2009, p.4). At the same time, as documents of political nature, they do not require ratification and implementation in partner countries, which significantly shortens the entry into force of the agreements. At any moment, the project may be joined by interested countries, which was the case with the Netherlands, that joined the partnership several months after signing the declaration with Cape Verde.

According to the Commission, the signed agreements are the most innovative and highly developed instrument for implementation of the global approach to migration. It is estimated that the partnerships meet the assumptions and priorities of both the EU and partner countries. The only risk involved in this form of cooperation is the collection of actions taken individually by the Member States in the framework of their existing cooperation and their replication in the partnership.

This argument is quite often quoted in the literature, as Member States are reluctant to duplicate their actions, especially when the existing forms of cooperation function well (Reslow, 2010a, p.17). In its evaluation of Mobility Partnerships, the Commission emphasizes the fact that this mechanism is versatile and comprehensively reflects all elements of the global approach to migration, whereas the instruments used so far have focused only on its selected aspects (European Commission, 2009, p.6).

The advantage of the partnerships is their complementarity with other Community policies, instruments and the EU measures in the areas of migration and their positive impact on strengthening ties with partner countries. The EU joint activities in the sphere of migration strengthens the national migration policy whose implementation only at the national level is increasingly difficult (Reslow, 2010b, p.4). The evaluation of the agreements given by the Commission is, therefore, definitely positive, and the institution seems to be full of optimism when it comes to the future of the partnerships.

The European Commission focuses mainly on the positive aspects of the Mobility Partnerships, however, the objective assessment of the agreements is not clear. Above all, the question arises as to the actual promotion of legal migration to the EU. It is quite difficult to conclusively assess the impact of the legal migration initiatives on the actual increase in labour migration from the partner countries to the EU. Currently, statistical data is the only way to evaluate the effectiveness of the partnerships. This method is not conclusive, as it does not indicate the extent to which the signed agreements have contributed to changes in the flow of the partner countries nationals to the Member States. In addition, most of the statistical data does not cover temporary migrants. Despite these difficulties, it is worth having a look at statistics reflecting the number of migrants in particular countries. The analysis of Eurostat statistical data conducted by N. Reslow points to the lack of impact of the partnerships signed with Moldova, Armenia, Georgia and the Republic of Cape Verde on the number of short-stay visas issued to nationals of these countries or residence permits in the Member States (Reslow, 2015, p.119-120).

The statistical data presented by the OECD gives similar conclusions as to the changes in the number of immigrants from Moldova, the Republic of Cape Verde, Georgia and Armenia, which occurred since the conclusion of the individual partnerships until 2014 (OECD, 2016). As in the case of the Eurostat data, it is difficult to identify a clear impact on the scale of migration to the Member States that are parties to the partnerships. In the case of Moldova, only in Germany it was noted an increase in the number of immigrants in 2008-2013 (699 people in 2008, 1039 in 2013). Other EU countries noted in that time significant declines in the influx of citizens of Moldova (for example in Italy the decline from 22 000 in 2008 to 3 700 in 2014). A similar situation concerns citizens of the Republic of Cape Verde - the increased inflow was noted in France, whereas in Spain and Portugal the number of Cape Verdeans has decreased. Growth trends are more pronounced in the case of Georgia, as in most of the partner countries the number of immigrants from this country increased (particularly in Germany and Italy). Mixed trends are also visible in statistics for Armenia. In several Member States, including

Belgium, France and in particular Germany, the number of immigrants from Armenia has increased since the Mobility Partnership was signed. There are also countries such as the Czech Republic and Poland, where these numbers fell, as well as those where major changes in the number of citizens from Armenia were not observed (Italy).

Hence, it is difficult to talk about the real impact of the partnerships on mobility. However, it should be stressed that these statistics may change in the long term. What is more, the mobility of migrants is affected by various factors which might not be related to the signed declarations, for example the economic and political situations or social moods. Reliable sources showing a direct impact of the signed declarations on the increase in immigration to the Member States do not exist, which unfortunately hiders research in this area.

Too much focus on the obligation to readmit its citizens and better border controls, imposed on third countries by Member States, is a strong objection to Mobility Partnerships. One may get the impression that readmission and fight against illegal immigration (and not legal immigration or mobility)are the core of these agreements. Such an approach stems from the fact that only in such a way, i.e. offering to partner countries certain facilitations and aid in the management of migration and the obscure promise of legal migration, the EU is able to gain consent to the readmission of citizens of these countries (Carrera, Hernandez, Sagrera, 2009, p.19). Third countries have a negative attitude to the condition of readmission, in which they can see benefits only for the EU (Cassarino, 2008, p.8). This reluctance stems from costs and financial burden associated with the implementation of the readmission agreements. This procedure is not in the interest of third countries whose economies benefit from money transfers sent by migrants, regardless of whether their stay is legal or not. A. Triandafyllidou rightly notices that it is hard to believe that the partner countries are able to meet the demanding expectations of the EU (Triandafyllidou, 2009, p.2). A long list of requirements that third countries must fulfil to win "the prize" in the form of a Mobility Partnership, such as boarder control, readmission agreement or fight against illegal immigration, may make their provisions not viable.

Mobility Partnerships, despite a positive implication of their name, are not entirely based on cooperation between equal partners sharing the same objectives (Kunz, Maisenbacher 2013, p.201). A negotiating position of European countries is certainly stronger, especially if the declaration is to be signed by a few or a dozen of EU countries. The real contribution of third countries in the creation of the projects is then thought-provoking. For example, Georgia or Morocco did not propose any initiatives contained in the agreement on their own. J.P. Cassarino drew attention to double selectivity of the partnerships (Cassarino, 2009). On the one hand, they are signed by countries which undertake to implement conditions set by the EU (concerning readmission, border protection, etc.). On the other one, they only apply to certain categories of immigrants, who have the possibility to take advantage of the proposed forms of arrival to the EU Member States. Moreover, provisions of the partnerships bind only the Member States which signed them, while the readmission agreements apply to the whole territory of the EU (Martin, 2012, p.313-314).

The fact that the partnerships are not legally binding and participation in them depends solely on the will of the Member States, , can be an advantage, but on the otherhand, may adversely affect the integrity and legitimacy of the EU policy (Carrera, Hernandez, Sagrera, 2009, p.36). It suffices to look at the number of the EU countries which joined the partnerships. Many countries signed the declaration with Georgia (16) and Moldova (15), while only five are parties to the agreement with the Republic of Cape Verde.[1] There are countries that are involved in several partnerships (France, Poland, Belgium) and those that do not participate in any project (Austria, Finland, Malta). Countries decide to sign a declaration when cooperation with the given country is in their national interest and is consistent with their policy (Reslow, 2010a). Hence, we can see the clear division: states from the southern regions of Europe are interested in cooperation with the Mediterranean countries and Africa while other Member States prefer cooperation with the region of Eastern Europe.

It seems that voluntary participation in the partnerships is after all a good idea. In this case, they are joined by states which really seek cooperation, which greatly increases the likelihood of compliance with the commitments. The aspect which has already been raised is the actual added value of Mobility Partnerships. In the case of the declaration with the Republic of Cape Verde, whose signatories are Portugal, Spain, France and Luxembourg, most of the initiatives contained in the document are proposals made by one of the EU countries. It should be noted that these initiatives had been expressed before in bilateral agreements concluded between the Member States and the Republic of Cape Verde (Chou, Gibert 2010, p.10). Therefore, the question arises, to what extent it is a new form of multilateral cooperation, and to what it is simply gathering together projects that had existed before. It is also wondering why proposals for specific measures to be undertaken by individual Member States were skipped in the recent declarations.

Recommendations

The analysis of the Mobility Partnerships assumptions in terms of legal migration and their actual presence in the signed declarations allows to put forward several recommendations, whose aim is to increase the effectiveness of the partnerships in the promotion of legal movements to the EU. Above all, the partnerships lack a multilateral dimension. The vast majority of initiatives comes from individual entities rather than several states, which makes the declarations look as a few or a dozen bilateral agreements contained in one document. Therefore, it is worth putting more emphasis on taking a joint action. Many times Member States had the opportunity to realise that enhanced cooperation between countries yields tangible results. A near-ideal situation would be the creation of a partially open labour market for third-country nationals in the Member States that have decided to join the partnership with a given country. Migrant workers could then move freely between the Member States in search of work, and they could also enjoy the same rights everywhere.

Practice shows that the implementation of visa facilitations, although

---

[1] The Netherlands joined the partnership a few months after it was signed.

emphasised in most of the adopted declarations, is not too successful in reality. In contrast to the European Commission, the EU Council highlights that visa facilitation should be conditional upon concluded readmission agreements (Angenendt, 2014). Short-term visas for temporary and circular migrants should be one of the main instruments supporting mobility between the signatories of the partnerships. There is still a lot to be done by the Member States.

In order to be able to draw on experience, the EU institutions, particularly the European Commission, should evaluate the partnerships on an ongoing basis and adapt them to the current needs. The partnerships were supposed to be inherently flexible, "living" documents, to evolve over time. So far, the evaluation of the signed partnerships is missing (apart from the declarations with Moldova and Cape Verde). In addition, none of the signed declarations has changed its content since they were signed, which clearly shows that these are not specifically flexible acts. It is not only about the evaluations carried out by the European Commission itself but also about more extensive evaluations carried out in cooperation with signatory states, and even with individual national actors directly involved in the implementation of the partnerships, such as ministries, government agencies, etc.

Last but not least, Mobility Partnerships also lack good publicity. The signed declarations should be implemented and recognized as flagship projects and, therefore, ought to encourage other third countries to sign similar declarations with EU countries. One of the arguments why partnerships lack positive publicity may be as follows. For an effective promotion of partnerships, it is necessary to enjoy specific, measurable results and benefits resulting from their adoption. For now, however, the hard evidence of such results has not been found.

Conclusion

Cooperation in the field of legal migration may lead to better coordination and coherence of activities, but looking at the signed declarations certainly we cannot talk about revolutionary changes. Due to not very advanced stage of implementation of the agreements and the lack of their thorough evaluation by the EU, it is difficult to clearly indicate positive effects noted by the participating states. However, we should hope that in the face of the current immigration crisis, the European Union will finally take concrete actions in terms of effective migration management at European level. The analysis of the Mobility Partnerships carried out in this article points to the untapped potential of this instrument, which despite its weaknesses, may positively affect the European immigration policy.

References

Angenendt S. (2014). EU Mobility Partnerships: the „most innovative and sophisticated tool" of European migration policy?, Migration Strategy Group on Global Competitiveness.

Borawska-Kędzierska E., Strąk K. (2011). Przestrzeń Wolności, Bezpieczeństwa i Sprawiedliwości. Zarządzanie granicami, polityka wizowa, azylowa i imigracyjna, Instytut Wydawniczy EuroPrawo, Warsaw 2011: 10.

Carrera, S., Hernandez, Sagrera, R. (2009). The Externalisation of the EU's Labour Immigration Policy. Towards Mobility or Insecurity Partnerships?, Centre for European Policy Studies, Working Document No. 321/2009: 19.

Cassarino, J.P. (2008). Patterns of Circular Migration in the Euro – Mediterranean Area: Implications for Policy – Making, CARIM 2008/29: 8.

Cassarino, J.P. (2009). EU Mobility Partnerships: Expression of a New Compromise, received from:

http://www.migrationinformation.org/Feature/display.cfm?ID=741 (date: January 27, 2014).

Chou, M.H., Gibert, M. (2010). From Cotonou to Circular Migration: the EU, Senegal, and the "Agreement Duplicity", Paper for "Migration: A world in Motion", Maastricht, the Netherlands, 18 – 20 February 2010: 10.

Council of the European Union (2008). Joint Declaration on a Mobility Partnership between the European Union and the Republic of Moldova, 9460/08 ADD 1, Brussels 2008.

Council of the European Union (2008). Joint Declaration on a Mobility Partnership between the European Union and the Republic of Cape Verde, 9460/08 ADD 1, Brussels 2008.

Council of the European Union (2011). Joint Declaration on a Mobility Partnership between the European Union and Armenia, 14963/11 ADD 1, Brussels 2011.

European Commission (2001). A common policy on legal illegal migration, COM (2001) 672.

European Commission (2006). Global Approach to Migration a Year Later: Towards a Comprehensive European Migration Policy, COM (2006) 735.

European Commission (2007). Communication on Circular Migration and Mobility Partnerships between the European Union and Third Countries, COM (2007) 248.

European Commission (2009). Commission Staff Working Document Mobility partnerships as a tool of the Global Approach to Migration, SEC (2009) 1240.

European Council (2005). Presidency Conclusions, 15-16 December 2005, European Council Summit in Hampton Court.

European Policy Center (2012). Mobility partnerships - An effecitive tool for EU external migration policy?, received from: http://www.epc.eu/events_rep_details .php?cat_id=6&pub_id =2696 (date: January 25, 2014).

Kunz, R., Maisenbacher, J. (2013). Beyond conditionality versus cooperation: Power and resistance in the case of EU mobility partnerships and Swiss migration partnerships, Migration Studies, Vol. 1 No. 2/2013: 201.

Martin, M. (2012). Extension des partenariats pour la mobilite avec les partenariats euro –mediterraneens, received from: http://www.iemed.org/observatori-fr/areesdanalisi arxiusadjunts/anuari /med..2012/ martin_fr.pdf (date: January 30, 2014).

Organisation for Economic Cooperation and Development (2016). https://stats.oecd.org/ Index. aspx? DataSetCode= MIG (dostęp: 6 października 2016 r.).

Parkes, R. (2009). Mobility Partnerships: valuable addition to the ENP repertoire? A checklist for revitalising ENP, German Institute for International and Security Affaires, Working Paper FG 1, No. 03/2009, SWP Berlin.

Reslow, N. (2010a). The new politics of EU migration policy: analysing the decision – making proces of the Mobility Partnerships, Maastricht University, the Netherlands: 17.

Reslow, N. (2010b). Explaining the development of EU migration policy: the case of Mobility Partnerships, Paper prepared for the fifth Pan-European Conference on EU Politics, Porto, Portugal: 4.

Reslow, N. (2015). EU „Mobility" Partnerships: An initial assessment of implementation dynamics, Politics and Governance, Vol. 3, No. 2/2015: 119-120.

Triandafyllidou, A. (2009). Attemping the Impossible? The Prospects and Limits of Mobility Partnerships and Circular Migration, received from: http://www.eliamep.gr/wp-content/uploads/en/2009 /02/eliamep-thesis-1-2009-triandafyllidou.pdf (date: January 27, 2014).

DEVELOPING THE UNDERSTANDING OF MIGRANT INTEGRATION IN THE EU: IMPLICATIONS FOR HOUSING PRACTICES

Maria Psoinos[*] and **Orna Rosenfeld**[**]

Introduction: Mapping the Field of Migration, Housing and Integration

Integration has been persistently difficult to define across mobile populations (e.g. refugees, economic migrants, internally displaced persons) and across disciplines (Bretell & Hollifield, 2000). What is for sure is that it has been recently and unanimously changing from a rather static and one-sided phenomenon, where migrants have to shed their 'cultural distinctiveness' in order to blend into the majority culture (Heissler, 2000: 77), to an increasingly dynamic and multi-level process, owing to today's migrants' diverse characteristics and the social contexts they join.

As far as integration and housing is concerned: There is relative paucity of literature and policy in relation to the housing dimension of migrants' integration. While integration literature and strategies generally focus on issues related to migrants' citizenship, health provision, employment and education, housing as a central element of integration has received limited attention. This may be because housing is a taken-for-granted aspect of integration in the sense that everyone has to have a roof over their heads, but there are still important issues to be addressed when thinking about how housing conditions and location can affect the process of integration (Craig, 2015). Indeed, Phillimore (2013) has pertinently outlined the four roles that housing plays in the lives of migrants: as shelter, status and identity; as a nexus for social relationships; as a provider of safety and freedom; and as the site of the integration process.

In this context the present chapter is instrumental in clarifying the term 'integration' so that this can be realistically linked to the housing sector. The main aim of this chapter is to explore recent developments and aspects of the concept of 'integration' and examine critically how these aspects can be implemented (or not) in existing housing strategies for migrants. This can give insight to a better monitoring and understanding of migration and integration processes and ultimately to a greater effectiveness of these aspects of practices (and wider policies)

---

[*] Maria Psoinos, Visiting Research Fellow, Faculty of Health and Wellbeing, Canterbury Christ Church University, North Holmes Road, Canterbury, Kent, CT1 1QU, United Kingdom.
E-mail: m.psoinos471@canterbury.ac.uk.

[**] Orna Rosenfeld, Visiting Lecturer, Urban School –GLM, Sciences Po - Paris Institute of Political Studies, 117 Boulevard Saint-Germain, Paris 6, France. E-mail: orna.rosenfeld@sciencespo.fr and orna.rosenfeld@gmail.com.

in the housing sector.

Main Challenges in the Housing Sector in the EU

It is important to note the ongoing but also new challenges which affect housing in the EU: the economic downturn and recession in Europe has had a critical impact on the housing sector: over 80 million people in the region are housing cost overburdened (Eurostat, 2017). As a result of this crisis, the social and affordable housing sector faces two challenges: increased need and reduced funds (Rosenfeld, 2015).

Another challenge for many countries is understanding how to adapt to rapid demographic changes to ensure access to affordable housing, more inclusive neighbourhoods and higher quality of life (Tsenkova, 2016). By demographic changes we refer both to sheer numbers of people who migrate but also characteristics of newly arrived populations:

First, there is the fact that every month, 1 million people are added to the urban population globally (Tsenkova, 2016). In addition, this inflow of populations to urban centres has been dramatically increasing since 2015, due to the evident increase in global forced displacement with record-high numbers (UNHCR, 2015) (the ongoing influx of migrants and refugees from Syria and other conflict zones to the region is one such manifestation of the increase in forced migration).

Second, today's migrants and refugees emerge as more different from those of previous decades because they are very diverse in terms of country of origin, profile and motivation (OECD, 2015). They are also quite different from host populations when it comes to cultural background/language/education (Aiyar et al., 2016). This means that the ways in which they resettle and integrate (or not) in the society where they arrive are new and dynamic.

It is clear then that the rising numbers of newcomers and their changing demographic profile bring new and pressing challenges to the places they resettle in and consequently to an already pressurized housing sector. The inflow of migrants and refugees is already reported as currently putting pressure on the market for affordable housing in Europe (Aiyar et al., 2016). It is well-known from the literature that various barriers prevent migrants from accessing and securing affordable and decent housing in the societies where they resettle, impeding therefore their integration. Typical barriers include a limited command of the language of the receiving country, a lower socio-economic status, social exclusion, lack of knowledge on housing-related rights and responsibilities, as well as discrimination and exploitation on the housing market (European Foundation for the Improvement of Living and Working Conditions, 2007). Nowadays, this context where specific groups had rather predictable housing needs, has changed significantly as major societal trends such as increasing urbanization, population ageing, global migration of a massive scale and ethnic diversity are happening across the world (van der Greft & Droogleever Fortuijn, 2017). Adjustments in local housing practices are therefore needed in order to support the provision of adequate housing as well as the smooth integration of migrants in the host communities and their labour markets.

Definitions

For the purposes of this chapter, a brief description follows for the terms used throughout the text.

'Migrant populations'- issues of definition and measurement

The concept of 'migrant' is not a simple one. Many typologies have been suggested, normally based on country of origin, distance moved, reasons for moving away or time spent away from one's home country. There is no consensus on what migration is, although most definitions assume a move of home. Furthermore, types of migration are not immutable. Individuals classed as one type of migrant may become another and, perhaps, back again. For example, labour migrants move in and out of the labour market, migrants coming for family reunions go to work and refugees naturalise and settle down thus the permutations are endless (Glover et al., 2001).

Against a background of changing concepts, lack of commonly agreed legal definitions of 'migrant' and inadequate statistical sources, some categories are more clearly described than others. In the international sphere for instance, in the UN Refugee Convention of 1951, Article 1 Paragraph (2), the term *Refugee* is defined as any person:

> *Who owing to well-founded fear of being persecuted of reasons of race, religion, nationality, membership of a particular social group or political opinion, is outside the country of his nationality and is unable or owing to such fear is unwilling to avail himself of the protection of that country, or who not having a nationality and being outside the country of his former habitual residence, is unable or owing to such fear is unwilling to return to it. (UN, 21 July 1951).*

A distinction is frequently drawn between refugees and migrants, in terms of their *motivation* to migrate, that is, the movement of migrants unlike refugees is triggered by socio-economic push or pull factors (Bhugra & Jones, 2001).

The lack of a commonly agreed upon definition of who constitutes a migrant at the intranational and international level is likely to continue being an ongoing problem, especially with the recent migration crisis. Although the UN aimed to establish a set of common definitions of migratory movements, data collection is still guided by national legislative, administrative and policy needs. Therefore, as countries define migrants in many different ways, it also becomes particularly challenging to measure international migration, not to speak of monitoring specific aspects of migrants' lives, for instance their health (Rechel et al., 2012: 11) or their rights to access services- including housing- and benefits (Oliver et al., 2103).

This chapter does not refer to refugees who have a clear political status, nor to 'stranded migrants', which is a definition -for those migrants who have particular vulnerabilities and needs- that gained renewed attention by international actors, and especially in relation to the 2011 uprising and consequent conflict in Libya and the current crisis in Syria (Chetail & Braeunlich, 2013). Reference here is made only to 'migrants', a term that will be used throughout the following pages.

'Migration Crisis'

In 2015 there was an evident increase in global forced displacement with record-high numbers. On a global scale, 86 per cent of migrants and refugees are currently hosted in the developing world, which is rife with its own economic and political challenges (Banulescu-Bogdan & Fratzke, 2015).

In the EU, during the same year that is, 2015, 1 million migrants and refugees made the dangerous journey across the Mediterranean into Europe. The majority – or 850,000 – crossed from Turkey to the Balkans, a movement which constitutes one of the largest movements of forcibly displaced people through European borders since World War II (UNHCR, 2016). Thousands of migrants and refugees travelled towards western and northern Europe, passing through Balkan and Central-European countries such as Greece, the Former Yugoslav Republic of Macedonia, Serbia, Hungary and Austria (Gulland, 2015). EU countries in the north such as Sweden and Germany have been receiving almost half of all EU asylum applications and despite their very good economic state when compared to southern Europe they are nevertheless struggling to accommodate the complex needs of the incoming populations. The heterogeneity of arriving migrants who, much more than in previous migration crises, are very diverse in terms of profile and move motivation has been already noted in the previous pages.

The sheer numbers of migrant inflows and resettlements, the increasing diversity of incoming populations, and the recently increased anti-immigration sentiment across Europe (Mladovsky et al., 2012) have undoubtedly put under immense pressure the protection, healthcare, legislative, housing, educational and other systems. In this volatile context, there is a clear need for better understanding of the concept of migrant integration and for effective practices in the reception societies and their local communities.

'Housing Disadvantage for Migrants'

Research consistently shows that housing disadvantage, that is, difficulties in housing access and poor housing conditions, for migrants is widespread and often severe (Law, 2010: 189). Extensively reported and well-known factors which feed this disadvantage include: real or perceived discrimination (Teixeira, 2008); poor employment and income prospects, language barriers and lack of knowledge about housing services (Ray et al., 2004); and a shortage of social and other forms of affordable housing that severely affects local populations (Rosenfeld, 2015). It should be noted that the processes and patterns of discrimination and exclusion are not random, but have a systematic and persistent character. This is evident from the fact that similar practices occur in the housing field within countries that are very different (Harrison et al., 2005: 14).

There have been measures for facilitating migrants' access to housing, such as the example the European Investment Bank who support EU countries in providing funding to migrants for adequate and affordable long-term social housing, and indirectly by the EU Commission through other services such as healthcare, education and employment.

However, integration has always been an issue that goes beyond mere participation in the housing market. As pointed out by the EU Commission (2016) housing is undoubtedly important for migrants' well-being but integration is most effective when it is anchored in what it means to live in diverse European societies. This is why before amending the policies that will address better the aforementioned barriers to housing and implementing the practices that may remove them, the classic concept of integration needs to be revisited and understood through a lens more suitable to the contemporary societal context.

Integration of Migrants: Moving Towards a More Dynamic and Multi-Level Conceptualisation in Social Sciences

'Integration of migrants' as a social issue and also as a social-psychological phenomenon or outcome has been present in the social sciences for quite a few decades. We review how scholars from the disciplines of sociology, psychology and human geography have approached it.

Sociology

Sociologists such as Granovetter (1973) talked early about the various dimensions of migrants' integration: first there is the 'incidence' dimension which includes frequency and intensity. Frequency relates to the number of ties with their surroundings that an individual or group maintains and to the numbers of actual contacts with others. Intensity relates to the nature of these contacts and thus to feelings of belonging and familiarity. Then there is the 'identification' dimension- the more one identifies with others, the closer ties tend to be. But a strong identification does not necessarily presuppose frequent or intense contacts- for example many migrants strongly identify with their home country, even though the bulk of their contacts may lie in the country of residence (Entzinger & Biezeveld, 2003: 6).

Other authors (e.g. Engbersen & Gabriëls, 1995) distinguish between different spheres of integration and point out how a migrant who is well integrated into one sphere, may not be equally integrated into another. Entzinger & Biezeveld (2003) use the example of an educated migrant having employment in a 'good' mainstream company, while at the same time only having all of his social relationships with people originating from his own ethnic community. In this example, they argue that *"at the level of personal friendships this person is well integrated into his own community"* (p. 8).

On a similar note Spencer & Cooper (2006) have challenged the primacy of economic indicators which cannot tell the full story of integration. These authors note that migrants can have strong transnational links and be well integrated into the host society. They can also be well integrated into one sphere such as intermarriage but not in another sphere such as education. As Niessen & Huddleston (2009) point out: *"integration must be captured as a multi-dimensional process revealing strengths and weaknesses across areas of life"* (p. 32).

The analysis of 'incidence' and 'identification' by sociologists as well as the distinction between spheres of integration highlight the gradual acknowledgement that integration is not a one-dimensional and predictable outcome but rather a multi-faceted and dynamic process.

More recently, Lee (2009) carried out a comprehensive review of sociological theories of migrant integration: starting from classical assimilation theory in the 1920s and then moving to more sophisticated theories of integration in the 1960s, he then discusses the theory of spatial assimilation (the phenomenon of migrants moving away from ethnic enclaves and into areas occupied predominantly by the majority group of the host society) and the theory of transnationalism (where migrants invest in the new host environment but also continue to participate in activities and relationships from their country of origin). He concludes that *"migrant integration is not only a multi-faceted process but an ever-evolving one as sociologists develop new theories to explain the migration integration process"* (p. 743).

Psychology

In the field of psychology too, a gradual move from rather one-dimensional views to more complex ones has occurred.

Berry's (1980, 1997) acculturation theory and its uptake by other scholars (e.g. Ward & Kagitcibasi, 2010) have been widely applied for examining migrants' adaptation to the host society and overall well-being. Acculturation can be defined as *"the process of cultural change and adaptation that occurs when individuals from different cultures come into contact"* (Gibson, 2001:19). At the group level, it involves changes in social structures, institutions and cultural practices. At the individual level, it involves changes in a person's behavioural repertoire.

Berry (1997) pointed out that acculturation is determined by the extent to which an individual is willing to retain an old culture and adopt a new one. This results in four types of acculturation attitudes: integration (accept both old and new culture); assimilation (reject old culture, accept new); separation (accept old culture, reject new); and marginalisation (reject both). Many studies have implied that integration is the 'best' acculturation attitude a migrant could adopt, in the sense of being associated with the most favourable psychosocial outcomes (Coatsworth et al. 2005; Chen et al., 2008).

Due to this approach, the longstanding assumption held by psychologists and other social scientists has been that when the host society is positively oriented towards migration and cultural diversity, then migrants have high chances of successfully integrating. Yet this assumption has been challenged, as it conveys a rather two-dimensional view of acculturation, according to which migrants find themselves either in a positive new context, thus integrate easily, or in a negative context which thwarts their opportunities for smooth integration (Wilczek et al., 2009).

Berry (2008) in his work on globalisation and acculturation, recognised how processes of acculturation today change as globalisation unfolds and migrants' profiles are diverse and addressed the above criticisms by supporting that high degrees of intercultural contact actually have *highly variable outcomes* for communities and their members: some migrants may remain strongly attached to their heritage culture, while others from the same community may keep some things from their own culture or prefer to assimilate to the new society. Therefore, he enriched his theory with a dynamic dimension which avoided either-or generalisations about migrants' acculturation and well-being.

While Berry's theory to understanding acculturation has been undoubtedly influential, it received additional criticisms such as Sakamoto's (2007) point that the theory focuses too much on intra-individual or interpersonal states and ignoring structural issues affecting individuals (p. 520) (characteristics of the country and local community where migrants resettle) and their ability to integrate or not; as well as criticisms referring to the lack of a view on the various reasons why people adopt certain acculturation strategies over others (e.g. due to personality traits, pre-migration experiences such as trauma, fluency in the language of the host country, age when one migrates to a new country etc) (Schwartz et al., 2010; Sleijpen et al., 2015) and whether these change over time (Navas et al., 2005).

The aforementioned criticisms to the classic psychological acculturation theory clearly suggest that 'integration' is neither the same simple process for all migrants, nor necessarily the guaranteed 'linear' way to attaining positive well-being outcomes while resettling in the new country.

Human Geography

In disciplines such as human geography and human development there is also a rethinking of acculturation and of the universalist assumption that all migrants undergo the same processes when resettling in a new society (Bhatia & Ram, 2001). The concept of 'integration strategy', developed- as already discussed- by cross-cultural psychologist John Berry and further used by many other scholars is also put under a critical lens. This is because the migrants of the 21st century are regarded as transnational peoples *"whose lived experiences and every day activities are shaped by multiple connections and linkages to several nations and cultures through travel, technology and media"* (Glick-Schiller et al. 1995: 48 in Bhatia (2007). Of course, transnationalism varies across and within migrant groups with significant differences in the scope and range of transnational activities (Lima, 2010). For example, Portes (2007) found, that it is the better educated and the more comfortably established migrants who are most likely to engage in transnational activities.

Nevertheless, if contemporary migrants are then regarded as dynamic groups who keep active ties both with their country of origin and the host country, and choose to draw more resources (e.g. ethnic and family ties) from one rather than the other (e.g. employment), 'integration' in Berry's traditional sense of accepting equally both old and new culture, is clearly not the only way in which one can better acculturate. This is why Lima (2010) discusses how integration represents overlapping relationships- migrants becoming part of the host society and its institutions and transforming them, while simultaneously maintaining and strengthening their ties to their countries of origin and defines integration as a *"sociopolitical process by which migrants negotiate the terms of membership and belonging in their new countries"* (p. 9).

Integration of Migrants as an 'Agency-Oriented Process'

The aforementioned renewed approaches to the concept of integration from the fields of sociology, psychology, and human geography showcase this gradual shift from looking at integration as a one-sided phenomenon which follows a linear route, to an increasingly dynamic and multi-level process, where risk and protective factors for migrants' well-being constantly interact at various levels (individual migrant, sending and receiving community, society) (Prilleltensky, 2008).

Another recent shift in conceptualising migrant integration is also worth to note. Migrant integration is recently being regarded as an agency-oriented and liberating act for migrants who can overcome the typical disadvantages they face for example, having on average lower participation rates, employment rates and wages than natives, as has been observed in Europe and other advanced economies (Kerr & Kerr, 2011 in Aiyar et al., 2016).

Moreover, when viewing integration through the agency-oriented lens it emerges that migrants may even bring positive change to the new societies they reside in, for example migrant small business is an important economy sector, and has brought positive change especially for certain niches. As noted by the European Migration Network (2006)

> *"In most European countries, various opportunities exist for migrants to develop small businesses, for example, the existence of Diaspora network capital and family labour... Thus the so-called 'ethnic entrepreneurship' has greatly influenced European economies and has played a major role in the renewal of urban neighbourhoods"* (p. 9).

Specific theoretical approaches have since been formulated, such as the acculturative integration framework of García- Ramírez et al., (2010) which supports that integration without agency and empowerment is not real integration.

According to this framework, acculturative integration implies a self-construction process linked to the capacity of human beings to a) create meaning and act with intentionality; b) show reflexivity or the capacity of thinking of oneself and society as a whole; and c) maintain one's culture, which provides a symbolic system necessary to make sense of new encounters (De la Mata & Cubero, 2003 in García- Ramírez et al. (2010). As migrants resettle in the new society and provided the latter favours migrants' integration, then they reconstruct themselves and their relations and in turn may bring changes to the existing society (see example above regarding small businesses).

The above framework expands classic acculturation approaches by including a self-construction process where it is shown how migrants despite experiencing vulnerability and risk of social exclusion, may also critically view injustices, build up niches and develop resources to protect themselves, and overcome disadvantage (Sonn and Lewis, 2009 in García- Ramírez et al. (2010). Access to housing, to a safe place to live, is essential element enabling the migrants to start and advance the process of self-construction in the new society.

Observations Drawn from the New Concept of Migrant Integration for Theory and Practice

In the previous pages various updated approaches to the concept of integration from the fields of sociology, psychology, and human geography were discussed, as well as the specific shift to viewing migrant integration as an 'agency-oriented process'. The main observations to be derived from this discussion are the following:

- Integration is a dynamic and complex process, where risk and protective factors for migrants' well-being constantly interact at various levels

- Migrants today are transnational as they invest in the new host society but also continue to participate in activities and relationships from their country of origin. This transnationalism, facilitated and sustained through travel, technology and media, means that co-ethnic communities both in the host society but also in the country of origin matter a lot for migrants' integration

- Migrants who are in the process of integrating in the new society are increasingly viewed as agents who are in control of their lives and try to overcome the disadvantages they face when compared to native populations

- As migrants resettle in the new society and provided the latter favours migrants' integration, then they reconstruct themselves and their relations and in turn may bring changes to the host society (e.g. developing small businesses which in turn boost local economies and renew urban neighbourhoods)

The above points which highlight the multi-level and dynamic qualities of migrant integration undoubtedly have implications for the key actions needed to facilitate integration at different fields (e.g. healthcare, housing, employment, education) and at various stages of this ongoing process. However, despite these new understandings of migrant integration, it is admittedly difficult to change practices and policies. Indicatively, as Lima (2010) points out:

> *"Present-day policies, at the national and local levels, while displacing conventional assimilation models for multicultural ones, still do not take into consideration the transnational character of immigrant life and its far-reaching consequences for integration policies…" (p.9).*

In the following section, the implications of the renewed understanding of migrant integration related to housing provision and associated services are discussed. The ongoing issue of effectively changing practices and policies is also discussed in the closing sections.

Implications of The New Concept of Migrant Integration for Housing Provision and Associated Services in the EU

In the past, social housing may have provided a home for the vulnerable and poor. However, due to the recent economic and consequently socio-economic crisis, the social and affordable housing sector faces two challenges: increased need and reduced funds (Rosenfeld, 2015: xii). In this ongoing climate of uncertainty and .and volatility for the local population, exacerbated by the dramatic increase of the inflows of massive and diverse migrant populations since 2015, various strategies are being applied for helping migrants secure housing that is- to varying degrees- affordable, inclusive and of good quality.

Housing Solutions for Accommodating New Migrants

Under this strategy we find different initiatives that fall under *solidarity practices.*

By *solidarity practices* we mean local voluntary initiatives by local civil society members and their networks that focus on enabling access to existing local housing directly (e.g. housing cooperatives, interethnic housing projects) and through intermediaries (e.g. online networks for matching migrants and people or organisations willing to host them).Integration here is assumed to develop due to the direct contact with local population. For instance, cohabitation or flat share with the local residents in case of interethnic housing projects as well as online networks. In case of solidarity practices integration is understood as a smoother adjustment to the host society because migrants can use existing housing units (or their parts – rooms) in local neighborhoods. Co-habitation or living in close proximity to the majority local population enables them an everyday contact. In certain contexts, (i.e. housing cooperatives) migrants may even be empowered as they have the ongoing opportunity to get involved in the cooperatives' daily operation.

However, when considering integration under the new lens of an 'agency-oriented process', it emerges that solidarity practices may not really assist migrants build up niches and develop resources to protect themselves, nor overcome chronic disadvantage they may be facing. This is because solidarity practices in the housing sector- even though they may be supportive of the beneficiaries- have a short life-span, are small scale and not comprehensive comprehensive enough because of their very nature. In other words, while the accommodation is secured further resources essential for integration in host society, such as social support, education and employment-related information are often not envisaged beyond the hosts' willingness (and knowledge) to acquire and provide them to their 'guests'. In this sense both the migrant and the host may need further support to ensure integration of new migrants takes place.

Other initiatives, under this strategy, link migrant housing with *neighbourhood revitalization*. Rosenfeld (2015) emphasized that the lack of housing affordability and housing shortage in one region often co-exists with the empty housing in other parts of the same country. *Neighbourhood revitalization* has been highlighted as good practice in localities experiencing over-supply of housing but lack of affordable housing for new migrants. *Neighbourhood revitalization* practices make use of empty properties to accommodate migrants or refugees who often struggle to find a housing solution on their own. Theoretically this practice could help migrants gradually integrate in the new society, as they will have housing- that is, one major need- addressed. Selected practices among these involve new migrants in the process of regeneration and refurbishment of empty properties (their future homes). In these cases integration seems to evolve more efficiently as the migrants work and collaborate with the local labour. However, when we consider the long term and real sense of integration, these practices may be limited still.

What is needed is that host communities and migrants systematically collaborate for addressing the ongoing complex needs of integration. This means looking beyond housing to navigation in the new neighbourhoods and community, social care, education and employment. Collaborations can be launched first via organising awareness-raining campaigns (e.g. information days, workshops for professionals from various fields working with migrants), and second by establishing a participatory culture of mutual understanding and dialogue between migrants and the local community (e.g. running several consultation meetings with participants from both the local and migrant communities) so that complex needs are gradually addressed and stereotypes vilifying migrants for not contributing to host societies (Castles & Miller, 2009) are steadily dissipated. Informative material can be produced after the completion of each consultation meeting in which migrants have an active role regarding the drafting and the translation of the emerging material.

The motive for such collaborations between migrant and host populations is of course humanistic, that is, the importance of cultivating harmonious relations thus not only 'community cohesion but also broader social cohesion' (Ratcliffe & Newman, 2011). But there is also a practical motive driving both populations to collaborate: as migrants engage in transnational activities they create 'social fields' that link the country of origin with the new country of residence (Lima, 2010). And as already discussed, in these fields new small businesses or creative enterprises may arise, thus giving new life to local sectors and neighbourhoods which have been in decline.

Eliminating/Removing Barriers for Securing Independent Accommodation

One of the identified barriers preventing migrants from accessing and securing affordable and decent housing is the lack of sufficient resources and the inability of especially new migrants to access the housing finance system in the host country. There have been initiatives in several countries in Europe which aim either to subsidize migrants' rent or help them access or lower the cost finance to purchase a home. Such initiatives undoubtedly take an important step towards enabling better access to housing for migrants.

However, if these practices are not accompanied with the initiatives addressing barriers affecting migrants such as the language barriers and discriminatory and exclusionary practices as well as the lack of information on housing rights and obligations, they may be of limited effect. Most importantly, they may impede migrants access to housing, while leaving the financial tools unused. The provision of funding is undoubtedly important but in addition, several information and mediation services need to be available at the local community level, if migrants are to access and sustain housing in the private sector long term.

It should be emphasized however, that after barriers to access to housing in the private sector have been addressed, integration in the host country is yet additional issue to be resolved. This process requires additional resources that should be accessible to migrants. For example, multidisciplinary teams (e.g. social scientists, cultural mediators, experts from civil society organisations) could be established in order to provide migrants with psychosocial, legal, support and networking via specific referral pathways. Such support is vital especially during the early stages of resettlement and first steps of integration in the host society.

Only when services offered to migrants are multi-level we can consider that progress is made towards their empowerment, which the renewed sense of integration entails.

Improving Standard Housing Solutions for Migrants

Finally, a commonly known strategy for housing migrants is access to social housing especially in the European countries with mature social housing sector. Here it is worth pausing to stress that the shortage of social housing as an affordable housing option is a concern that presents a challenge not only to migrants but also the local population (Rosenfeld, 2015). Due to the increased housing need since the global financial crisis, in addition to the barriers in access to affordable housing noted in the previous section, the concerns raised in international literature related to access of migrants to this housing tenure are eligibility criteria and time spent on waiting lists.

Notably, a common challenge for new migrants is the requirement to reside in a specific locality for a defined period to be eligible to apply for the local social housing waiting list. In building the application file, practices requiring marriage, divorce, birth certificates as a standard part of the application procedure (UNHCR, 2013) may present an obstacle for migrants escaping conflict zones. Finally, once eligibility is established, the waiting period may still be relatively long - two to ten years depending on the country - unless there are special arrangements and regulations that put this group on a priority list.

While access to affordable housing is recognised to be paramount in securing a stable housing situation, it has been increasingly recognised that 'a roof over one's head' is not sufficient for new migrants to integrate into a host society nor for society to absorb migrants. For instance, establishing priority lists requires strategies to address possible tensions between local vulnerable groups in housing need and migrants. Additional challenge in terms of integration prospects of migrants in social housing are allocation procedures.

One danger may be that social housing providers 'cluster' migrants as one category of people without taking into account their particularities, e.g. their diverse cultural origins, their various educational and socio-economic backgrounds, their different resettlement experiences, or yet the different extent to which they cultivate their transnational ties etc.

Initiatives depending on standardized allocation practices as well as those failing to address potential tensions between the migrants and local population, may turn into rather tokenistic practices which again promote a superficial type of integration where locals and migrants just live side by side.

Improving standard social housing solutions for migrants requires addressing issues related to integration in the waiting period that may be substantial, addressing potential tensions between the migrant and local population in housing need and specific needs of the integration of migrants in the host society once migrants are allocated social housing.

Multi-dimensional integration in this context requires practices supporting migrants to address the disadvantageous situations they may be in and become more actively involved in the local community life, as well as supporting the local, often disadvantaged population, residing in social housing in accepting migrants.

The creation of regular common activities between migrants and local community members residing in social housing is recommended so that the active participation of migrants in the local social life is promoted. Such activities can be implemented gradually, beginning with familiarizing new migrants with the basic points in the city they are resettling (e.g. with planned visits in main services of concern), with its history and culture and finally with the people living in it. These practices should go hand in hand with support to the local community (in social housing - the immediate neighbors) and familiarization of thereof with the background of migrants, their culture and story of migration. These parallel efforts could support developing sustainable bonds and constant participation of migrants (e.g. as members of associations, as volunteers etc) in the local community life.

In summary, even though in many countries there are noteworthy strategies and practices for helping migrants access housing that is affordable, and of good quality, these strategies do not necessarily go beyond 'aid' and 'helping'; indeed, housing solutions based on solidarity practices, the removal of barriers for securing independent accommodation, and investing on improving social housing are all undoubtedly necessary to prevent extreme housing exclusion among migrant population (Netto et al., 2015) in the sense that they secure a secure home for migrants. Yet more steps need to be taken for promoting agency in migrants and addressing their own integration needs long term.

Conclusions

In 2001, a study by Niessen for the Council of Europe found a surprising number of similarities among EU Member States in their efforts to promote migrants' integration. According to Entzinger and Biezeveld (2003) who commented on Niessen's study, *"in all countries measures have been adopted by now that aim at securing legal residence rights- at facilitating equal access to employment, housing, education and political decision-making"* (p. 16). Fifteen years later we support that despite adopting the above measures, migrants' integration in Europe is still contested as a concept and far from attained as a reality.

This chapter presented how the concept of migrant integration has been developing in the past decades. From the time John Berry (1980, 1997) and his supporters in the field of Psychology claimed that integration is the 'best acculturation attitude' a migrant could adopt in the receiving country, we have come a long way. Indeed, the recent reconceptualising of integration shows the shift from looking at integration as a one-sided phenomenon which follows a linear route, to an increasingly dynamic and multi-level process, where risk and protective factors for migrants and host communities constantly interact at various levels (individual, collective, societal).

The first part of the chapter presented in detail how approaches to migrant integration have been evolving in the aforementioned manner. This conceptual evolution unfolding in the disciplines of Sociology, Psychology, and Human Geography was discussed. Particular emphasis was given on the rather recent 'agency-oriented' notion of integration, which supports that migrants despite experiencing vulnerability and various risks, may also critically view injustices, build up niches and develop resources to overcome disadvantage.

The remaining section highlighted the complexity of implementing this new

127

understanding of integration into the housing area, where practices often focus on housing provision and may operate in a tokenistic manner, which assumes that by helping migrants live side by side the local population, integration will automatically occur. Recommendations were made with regards to what actions can be taken to ensure that integration -from the sense of a multi-dimensional and 'agency-oriented process'- can happen.

The main aim of this chapter therefore was to explore developments of the concept of integration and examine critically how these aspects can be implemented (or not) in existing practices for housing migrants. This can give insight to a better monitoring of migration and to greater effectiveness of housing practices in promoting migrant integration and social cohesion overall.

It is important to point out there are big differences between EU countries in how they approach issues of migration and integration. The housing systems in the EU member states are also varied and diverse. So it would be impossible to talk about a homogeneous 'ideal' type of integration of migrants, or their housing in this context, given the wide variety of factors influencing migration and integration, the diversity of migrants and the huge difference in approach of these matters across regions, and also among policy makers.

In some cases even the understanding of related issues such as community cohesion and factors that break it may also differ significantly (Diaz et al., 2003). Also, there are ongoing measurement issues when it comes to capturing whether and to what extent integration unfolds (Niessen & Huddleston, 2009).

We are in the process of developing a more solid grasp on the concepts of community participation, social cohesion and integration and on refining indicators for measuring these overtime. Only then the details of which aspects of housing policies for migrants should be further supported will also become much clearer. This awareness is an important basis for exchange of information, policy initiatives and best practices (Entzinger & Biezeveld, 2003).

In conclusion, the undoubtedly more sophisticated approach to migrant integration that has been unfolding, is worth housing policy-makers' attention because it may trigger more well-informed actions to facilitate not only migrants' integration in the best and fairest possible way but also enhance the quality of life and well-being of both migrants and host communities.

References

Aiyar, S. et al. (2016). *The refugee surge in Europe: Economic challenges*. Washington, DC: International Monetary Fund.

Banulescu-Bogdan, N. & Fratzke, S. (2015). *Europe's migration crisis in context: Why now and what next?* Washington, DC: Migration Policy Institute.

Berry, J.W. (1980). Acculturation as varieties of adaptation. In: A.M. Padilla (ed.) *Acculturation: Theory, models, and some new findings*. Boulder, CO: Westview, pp.9-25.

Berry, J.W. (1997). Immigration, acculturation and adaptation. *Applied Psychology: An International Review, 46*, 5-34.

Berry, J. W. (2008). Globalisation and acculturation. *International Journal of Intercultural Relations, 32*, 328-336.

Bhatia, S. (2007). Rethinking culture and identity in psychology: Towards a transnational cultural psychology. *Journal of Theoretical and Philosophical Psychology, 27-28*(2-1), 301-321.

Bhatia, S. & Ram, A. (2001). Rethinking 'acculturation' in relation to diasporic cultures and postcolonial identities. *Human Development*, *44*(1), 1-18.

Bhugra, D. & Jones, P. (2001). Migration and mental illness. *Advances in Psychiatric Treatment*, *7*, 216-223.

Bradby, H., Humphris, R., Newall, D. & Phillimore, J. (2015). *Public health aspects of migrant health: a review of the evidence on health status for refugees and asylum seekers in the European Union.* Copenhagen: WHO Regional Office for Europe (Health Evidence Network synthesis report 44).

Bretell, C. & Hollifield, J.F. (Eds.). (2000). *Migration Theory: Talking across disciplines.* New York: Routledge.

Castles, S. & Miller, M. (2009). *The age of migration: International population movements in the modern world* (4th edn). Basingstoke: Palgrave Macmillan.

Chetail, V. & Braeunlich, M.A. (2013). *Stranded migrants: Giving structure to a multifaceted notion.* Global Migration Research Paper, No 5. Geneva: Global Migration Centre.

Chen, S.X., Benet-Martínez, V. & Bond, M.H. (2008). Bicultural identity, bilingualism, and psychological adjustment in multicultural societies: Immigration-based and globalization-based acculturation. *Journal of Personality*, *76*, 803–838.

Coatsworth, J.D., Maldonado-Molina, M., Pantin, H. & Szapocznik, J. (2005). A person-centered and ecological investigation of acculturation strategies in Hispanic immigrant youth. *Journal of Community Psychology*, *33*, 157–174.

Craig, C. (2015). *Migration and integration: A local and experiential perspective.* IRiS Working Paper Series, No. 7/2014. Birmingham: Institute for Research into Superdiversity.

De la Mata, M.L., & Cubero, M. (2003). Psicología cultural: Approximaciones al studio de la relación entre mente y cultura. *Infancia y Apprendizaje*, *26*(2), 181-199 (in Spanish).

Diaz, P., Widdis, R. & Gauthier, D. (2003). Social cohesion and the rural community. In Blake, R. and Nurse, A. (eds.) *The trajectories of rural life: New perspectives on rural Canada.* University of Regina: Saskatchewan Institute of Public Policy, pp. 123-137

Engbersen, G. & Gabriëls, R. (Eds.) (1995). *Sferen van integratie: Naar een gedifferentieerd allochtonenbeleid.* Amsterdam: Boom.

Entzinger, H. & Biezeveld, R. (2003). *Benchmarking in immigrant integration.* Rotterdam, Erasmus University: European Research Centre on Migration and Ethnic Relations (ERCOMER).

European Commission. (2016). *Action Plan on the integration of third country nationals.* Brussels: 7.6.2016, COM (2016) 377 final.

European Foundation for the Improvement of Living and Working Conditions. (2007). *Housing and integration of migrants in Europe.* Strasbourg: Council of Europe.

European Migration Network. (2006). *Impact of immigration on Europe's societies.* Luxembourg: Office for Official Publications of the European Communities.

Eurostat. (2017). *Housing costs - an excessive burden for 11 % of Europeans.* Brussels: Eurostat.

García- Ramírez, M., de la Mata, M., Paloma, V. & Hernández-Plaza, S. (2010). A liberation psychology approach to acculturative integration of migrant populations. *American Journal of Community Psychology*, *47*(1-2), 86-97.

Gibson, M.A. (2001). Immigrant adaptation and patterns of acculturation. *Human Development*, *44*, 19–23.

Glick-Schiller, N., Basch, L., & Szanton-Blanc, C. (1995). From immigrant to transmigrant: Theorising transnational migration. *Anthropological Quarterly*, *68*, 48-63.

Glover, S., Gott, C., Loizillon, A., Portes, J., Price, R., Spencer, S., Srinivasan, V., & Willis, C. (2001). *Migration: An economic and social analysis.* RDS Occasional Paper, No 67. U.K. Home Office: Research Development and Statistics Directorate (RDS) Publications.

Granovetter, M. (1973). The strength of weak ties. *American Journal of Sociology*, *78*, 1360-1380.

Gulland, A. (2015). Refugees pose little health risk, says WHO. *British Medical Journal*, *351*, h4808.

Harrison, M., Law, I. & Phillips, D. (2005). *Migrants, minorities and housing: exclusion, discrimination and anti-discrimination in 15 Member States of the European Union.* Vienna: European Monitoring Centre on Racism and Xenophobia (EUMC).

Heissler, B. (2000). The sociology of immigration: From assimilation to segmented integration, from the American experience to the global arena. In Bretell, C. and Hollifield, J.F. (eds.) *Migration Theory: Talking across disciplines.* New York: Routledge. pp. 77-96.

Kerr, S.P., & Kerr, W. (2011). Economic Impacts of Immigration: A Survey? *Finnish Economic Papers, 24* (1), 1–32.

Law, I. (2010). *Racism and ethnicity: Global debates, dilemmas, directions.* London: Pearson Education.

Lee, C. (2009). Sociological theories of immigration: Pathways to integration for U.S. immigrants. *Journal of Human Behavior in the Social Environment, 19*(6), 730-744.

Lima, A. (2010). *Transnationalism: A New Mode of Immigrant Integration.* University of Massachussets: The Mauricio Gaston Institute for Latino Community Development and Public Policy.

Mladovsky, P., Ingleby, D., & Rechel, B. (2012). Good practices in migrant health: The European experience. *Clinical Medicine, 12*(3), 248-252.

Navas, M., Garcia, M. C., Sanchez, J., Rojas, A. J., Pumares, P., & Fernandez, J. S. (2005). Relative acculturation extended model (raem): New contributions with regard to the study of acculturation. *International Journal of Intercultural Relations, 29* (1), 21-37.

Netto, G., Fitzpatrick, S., Sosenko, F., & Smith, H. (2015) *International lessons on tackling extreme housing exclusion.* London: Joseph Rowntree Foundation.

Niessen, J. (2001). *Diversity and cohesion: New challenges for the integration of immigrants and minorities.* Strasbourg: Council of Europe.

Niessen, J. & Huddleston, T. (Eds). (2009). *Legal frameworks for the integration of third-country nationals.* Leiden and Boston: Martinus Nijhoff Publishers.

OECD (2015). *Is this humanitarian migration crisis different?* Migration Policy Debate No 7.

Oliver, C., Spencer, S., Jayaweera, H. & Hughes, V. (2013). *Post-entry restrictions and entitlements: What are the consequences of changing policies for family migrants within the UK?* COMPAS Breakfast Briefing 27, 12 July 2013. Oxford: COMPAS.

Phillimore, J. (2013). Housing home and neighbourhood in the era of superdiversity. *Housing Studies, 28*(5), 682-700.

Portes, A. (2007). Migration, development, and segmented assimilation: A conceptual review of the evidence. *The Annals of the American Academy of Political and Social Science, 610* (1), 73-97.

Prilleltensky, I. (2008). Migrant well-being is a multilevel, dynamic, value dependent phenomenon. *American Journal of Community Psychology, 42*(3-4), 359-364.

Ratcliffe, P. & Newman, I. (Eds.). (2011). *Promoting social cohesion: Implications for policy and evaluation.* Bristol: Policy Press.

Ray, B.K., Papademetriou, D., & Jachimowicz. (2004). *Immigrants and homeownership in urban America: An examination of nativity, socio-economic status and place.* Washington, DC: Migration Policy Institute.

Rechel, B., Mladovsky, P. & Devillé, W. (2012). Monitoring migrant health in Europe: A narrative review of data collection practices. *Health Policy, 105,* 10-16

Rosenfeld, O. (2015). *Social housing in the UNECE region: Models, trends and challenges.* Geneva: UNECE.

Rosenkranz, H. (2000). *A concise guide to Refugees' Education and qualifications.* London: World University Service/ RETAS.

Sakamoto, I. (2007). A critical examination of immigrant acculturation: Toward an anti-oppressive social work model with immigrant adults in a pluralistic society. *British Journal of Social Work, 37,* 515-535.

Schwartz, S.J., Unger, J.B., Zamboanga, B.L., & Szapocznik, J. (2010). Rethinking the concept of acculturation. *American Psychologist, 65*(4), 237-251.

Sleijpen, M., Boeije, H.R., Kleber, R.J. & Mooren, T. (2016). Between power and powerlessness: A meta-ethnography of sources of resilience in young refugees. *Ethnicity and Health, 21*(2), 158-180.

Spencer, S. & Cooper, B. (2006). *Social integration of migrants in Europe: A review of the European literature 2000-2006.* Paris: OECD.

Sonn, C.C., & Lewis, R.C. (2009). Immigration and identity: The ongoing struggles for liberation. In Montero, M. & Sonn, C.C. (eds.) *Psychology of liberation. Theory and applications.* New York, NY: Springer, pp. 115-133.

Teixeira, C. (2008). Barriers and outcomes in the housing searches of new immigrants and refugees: A case study of 'Black' Africans in Toronto's rental market. *Journal of Housing and the Built Environment, 23*(4), 253-276.

Tsenkova, S. (2016). Sustainable housing and liveable cities. *Urban Research and Practice, 9* (3), 322-326.

UNHCR- United Nations High Commissioner for Refugees. (2016). *RRMRP-Regional Refugee and Migrant Response Plan for Europe. Eastern Mediterranean and Western Balkans Route, January-December 2016.* Geneva: UNHCR.

UNHCR- United Nations High Commissioner for Refugees. (2015). *Global trends-Forced Displacement in 2015.* Geneva: UNHCR.

UNHCR- United Nations High Commissioner for Refugees. (2013). *A New Beginning, Refugee Integration in Europe.* Geneva: UNHCR.

van der Greft, S. & Droogleever Fortuijn, J. (2017). Multiple disadvantage of older migrants and native Dutch older adults in deprived neighbourhoods in Amsterdam, the Netherlands: A life course perspective. *GeoJournal, 82*(3), 415-432.

Ward, C. & Kagitcibasi, C. (2010). Applied acculturation research: Working with, for and beyond communities. *International Journal of Intercultural Relations, 34,* 186-189.

IMMIGRATION AND ELECTORAL SUPPORT FOR THE RADICAL RIGHT: EVIDENCE FROM DUTCH MUNICIPALITIES

Panagiotis Chasapopoulos*, Arjen van Witteloostuijn* and Christophe Boone**

Introduction

Throughout Europe in recent years, a considerable number of 'extreme-right' parties, as they are most often referred to, have been gaining popularity and influencing the formation of public opinion. In France, the far-right '*Front National*' party of Marine Le Pen scored its highest ever percentage of votes when it won through to the second round of the presidential elections in the spring of 2017. Shortly before that, at the national elections taking place in the Netherlands, the populist radical-right '*Party for Freedom*' of Geert Wilders came second, increasing its previous number of seats in the parliament. Only a few months earlier, in summer of 2016, the right-wing populist '*UK Independence Party*' had managed to play a major role in the 'Brexit' referendum by promoting itself as a nativist nationalist political movement.

In Italy, the right-wing anti-immigrant parties '*North League*' and '*Brothers of Italy*' have been among the big winners in the recent general election of 2018, gaining significant political power in parliament. The increasing popularity of the xenophobic party '*Alternative for Germany*' in the last German federal elections of 2017 is a further typical example of the radical right's electoral success in Western Europe. In addition, in the same year, the right-wing populist '*Freedom Party of Austria*' finished third in the Austrian legislative elections, only one parliamentary seat behind the party who came second. In Scandinavia three out of four countries, Denmark, Finland and Norway, have formed coalition governments with the support of right-wing populist parties, whilst in Sweden the nationalist party '*Sweden Democrats*' impressively jumped to third place at the last general election in 2014.

---

* Panagiotis Chasapopoulos is a joint PhD candidate at the Antwerp Centre of Evolutionary Demography (ACED) of the Faculty of Applied Economics at the University of Antwerp in Belgium and at the Tilburg Shool of Economics and Management (TiSEM) of Tilburg University in the Netherlands.

* Arjen van Witteloostuijn holds a PhD in Economics from Maastricht University (1990) and currently is a Full Professor of Business and Economics at the VU University Amsterdam. He is also Dean of the VU School of Business and Economics (SBE) in Amsterdam.

** Christophe Boone holds a PhD in Applied Economics from the University of Antwerp (1992) and currently is a Full Professor of Organization Theory and Behavior at the same university. He is also co-founder and co-director of the Antwerp Centre of Evolutionary demography (ACED).

The summary of electoral outcomes presented above highlights that the success of radical right parties is an ongoing reality in the political landscape of Europe. One way to explain this growing phenomenon is to assume that the high concentration of foreigners and the rising immigrant inflows to European countries in recent years have led to electoral support for parties with strong anti-immigrant political agendas (Lubbers *et al.*, 2002; Golder, 2003; Van der Brug and Fennema; 2009). Additionally, others might argue that increasing inequality in Western democracies and the economic recession that followed the recent financial crisis in many European countries have tended to sharpen the existing negative attitudes toward foreigners. They may also have acted to enlarge the perceived threat of immigration because of the significant impact of migrants on the labour market and welfare state (Card, 2001; Borjas, 2003; Facchini and Mayda, 2009; Dustmann *et al.*, 2010). A more complex reasoning attempts to link the increasing popularity of radical right parties with a general disaffection from the traditional political system or with the rising trend of Euroscepticism and ethnic exclusion in the continent that stems from intensive globalization (Norris, 2005; Werts *et al.*, 2013, Hatton, 2016).

The purpose of this study is to empirically examine the impact of international immigration on political outcomes in the Netherlands. More precisely, we investigate how the stock of immigrants and the immigrant inflows to Dutch municipalities affect electoral support for the radical right parties in the country. Thus, our work contributes to the growing literature on immigration and political preferences by providing empirical evidence from the Netherlands. Additionally, in this study we differentiate ourselves from previous empirical research by exploring and comparing the short-term effect of immigration (immigrant inflows) and its longer-term impact (immigrant stock) on the vote share of the radical right. Finally, to the best of our knowledge, the current work is the only empirical study of the related literature that distinguishes first- and second-generation immigrants. Our dataset consists of 338 Dutch municipalities and covers the four national elections that took place in the country during the decade 2003-2012.

The results of this study indicate that, although an increase in the share of foreign-born immigrants within a municipality does not increase the vote share of the radical right, increases in immigrant inflows have a positive and statistically significant effect on voting in support of radical right parties. Our empirical analysis leads to several other findings including that the share of second-generation immigrants negatively affects anti-immigrant votes, while similarly to previous studies, cultural distance between natives and immigrants is a significant determinant of the electoral support for the radical right.

This study is organized as follows: firstly, we will provide the theoretical background of our study and review the related literature. Afterwards, we will describe our dataset and explain the methods used to perform the analysis. Then, the results of our empirical analysis will be presented. Finally, we provide a discussion of our findings and offer some conclusions.

Theoretical Framework

Identify radical right parties

As implied by the previous section, different labels such as 'extreme-right', 'right-wing populist', 'far-right' and 'radical-right' are used to refer to the same family of parties in both the academic and pubic spheres of political discourse. Although an in-depth discussion about this battle of terminology is beyond the scope of this study, one question that needs to be answered is how the ideology, and thus the classification of a political party, is determined. As proposed by Mudde (2007), all members of the populist radical right party family share some core ideological features. According to the author, these parties are characterized first by a strong nationalist orientation, second by xenophobia, third by an authoritarian attitude and finally by a populist rhetoric.

In this study, we follow Wagner and Meyer (2017) to identify which political parties may be classified as radical right in the Netherlands. The authors based their classification on information derived from the Manifesto Project[1], which analyzes parties' electoral manifestos and categorizes them according to their policy preferences and positions. According to Wagner and Meyer (2017), there are two parties that may be classified as members of the radical right party family for the time period that our sample covers. These parties are the *Lijst Pim Fortuyn* (LPF) and *Partij Voor de Vrijheid* (PVV)[2]. For the rest of this study, we use the term 'radical right' to refer to these political parties.

Explanations of voting for radical right parties

There are several demand-side and supply-side explanations of the electoral success of radical right parties (Norris, 2005; Koopmans *et al.* 2005; Van der Brug and Fennema; 2007 & 2009; Golder, 2016). Demand-side explanations focus on individual-level factors that determine voting in support of these parties, whereas supply-side explanations highlight the importance of a strong party organization and other external factors such as political opportunity structures. According to the literature, a 'demand' for radical right parties can be generated as a reaction to the transition to a post-modern society (Ignazi, 1992). This argument claims that support for the radical right can be derived from people with strong conservative moral values who are against post-materialist values such as gender equality, sexual freedom and cultural pluralism, or from individuals who are opposite to the general trend of globalization.

Another demand-side explanation of the radical right's success emphasizes the role of ethnic competition between natives and immigrants. First, competition over scarce economic sources becomes quite intense when there is an increasing number of immigrants, and generates strong anti-immigrant attitudes within a society (Scheve and Slaughter, 2001; Mayda, 2006). These attitudes can become even more negative during periods of economic recession, which are characterized by high unemployment or increasing inequality, as the local population blame the 'out-

---

[1] More information about the Manifesto Project can be found at https://manifesto-project.wzb.eu/.
[2] For a more detailed discussion on the historical background and the organizational structure of the contemporary radical right in the Netherlands see Van Holsteijn (2018).

group' members for the poor economic conditions (Lubbers *et al.* 2002; Golder, 2003). Second, ethnic competition between natives and immigrants might be motivated by differences in social norms and cultural values, including religious beliefs and customs. Thus, the socio-cultural aspect of ethnic competition supports the idea that immigration can be perceived as a threat to the ethnic identity and social cohesion of the native population (O'Rourke and Sinnott, 2006; Dustmann and Preston, 2007).

Finally from the demand-side, the electoral success of radical right parties can be explained as a result of strategic voting. This can encourage particular coalition-building (Givens, 2005), and is often a protest vote based on the assumption that voters for these parties are against the political regime or generally disaffected from the established political elites (Van den Brug *et al.*, 2005; Norris, 2005).

Although sufficient demand is an important prerequisite for the radical right parties to succeed, supply-side factors can further explain why some of those parties eventually perform better than others. First, internal supply-side explanations include party-specific characteristics and organizational features. More specifically, a charismatic leadership or the ability of the party to effectively link crucial socio-economic issues, such as security concerns and high unemployment, to immigration appears to play a crucial role in the success of radical right parties and the consolidation of their political power (Williams, 2006; Mudde, 2007).

External supply-side explanations focus on exogenous factors, particularly on political opportunity (Van den Brug *et al.*, 2005; Mudde, 2007; Golder, 2016). Kitschelt (1995) argues that the radical right parties can perform well when the mainstream right parties converge to the centre, thereby providing available political space for the radical right to occupy. Electoral rules, too, can create favourable political conditions for the emergence of radical right parties. Electoral systems that translate votes proportionately into parliamentary seats encourage both the formation and success of small political parties such as the radical right (Norris, 2005; Givens, 2005). Koopmans *et al.* (2005) contend that institutional opportunities offered by citizenship regimes and other integration politics can also significantly affect the mobilization of radical right parties. Finally, another external factor that might influence the support of these parties is their media coverage. The way that the media frames the position of the radical right in the public sphere can be critical in determining its electoral success (Mudde, 2007; Ellinas, 2010; Golder, 2016).

As presented above, immigration can be part of both demand-side and supply-side explanations of the radical right's success. The subsection that follows provides the framework for understanding further how immigration determines the success of radical right parties, both directly through the ethnic competition between natives and immigrants and indirectly by immigration being used as a scapegoat by political actors.

Natives' attitudes towards immigration

The existing literature distinguishes between economic and non-economic channels through which are determined both the attitude of individuals towards immigrants and thus demand for the radical right. In particular, public opinion on immigration seems to be shaped by both labour market conditions and welfare system characteristics (Scheve and Slaughter, 2001; Hanson *et al.* 2007; Dustmann and Preston, 2007; Facchini and Mayda, 2009), and by social or cultural factors within the local community (Mayda, 2006; O'Rourke and Sinnott, 2006).

Economic theory suggests that immigration has a profound impact on the labour market by affecting the potential wages and the employment opportunities of natives. On one hand, immigration may depress the wages and decrease the job opportunities of some unskilled natives or those workers for whom migrants' labour can be considered a possible substitute (Card, 2001; Borjas, 2003; Card, 2005; Dustman *et al.*, 2013). On the other hand, immigration can have a positive effect on the average wage of native workers as many of them benefit from task specialization and skill complementarities among natives and immigrants (Peri and Sparber, 2009; Ottaviano and Peri, 2012; Docquier *et al.*, 2013; Peri, 2014).

In addition, because of the redistributive effects of taxes and benefits there are important fiscal consequences of immigration in receiving countries. The participation of immigrants in the social security system and welfare programs may have significant fiscal spillover effects through the contributions that foreigners pay and the public benefits they receive (Lee and Miller, 2000; Dustmann *et al.*, 2010; De la Rica *et al.*, 2015). Consequently, natives who benefit economically from the presence of immigrants in the country are likely to support more open immigration policies, while those who are negatively influenced by them tend to prefer the restriction of immigrant inflows (economic competition theory).

Beside the economic determinants, the literature emphasizes the importance of social and cultural factors in shaping public attitudes. Increasing immigration imposes non-economic negative externalities on the local society by changing the composition of the host country's population. Therefore, natives' attitudes toward immigrants are likely to be influenced by concerns about 'compositional amenities' associated with immigrants having common language, customs and religion within their neighborhoods or workplaces (Card *et al.*, 2012). Furthermore, racial prejudices that claim immigrants are more likely than natives to be involved in criminal activities have been a cause for additional security concerns (Mayda, 2006).

Cultural distance between natives and immigrants may also affect individual attitudes toward immigration. The different values and perceptions held by people coming from other ethnic backgrounds can be perceived as a threat to the national identity and culture of the native population (O'Rourke and Sinnott, 2006; Dustmann and Preston, 2007). As stated by Dustmann and Preston (2001), increasing immigrant inflows can determine individual attitudes toward immigration in two different ways. According to the authors, frequent contact and social interaction with immigrants could eliminate the existing racial prejudices of natives (contact theory). But a high concentration of immigrants in local society is also likely to be perceived as a threat to ethnic identity and cultural values of the indigenous population (conflict theory).

Additionally, natives' attitudes toward immigrants, which in turn determine their political preferences and voting behaviour, can be also indirectly shaped or manipulated by politics (Norris, 2005). Radical right parties often target immigrants as the cause of several problems such as high unemployment, increasing crime rates or other security threats such as terrorism (Williams, 2006). Therefore, public attitudes on immigration might be instrumentally shaped by the anti-immigrant rhetoric of some political actors. Consequently, as already suggested, ethnic competition between natives and immigrants can generate a direct demand for radical right parties. But at the same time, supply-side factors, such as the skill of political actors in associating immigration with many of the problems of society, can determine the extent to which public demand for the radical right is developed. In this way, the impact of international immigration on the electoral support of radical right parties can be seen as a result of inherent interaction between demand and supply factors. This might be a plausible explanation for any conflicting findings across case studies from different countries.

Empirical findings of prior research[3]

Previous research has shown that in recent decades in Europe the size of immigrant population has had a serious impact, in terms of both strength and significance, on radical right voting (Lubbers et al., 2002; Davis and Deole, 2017). Several recent empirical studies find a significantly positive effect of immigration on the electoral support for radical right parties in many European countries.

More specifically, Otto and Steinhardt (2014) find that an increase in the share of foreigners, defined by citizenship, within a city district of Hamburg is associated with an increase in electoral support for xenophobic extreme right-wing parties. Using data from the Austrian regions, Halla et al. (2017) find that the presence in one's neighborhood of immigrants, measured again as residents without Austrian citizenship, has a positive and significant effect on votes for the extreme right. Additionally, the authors find that this result is driven by the presence of low- and medium-skilled immigrants. Furthermore, Harmon (2017) shows a positive and significant effect for changes in the percentages of non-nationals in Danish municipalities on changes in the electoral support for the country's anti-immigrant nationalist parties. Similarly, the findings of Gerdes and Wadensjö (2010) for Danish municipalities indicate that increases in the share of non-Western immigrants (born outside the EU and OECD countries) within a municipality leads to the country's two anti-immigration parties winning votes in the local elections.

Using data from Swedish municipalities, Rydgren and Ruth (2011) also conclude that the proportion of foreign-born immigrants is positively related to electoral support for the radical right-wing party in the country. However, when the authors distinguish between EU and Non-EU immigrants, contrary to their expectations, they do not find any significant evidence that a higher proportion of Non-EU immigrants in a municipality increases electoral support for the radical right. In their recently published study for Switzerland, Brunner and Kuhn (2018) show that the share of culturally different immigrants, based on their country of origin, significantly affects voting in favour of that country's right-wing party, while the number of culturally similar immigrants does not seem to be a significant

---

[3] In this subsection, to maintain consistency with the terminology of the literature, we refer to the political parties with the same label that the authors use in their studies.

determinant of natives' voting behaviour in Swiss communities. In another study for Spain, Mendez and Cutillas (2014) find that in Spanish provinces changes in the foreign-born population, but only from African countries, are positively correlated with changes in the ratio of the vote for anti-immigration formations in the presidential elections.

Providing evidence from the municipalities of Italy, Barone *et al.* (2016) find that a higher share of foreign-born immigrants within the municipality increases votes at national elections for the centre-right coalition which has a political agenda less favourable to immigrants. In addition, the authors show that the positive effect of immigration on anti-immigrant voting is stronger in those municipalities where religious diversity is stronger. Finally, the results of Becker and Fetzer (2016) suggest that a UK district that experiences a large inflow of immigrants from Eastern European countries, due to accession of new members states to the EU, experiences a significant increase in the vote share of the anti-immigration UK Independence Party in European parliament elections.

From the findings summarized in the literature review above, it appears that both stock and inflows of immigrants (in terms of country of birth or nationality) are positively associated with electoral support for radical right parties. In addition, much of the prior empirical research has found that the type of immigrants (e.g. Western/Non-Western) significantly affects voting in favour of the radical right. In the case of the Netherlands, to the best of our knowledge, no other study has been conducted to empirically examine the impact of immigration on electoral support for the radical right.[4] Therefore, this study contributes to the existing literature by providing empirical evidence from the Dutch municipalities. The next section describes the data and methods used in the analysis.

Data and Methods

We use a panel dataset that covers 338 Dutch municipalities for which we observe the outcomes of national elections held in the Netherlands in 2003, 2006, 2010 and 2012. Our data are drawn from two different sources.

First, we use information on election results in Dutch municipalities from the Electoral Council (Kiesraad). We restrict our attention to the national elections where only Dutch nationals are eligible to vote.[5] Thus, our dependent variable is the share of votes that the radical right parties of the country, LPF in 2003 and PVV in 2006, 2010 and 2012, got in each municipality in national elections.

Our second source of data is the Central Bureau of Statistics (CBS) of the Netherlands from where we collected demographic data and the other socio-economic information use to construct our control variables. To measure the effect of immigration on election outcomes we use demographic data on both immigrant stock and inflows with respect to country of birth. Therefore, our main independent variables of interest include the stock of immigrants and the number

---

[4] A similar study is that of Koopmans and Muis (2009) which examines the effect of immigration on public opinion support for Pim Fortuyn in 2002. Contrary to what the authors expect, they conclude that immigration did not affect the opinion polls during the election campaign.

[5] According to the 'Maastricht Treaty' of European Union (EU) foreigners from EU countries who are residents of the Netherlands are also allowed to vote in local municipal and European Parliament elections.

of immigrant inflows, both as a share of total population in each municipality. In addition, we distinguish the stock of immigrants between first and second-generation immigrants. According to the CBS, a first-generation immigrant is defined as a person born abroad and having at least one parent born abroad. A second-generation immigrant is any person born in the Netherlands having at least one parent born abroad. Moreover, we further differentiate between western and non-western immigrants. This categorization of immigrants is made by CBS on the basis of their socio-economic and cultural characteristics. In particular, CBS counts as western immigrants those persons who come into the Netherlands from countries in Europe (excluding Turkey), North America, Oceania, Indonesia and Japan. Non-western immigrants are those individuals who migrate from countries in Africa, Latin America, Asia (excluding Indonesia and Japan) and Turkey.

Table 1. Descriptive Statistics

Variable	Mean	SD	Min	Max
Radical Right Vote share	9.09	5.46	1.68	38.70
Total Immigrants share	13.55	7.81	2.06	52.43
Foreign-Born share	6.40	4.49	1.00	36.80
Second-Generation share	7.15	3.61	1.06	21.89
Western Immigrants share	7.81	4.38	1.01	49.11
Non-Western Immigrants share	5.75	5.22	0.47	36.96
Foreign Born & Western share	3.07	2.37	0.38	34.14
Foreign Born & Non-Western share	3.32	3.03	0.29	21.03
Second-Gen. & Western share	4.73	2.36	0.63	16.58
Second-Gen. & Non-Western share	2.42	2.25	0.16	16.25
Total Immigrant Inflows share	0.44	0.48	0.00	4.93
Western Inflows share	0.25	0.29	0.00	2.53
Non-Western Inflows share	0.19	0.27	0.00	4.26
Pensioners share	15.67	3.11	6.53	27.70
Highly-Educated share	22.36	7.29	0.00	50.00
Unemployment rate	4.57	0.96	3.00	10.50
Population Density (inhabitants per km²)	776.54	913.50	3.50	5,115.70
Average House Value (in thousand Euro)	220.54	75.51	76.00	672.00
Crime Suspects (per 10,000 inhabitants)	105.52	37.94	23.00	295.00
Voter Turnout	79.90	5.43	62.63	100.00
Number of observations	1,352			

In addition, we introduce a set of control variables in our empirical analysis to account for differences between Dutch municipalities. Following previous literature (Gerdes and Wadensjö, 2010; Otto and Steinhardt, 2014; Harmon, 2017), first we use population density and share of pensioners as socio-demographic control variables. Moreover, to control for differences across municipalities in labour market conditions and the qualification levels of citizens, we include the unemployment rate and the percentage of the active and non-working population with higher levels of education. Furthermore, the average value of houses in each municipality is used as a proxy for its economic prosperity.

Finally, additional control variables are used as a robustness check. To capture the effect of crime on electoral support for the radical right, for each municipality we consider the number of suspects detained after a recorded criminal incident. In addition, voter turnout, which may affect election results through its disproportionate effect on different parties, is included in our robustness analysis. Table 1 provides descriptive statistics for all variables included in the analysis.

Empirical strategy

To empirically investigate the relationship between immigration and electoral support for radical right parties in Dutch municipalities we estimate the following linear regression model:

$$Y_{it} = \alpha + IM_{it}\beta + X'_{it}\gamma + v_i + \eta_t + \varepsilon_{it}$$

where i indicates municipalities and t indicates election year $(t = 2003, 2006, 2010, 2012)$. The dependent variable Y_{it} is the share of valid votes for radical right parties and the independent variable of interest IM_{it} is the share of immigrants over total population or alternatively the number of immigrant inflows, occurring during the election year,[6] as a share of total population. X'_{it} is a vector of control variables aim to capture economic and other socio-demographic differences across municipalities. In addition, the model includes municipality fixed effects v_i to control for all unobserved differences between municipalities that remain constant over the years, and time fixed effects η_t to account for potential cyclical trends such as changes in political preferences at the country level.[7] Finally, ε_{it} represents the error term of the regression which captures all other factors that might affect voting for radical right parties.

As we see above, our regression model includes two different measures to capture the effect of immigration on the vote share of radical right parties. The first measure is the total stock of immigrants that has accumulated over the years in Dutch municipalities and the second is the number of immigrant inflows to municipalities during the year of the election. Although the two measures are related (r=.53), they assess different aspects of the same phenomenon. The difference between them is that the stock variable measures the longer-term effects of immigration and the longer-term changes in stock of immigrants, whereas immigration inflows can capture the short-term effect of immigration on the electoral support for the radical right. As newcomers are more likely to generate stronger negative attitudes toward immigration, due to integration and assimilation issues, the two measures might generate different results.

So far, we have indicated that we focus our analysis on the national elections

---

[6] For the years 2006, 2010 and 2012 when the national elections took place in the second half of the year, or close it, we use the number of immigrant inflows occur during the election year. For the national elections of 2003 which held in late January, immigrant inflows of the year before the election year are used.

[7] Because to control for municipality-specific effects the use of a linear estimation model is required, we do not implement any non-linear estimation approach in our analysis.

because only Dutch nationals are eligible to vote in them. However, immigrants who have been naturalized and become Dutch citizens are also allowed to vote in these elections. The fixed effects setting of the model presented above allows us to assess variation within Dutch municipalities while accounting for stable unobserved heterogeneity. Therefore those immigrants who are naturalized, and thus eligible to vote, but who have been residing in the same municipality over the study period, will not directly impact the effect of the immigrant share on election outcomes. Thus, our fixed effects approach will minimize the potential confounding effect of the vote of the naturalized immigrant population that could otherwise skew the coefficient estimates. However, our estimates will capture the impact of the group of immigrants who obtain Dutch citizenship during the study period.

Results

Fixed-Effects Estimates of Immigrant Stock and Inflows

Table 2 reports the correlations of all variables used in the study. Table 3 presents the fixed-effects estimates of the effects of immigrant stock on electoral support for the radical right. All models are estimated with robust standard errors clustered at the municipality level to account for potential heteroscedasticity and within panel serial correlation of the idiosyncratic error terms. Model 1 includes control variables only. We see that the share of pensioners in the total population of municipality has a positive and statistically significant effect, at the two-sided one percent level of significance, on the success of radical right parties. More

Table 2. Correlations

	Variable	(1)	(2)	(3)	(4)	(5)	(6)	(7)	(8)	(9)	(10)
(1)	Radical Right Vote share	1.00									
(2)	Total Immigrants share	0.22	1.00								
(3)	Foreign-Born share	0.17	0.97	1.00							
(4)	Second-Generation share	0.28	0.96	0.86	1.00						
(5)	Western Immigrants share	0.25	0.77	0.72	0.78	1.00					
(6)	Non-Western Immigrants share	0.13	0.85	0.85	0.77	0.32	1.00				
(7)	Foreign Born & Western share	0.19	0.75	0.78	0.65	0.93	0.34	1.00			
(8)	Foreign Born & Non-Western share	0.10	0.85	0.87	0.76	0.34	0.99	0.37	1.00		
(9)	Second-Gen. & Western share	0.27	0.68	0.55	0.80	0.92	0.25	0.71	0.25	1.00	
(10)	Second-Gen. & Non-Western share	0.17	0.82	0.81	0.77	0.29	0.99	0.30	0.96	0.23	1.00
(11)	Total Immigrant Inflows share	0.07	0.53	0.62	0.38	0.43	0.44	0.54	0.49	0.25	0.35
(12)	Western Inflows share	0.14	0.52	0.60	0.38	0.51	0.35	0.64	0.38	0.29	0.30
(13)	Non-Western Inflows share	-0.03	0.38	0.45	0.26	0.21	0.40	0.26	0.46	0.12	0.30
(14)	Pensioners share	0.24	0.04	0.01	0.08	0.28	-0.18	0.24	-0.18	0.29	-0.17
(15)	Highly-Educated share	0.05	0.32	0.30	0.32	0.21	0.30	0.19	0.29	0.20	0.30
(16)	Unemployment rate	0.20	0.60	0.59	0.57	0.39	0.57	0.38	0.58	0.34	0.55
(17)	Population Density	0.11	0.64	0.62	0.61	0.34	0.67	0.32	0.67	0.31	0.66
(18)	Average House Value	0.21	-0.11	-0.13	-0.07	-0.02	-0.15	-0.02	-0.18	-0.01	-0.11
(19)	Crime Suspects	0.02	0.59	0.59	0.54	0.24	0.68	0.24	0.68	0.20	0.65
(20)	Voter Turnout	-0.61	-0.47	-0.44	-0.48	-0.34	-0.42	-0.31	-0.41	-0.33	-0.43

specifically, a one percentage point increase in the share of pensioners within a Dutch municipality increases the vote share of the radical right by .449 percentage points. Nevertheless, population density and the average value of houses, representing the economic prosperity of municipalities, are found to have the opposite effect. The magnitude of these estimated effects, however, appears to be negligible. Finally, the estimated impacts of the share of high educated and the unemployment rate appear to be insignificant.

In Model 2, the share of immigrants' variable is added to the regression. Nevertheless, we do not find any significant relationship between the total share of immigrants living in the municipality and electoral support for radical right parties. Models 3 and 4 include instead the shares of first- and second-generation immigrants, respectively. Our results show that although the share of foreign-born immigrants does not affect the electoral outcomes, the share of second-generation immigrants has a negative and strongly significant impact on the success of the radical right. More precisely, our estimate indicates that a one percentage point increase in second-generation share decreases the vote share of radical right parties by 1.103 percentage points.

Furthermore, in Model 5 we differentiate between western and non-western immigrants. We find that the share of western immigrants has a strong negative and statistically significant effect on voting for the radical right, at the two-sided one percent level of significance. In particular, a one percentage point increase in the share of western immigrants decreases the vote share of radical right parties by .771 percentage points. On the contrary, the share of non-western immigrants is found to have a weak but positive impact on the success of the radical right with a statistically significant coefficient of .185, at the two-sided ten percent level of

(11)	(12)	(13)	(14)	(15)	(16)	(17)	(18)	(19)	(20)		Variable
										(1)	Radical Right Vote share
										(2)	Total Immigrants share
										(3)	Foreign-Born share
										(4)	Second-Generation share
										(5)	Western Immigrants share
										(6)	Non-Western Immigrants share
										(7)	Foreign Born & Western share
										(8)	Foreign Born & Non-Western shar
										(9)	Second-Gen. & Western share
										(10)	Second-Gen. & Non-Western share
1.00										(11)	Total Immigrant Inflows share
0.86	1.00									(12)	Western Inflows share
0.84	0.44	1.00								(13)	Non-Western Inflows share
0.07	0.13	-0.00	1.00							(14)	Pensioners share
0.22	0.22	0.16	0.13	1.00						(15)	Highly-Educated share
0.34	0.29	0.29	0.16	0.09	1.00					(16)	Unemployment rate
0.29	0.26	0.23	-0.08	0.35	0.33	1.00				(17)	Population Density
0.00	0.11	-0.11	0.40	0.40	-0.29	-0.11	1.00			(18)	Average House Value
0.23	0.16	0.23	-0.26	0.03	0.48	0.47	-0.34	1.00		(19)	Crime Suspects
-0.20	-0.21	-0.12	-0.15	-0.03	-0.62	-0.25	0.09	-0.30	1.00	(20)	Voter Turnout

significance. Finally, in Models 6 and 7 we further distinguish the western and non-western immigrants into first- and second-generation, respectively. We find no significant correlation between the share of foreign-born western immigrants and voting for the radical right, although the coefficient has a negative sign. However, the results suggest that a one percentage point increase in the share of foreign-born non-western immigrants is associated with an increase of .428 percentage points in the electoral support for radical right parties. The results in the last column of the table demonstrate that the share of second-generation non-western immigrants has no significant impact on voting for the radical right, while the share of second-generation western ones has a very strong negative and statistically significant coefficient of about -3.8, at the two-sided one percent level of significance.

Table 3. Fixed Effects Estimates of Immigrant Shares

Dependent Variable: Radical Right Votes Share	Model (1)	Model (2)	Model (3)	Model (4)	Model (5)	Model (6)	Model (7)
Highly-Educated Share	.005	.004	.005	.002	.007	.006	.006
	(.015)	(.015)	(.015)	(.014)	(.015)	(.015)	(.014)
Pensioners Share	.449***	.392***	.480***	.207*	.370***	.448***	.286**
	(.120)	(.122)	(.121)	(.123)	(.118)	(.122)	(.114)
Unemployment Rate	-.099	-.003	-.154	.289	-.095	-.197	.168
	(.268)	(.247)	(.261)	(.230)	(.248)	(.265)	(.224)
Population Density	-.004*	-.003	-.004*	-.001	-.003	-.004*	-.002
	(.002)	(.002)	(.002)	(.002)	(.002)	(.002)	(.002)
Average House Value	-.056***	-.056***	-.056***	-.057***	-.052***	-.056***	-.046***
	(.007)	(.007)	(.008)	(.007)	(.006)	(.007)	(.006)
Total Immigrants Share		-.130					
		(.111)					
Foreign-Born Share			.142				
			(.136)				
Second-Generation Share				-1.103***			
				(.248)			
Western Immigrants Share					-.771***		
					(.288)		
Non-Western Immigrants Share					.185*		
					(.109)		
Foreign-Born & Western Share						-.248	
						(.315)	
Foreign-Born & Non-Western Share						.428**	
						(.180)	
Second-Gen. & Western Share							-3.775***
							(.661)
Second-Gen. & Non-Western Share							-.302
							(.202)
Constant	10.30***	12.02***	9.40***	18.00***	15.63***	10.32***	26.79***
	(3.37)	(3.79)	(3.54)	(3.98)	(4.30)	(3.73)	(4.30)
Number of municipalities	338	338	338	338	338	338	338
Observations	1,352	1,352	1,352	1,352	1,352	1,352	1,352
R-squared	.879	.880	.880	.884	.882	.880	.892

Robust standard errors, clustered on the municipality level, in parentheses *** $p<0.01$, ** $p<0.05$, * $p<0.1$; two-sided t-test. All models include municipality and time fixed effects.

Table 4 reports the fixed-effects estimates of the impact of immigrant inflows on electoral support for radical right parties. For ease of comparison, the first model of the table repeats the results from Model 1 of Table 3 including only control variables. Model 2 adds to the equation the number of immigrant inflows as a share of the total population of each municipality. We find that the share of immigrant inflows has a positive and statistically significant effect on voting for the radical right, at the two-sided one percent level of significance. In particular, our estimate indicates that a one percentage point increase in the share of total immigrant inflows increases the vote share of radical right parties by .657 percentage points.

Finally, in Model 3 we distinguish between western and non-western immigrant inflows. Our results suggest no significant association between the share of western immigrant inflows and electoral support for radical right parties. However, the share of non-western immigrant inflows is found to have a strong positive and statistically significant coefficient of about 1.02, at the two-sided five percent level of significance.

Table 4. Fixed Effects Estimates of Immigrant Inflows

Dependent Variable: Radical Right Votes Share	Model (1)	Model (2)	Model (3)
Highly-Educated Share	.005	.006	.006
	(.015)	(.015)	(.015)
Pensioners Share	.449***	.497***	.480***
	(.120)	(.120)	(.119)
Unemployment Rate	-.099	-.123	-.139
	(.268)	(.268)	(.266)
Population Density	-.004*	-.004*	-.003*
	(.002)	(.002)	(.002)
Average House Value	-.056***	-.056***	-.057***
	(.007)	(.007)	(.008)
Total Immigrant Inflows Share		.657***	
		(.242)	
Western Immigrant Inflows Share			.076
			(.445)
Non-Western Immigrant Inflows Share			1.017**
			(.424)
Constant	10.30***	9.42***	9.79***
	(3.37)	(3.37)	(3.38)
Number of municipalities	338	338	338
Observations	1,352	1,352	1,352
R-squared	.879	.880	.881

Robust standard errors, clustered on the municipality level, in parentheses *** p<0.01, ** p<0.05, * p<0.1; two-sided t-test. All models include municipality and time fixed effects.

Robustness Checks

To check the robustness of our results we first estimate alternative specifications of our model by including additional control variables. We introduce in our model controls for crime and voter turnout as described previously in subsection 3.2. Each variable is subsequently added to a separate specification, but we also test them jointly. Tables A1 and A2 in the Appendix present the results with additional controls. The magnitude and significance level of the estimates do not change much indicating that our results are robust to the inclusion of additional control variables.

Furthermore, as an additional robustness test the outliers are excluded from our sample. More precisely, we drop from our dataset the municipalities of Amsterdam, Ruchpen and Vaals as they appear to have highly disproportionate shares of immigrants or vote shares of radical right parties. Table A3 and A4 in the Appendix report the estimates obtained when we exclude the outliers. We see that our results hold also in a subsample that excludes the outlier municipalities. Consequently, both robustness checks we perform confirm the validity of our estimates.

Endogenous Location Decisions

Up to this point in our analysis we have not taken into consideration that the location decisions of both natives and immigrants are determined by individual preferences and thus are not exogenous. Natives are likely to react against increasing concentration of immigrants in their municipality by "voting with their feet" and moving to a different house. If this is the case, our results might underestimate the true effect of immigration on voting for radical right parties. To address for any potential bias arising from native relocation choices, we estimate a model of the internal migration decisions of natives as suggested by Peri and Spaber (2011). In their study, the authors introduce a microsimulation methodology to test for native displacement due to immigration. Following their approach, we estimate the following model:

$$\frac{N_{it} - N_{it-1}}{Pop_{it-1}} = \alpha + \beta \frac{(I_{it} - I_{it-1})}{Pop_{it-1}} + v_i + \eta_t + \varepsilon_{it}$$

where N_{it} and I_{it} is the number of natives and immigrants respectively, in municipality i at time period t, and Pop_{it-1} is the total population of municipality at time $t - 1$. The model is estimated using yearly changes between 2000 and 2012.

Table 5 presents our estimated results. As in the studies of Otto and Steinhardt (2014) and Halla *et al.* (2017), for the districts of Hamburg and Austrian regions respectively, we do not find any evidence for native displacement because of immigrant concentration. However, the results of both of our models indicate a positive and strongly significant correlation between immigration and natives' location choices. A more likely interpretation of these findings is that large or booming municipalities tend to attract both immigrants and natives (Card, 2007).

Table 5. Natives' Location Choices

Dependent Variable: $(N_{it} - N_{it-1})/Pop_{it-1}$	Total Immigrants	Foreign-born Immigrants
Explanatory Variable: $(I_{it} - I_{it-1})/Pop_{it-1}$	3.931***	4.539***
	(1.112)	(1.283)
Number of municipalities	338	338
Observations	4,056	4,056
R-squared	.227	.114
$F_{(12,337)}$	2.83	2.41

Robust standard errors, clustered on the municipality level, in parentheses *** p<0.01, ** p<0.05, * p<0.1; two-sided t-test. Both models include municipality and time fixed effects.

With respect to the location decisions of immigrants, as Otto and Steinhardt (2014) clearly state, there are two different trends. On one hand, immigrants are likely to relocate in more liberal municipalities that appear to be more open and friendly towards them and avoid areas where citizens hold xenophobic attitudes.

On the other hand, due to economic constrains they might be forced to move into poor suburb municipalities which traditionally constitute the core of strong anti-immigrant sentiments. Therefore, since the two effects could offset each other any potential bias in our estimation results is expected to be small.

Discussion and Conclusions

The purpose of this study is to examine the effect of immigration on electoral support for radical right parties in the Netherlands. We contribute to the existing literature by providing empirical evidence from 338 Dutch municipalities for which we observe the outcomes of national elections held in the Netherlands in 2003, 2006, 2010 and 2012.

Several theories seem to explain how individual attitudes towards immigrants, and thus demand for the radical right, is determined. First, economic competition theory suggests that natives who benefit from the presence of immigrants in the country are likely to support more open immigration policies, while those who are negatively affected by them tend to prefer the restriction of further immigration. Second, with respect to social and cultural considerations, conflict theory proposes that cultural distance and different values between natives and immigrants could be perceived as a threat to ethnic identity of the local population. Third, contact theory contends that frequent contact and more interaction with immigrants eliminate racial prejudices and cause natives to hold less negative attitudes toward them. Finally, some scholars argue that natives' attitudes toward immigrants, which in turn determine their political preferences and voting behaviour, might be instrumentally manipulated by the anti-immigrant rhetoric of some political actors. Based on these theories, we develop our empirical model to investigate how immigrant stock and inflows affect electoral support for the radical right in Dutch municipalities.

Among existing empirical literature there is none that differentiates between first- and second-generation immigrants. Apart from this contribution, as the literature indicates has been done before (Gerdes and Wadensjö, 2010; Rydgren and Ruth, 2011; Brunner and Kuhn, 2018), we also distinguish immigrants according to their ethnic background into western and non-western. Our results show that neither increases in the overall immigrant share nor increases in the share of foreign-born immigrants within a municipality affect voting for radical right parties. Similarly, Mendez and Cutillas (2014) find that increases in the total immigrant population within Spanish provinces do not have a significant impact on electoral support for the radical right. In addition, Brunner and Kuhn (2018) conclude that the total immigrant share does not affect the voting behaviour of Swiss citizens. Yet, previous research has found that a higher proportion of foreign-born immigrants (Barone *et al.*, 2016) or an increase in the share of non-nationals (Otto and Steinhardt, 2014; Harmon, 2017;) within a municipality or a city district increases anti-immigrant votes. The findings of some other studies are similar, showing that the presence of immigrants, defined by citizenship (Halla *et al.*, 2017) or country of birth (Rydgren and Ruth, 2011), in one's area is positively related to electoral support for the radical right party in the country. On the contrary, our results indicate that an increase in the share of second-generation immigrants within a Dutch municipality has a negative and substantial impact on voting for the radical right. This finding can provide some support for the contact hypothesis. However, another plausible explanation of this result could be that individuals with immigrant background, who obtain Dutch citizenship during the study period and are therefore eligible to vote, are much less likely to vote in favour of radical right parties.

Furthermore, our outcomes point out the importance of the country of origin of immigrants. In particular, we find a strong negative effect of growing shares of western immigrants on the support for radical right parties while an increase in the share of non-western immigrants within a municipality increases their electoral success. These findings can be explained by conflict theory which puts emphasis on the cultural differences between natives and immigrants. In addition, non-western immigrants are more likely to compete in the labour market with low-skilled natives who are inclined to vote in favour of the radical right, or to depend on welfare state provisions, and thereby generate stronger anti-immigrant attitudes toward them. Thus, economic competition theory can provide some additional explanations for these findings.

When we further distinguish the western and non-western immigrants into first- and second-generation, we find no significant association between rising concentration of foreign-born western immigrants and electoral support for radical right parties. However, our results suggest that an increase in the share of foreign-born non-western immigrants within a municipality leads to a higher share of the vote for the radical right. These findings are in line with those of Gerdes and Wadensjö (2010) who find that increases in the shares of non-western immigrants within Danish municipalities increase the votes of the two anti-immigration parties of the country. In addition, Mendez and Cutillas (2014) show that within Spanish provinces an increase in the foreign-born population, although only those from African countries, increases support for the anti-immigration formations of the country. Similarly, Brunner and Kuhn (2018) find that the presence of culturally different immigrants in Swiss communities affects voting in favour of the country's radical right party, while culturally similar immigrants have no effect on natives' voting behaviour. With respect to second-generation immigrants, we find that increases in the shares of those of western origin have a negative and substantial impact on voting for the radical right. And to the contrary, an increase in the share of second-generation, non-western immigrants within a Dutch municipality is not found to have any statistically significant effect. Thus, the overall negative effect of growing shares of second-generation immigrants on electoral support for the radical right seems driven by the western immigrants.

Finally, although as stated above we do not find any significant effect of an increase in the share of foreign-born immigrants on the vote in support of the radical right, our estimate suggests that an increase in immigrant inflows increases the vote share of radical right parties. This result implies that is not so much the longer-term effect of immigration but its short-term impact that is important for explaining anti-immigrant voting. In other words, it seems to be the increase in the number of newcomers, relative to the population size, that poses a greater threat to natives, and is in turn reflected in their voting decisions. Moreover, our results indicate that the positive effect on electoral support for the radical right of an increase in immigrant inflows seems to be driven mainly by the influx of non-western immigrants. This is similar to the findings of Becker and Fetzer (2016), which show that a UK district experiencing a large inflow of immigrants from Eastern European countries experiences a significant increase in the anti-immigration party's share of the vote.

The findings of this study might have important implications for immigration policy. The Netherlands is a country which is well known for its diverse and multi-ethnic population but also for its multicultural approach to immigrant integration (Duyvendak and Scholten, 2011). However, the Dutch government has a general integration policy framework which means that there are no specific strategies in place aimed at particular groups of immigrants or specific events (Fischler, 2015). Since our results indicate that it is mainly the non-western immigrants who lead to an increase in the vote for the radical right in Dutch municipalities, policy makers are advised to develop the existing immigration policies in a way that targets certain groups of immigrants, primarily those who are culturally different. We argue that this could not only facilitate integration of immigrants into Dutch society but also contribute to reducing xenophobia in local communities. In addition, as our findings show that increases in immigrant inflows lead to an increase in electoral support for radical right parties, we would recommend that policy makers reorganize the current system accordingly so as to be able to respond effectively to a potential large influx of immigrants in the future.

Of course, the present study is not without limitations. First, immigrants in this study are distinguished, with respect to their country of origin, between western and non-western immigrants. However, future work could break down the group of non-western immigrants further in order to investigate how our results might vary across different subgroups. For example, of particular interest would be attempts to examine the effect on electoral support for radical right parties of immigrants coming from Islamic countries, who traditionally have strong religious and cultural differences with the native population. Moreover, in terms of future research, it would be particularly helpful to systematically theorize and investigate how municipality characteristics moderate the impact of immigration on voting behaviour. For instance, it would be quite interesting to explore whether the prior political climate of the municipality affects the direction or strength of the relation between immigration and the vote in favour of the radical right. Since our results seem to be explained by several different factors, a further exploration of the mechanisms linking immigration to radical right voting can yield important insights into the interpretation of our existing findings. Finally, an interesting extension of this work would be to additionally assess the impact of the recent refugee crisis in Europe, which is not captured in our sample, on the vote share of the radical right.

To conclude, we believe that the research outcomes of this study make a significant contribution to the empirical academic literature. At the same time, since important implications emerge from these results, our findings could be a useful tool for policy making in Dutch municipalities,

References

Barone, G., D'Ignazio, A., de Blasio, G. and Naticchioni, P. (2016) 'Mr. Rossi, Mr. Hu and politics. The role of immigration in shaping natives' voting behavior', *Journal of Public Economics*, Vol. 136, pp. 1-13.

Becker, S. O. and Fetzer, T. (2016) 'Does Migration Cause Extreme Voting?', Warwick Working Paper Series 306.

Borjas, G. (2003) 'The Labor Demand Curve Is Downward Sloping: Reexamining the Impact of Immigration on the Labor Market', *The Quarterly Journal of Economics*, Vol. 118, No. 4, pp. 1335-1374.

Brunner, B. and Kuhn, A. (2018) 'Immigration, Cultural Distance and Natives' Attitudes Towards Immigrants: Evidence from Swiss Voting Results', *Kyklos: International review for social sciences*, Vol. 71, Issue 1, pp.28-58.

Card, D. (2001) 'Immigrant Inflows, Native Outflows, and The Local Market Impacts of Higher Immigration', *Journal of Labor Economics*, Vol. 19, No. 1, pp. 22-64.

Card, D. (2005), 'Is the New Immigration Really so Bad?', *The Economic Journal*, Vol. 115, pp. 300-323.

Card, D. (2007) 'How immigration affects US cities', CReAM Discussion Paper No. 11/07.

Card, D., Dustmann, C. and Preston, I. (2012) 'Immigration, wages, and compositional amenities', *Journal of the European Economic Association.*, Vol. 10, pp. 78–119.

Davis, L. and Deole, S. S. (2017) 'Immigration and the Rise of Far-right Parties in Europe', *ifo DICE Report*, Vol. 15, No. 4, pp. 10-15.

De la Rica, S., Glitz, A. and Ortega, F. (2015) 'Immigration in Europe: Trends, Policies and Empirical Evidence', *Handbook of the Economics of International Migration*, Vol. 1, pp. 1303-1362.

Docquier, F., Ozden, C. and Peri, G. (2013) 'The wage effects of immigration and emigration in OCED countries', *The Economic Journal*, Vol. 124, pp. 1106-1145.

Dustmann, C. and Preston, I. (2001) 'Attitudes to ethnic minorities, ethnic context and location decisions', *The Economic Journal*, Vol. 111, pp. 353–373.

Dustmann, C. and Preston, I. (2007) 'Racial and economic factors in attitudes to immigration', *The B.E. Journal of Economic Analysis & Policy*,Vol. 7, Issue 1, Article 62.

Dustmann, C., Frattini, T. and Halls, C. (2010) 'Assessing the Fiscal Costs and Benefits of A8 Migration to the UK', *Fiscal Studies*, Vol. 31, No. 1, pp. 1-41.

Dustmann, C., Frattini, T. and Preston, I. (2013) 'The Effect of Immigration along the Distribution of Wages', *Review of Economic Studies*, Vol. 80, No. 1, pp. 145-173.

Duyvendak, J. W. and Scholten, P. W. A. (2011) 'Beyond the Dutch Multicultural Model', *Journal of International Migration and Integration*, Vol. 12, Issue. 3, pp. 331-348.

Ellinas, A. (2010) *The Media and the Far Right in Western Europe: Playing the Nationalistic Card*, New York: Cambridge University Press.

Facchini, G. and Mayda, A. M. (2009) 'Individual attitudes towards immigrants: welfare-state determinants across countries', *The Review of Economics and Statistics*, Vol. 2, pp. 295–314.

Fischler, F. (2014) 'Integration Policies – Netherlands Country Report', INTERACT RR 2014/15.

Gerdes, C. and Wadensjö, E. (2010) 'The impact of immigration on election outcomes in Danish municipalities', SULCIS Working Paper 2010:3.

Givens, T. (2005) *Voting Radical Right in Western Europe*, New York: Cambridge University Press.

Golder, M. (2003) 'Explaining Variation In The Success Of Extreme Right Parties In Western Europe', *Comparative Political Studies*, Vol 36, No. 4, pp. 432-466.

Golder, M. (2016) 'Far Right Parties In Europe', *Annual Review of Political Science*, Vol. 19, pp. 477-497.

Halla, M., Wagner, A. F. and Zweimüller, J. (2017) 'Immigration and Voting for the Far Right', *Journal of the European Economic Association*, jvw003. doi: 10.1093/jeea/jvx003.

Hanson, G. H., Scheve, K. and Slaughter, M. J. (2007) 'Public finance and individual preferences over globalization strategies', *Economics and Politics*, Vol. 19, No. 1, pp. 1–33.

Harmon, N. A. (2017) 'Immigration, Ethnic Diversity, and Political Outcomes: Evidence from Denmark', *Scandinavian Journal of Economics*, Accepted Author Manuscript doi:10.1111/sjoe.12239.

Hatton, T. (2016) 'Immigration, public opinion and the recession in Europe', *Economic Policy*, Vol. 31, No. 86, pp.205-246.

Kitschelt, H. (1995) *The Radical Right in Western Europe: A Comparative Analysis*, MI: University of Michigan Press.

Koopmans, R. (2005) *Contested Citizenship: Immigration and Cultural Diversity in Europe*, Minneapolis: University of Minnesota Press.

Koopmans, R. and Muis, J. (2009) 'The rise of right-wing populist Pim Fortuyn in the Netherlands: A discursive opportunity approach', European Journal of Political Research, Vol. 48, Issue. 5, pp. 642-664.

Lee, R. and Miller, T. (2000) 'Immigration, Social Security, and Broader Fiscal Impacts', *American Economic Review*, Vol. 90, No. 2, pp. 350-354.

Lubbers, M., Gijsberts, M. and Scheepers, P. (2002) 'Extreme right-wing voting in Western Europe', *European Journal of Political Research*, Vol. 41, pp. 345–378.

Mayda, A. M. (2006) 'Who is against immigration? A cross-country investigation of individual attitudes toward immigrants', *The Review of Economics and Statistics*, Vol. 88, No. 3, pp. 510–530.

Mendez, I. and Cutillas, I. M. (2014) 'Has immigration affected Spanish presidential election results?', *Journal of Population Economics*, Vol. 27, pp. 135-171.

Mudde, C. (2007) *Populist Radical Right Parties*, Cambridge: Cambridge University Press.

Norris, P. (2005) *Radical Right: Voters and Parties in the Electoral Market*, Cambridge: Cambridge University Press.

O'Rourke, K. H. and Sinnott, R. (2006) 'The determinants of individual attitudes towards immigration', *European Journal of Political Economy*, Vol. 22, No. 4, pp. 838–861.

Ottaviano, G. and Peri G. (2012) 'Rethinking the Effect of Immigration on Wages', *Journal of the European Economic Association*, Vol. 10, No. 1, pp. 152-197.

Otto, A. H. and Steinhardt, M. F. (2014) 'Immigration and election outcomes – Evidence from city districts in Hamburg', *Regional Science and Urban Economics*, Vol. 45, pp. 67-79.

Peri, G. (2014) 'Do immigrant workers depress the wages of native workers?' IZA World of Labor 2014: 42 doi: 10.15185/izawol.42.

Peri, G. and Sparber, C. (2009) 'Task Specialization, Immigration and Wages', *American Economic Journal: Applied Economics*, Vol. 1, No. 3, pp. 135–169.

Peri, G. and Spaber, C. (2011) 'Assessing Inherent Model Bias: An Application to Native Displacement in Response to Immigration', *Journal of Urban Economics*, Vol. 69, No. 1, pp. 82-91.

Rydgren, J. and Ruth, P. (2011) 'Voting for the Radical Right in Swedish Municipalities: Social Marginality and Ethnic Competition?', *Scandinavian Political Studies*, Vol. 34, No. 3, pp. 202-225.

Scheve, K. F. and Slaughter, M. J. (2001) 'Labor Market Competition and Individual Preferences over Immigration Policy', *The Review of Economics and Statistics*, Vol. 83, No. 1, pp. 133-145.

Van der Brug, W., Fennema, M. and Tillie, J. (2005) 'Why Some Anti-Immigrat Parties Fail And Others Succeed A Two-Step Model of Aggregate Electoral Support', *Comparative Political Studies*, Vol. 38, No. 5, pp. 537-573.

Van der Brug, W., Fennema, M. (2007) 'Causes of Voting for the Radical Right', *International Journal of Public Opinion Research*, Vol. 19, No. 4, pp 474-487.

Van der Brug, W., Fennema, M. (2009) 'The Support Base of Radical Right Parties in the Enlarged European Union, *Journal of European Integration*, Vol. 31, No. 5, pp. 589-608.

Van Holsteijn, J. J. M. (2018) 'The Radical Right in Belgium and the Netherlands', *The Oxford Handbook of the Radical Right*, DOI: 10.1093/oxfordhb/9780190274559.013.24.

Wagner, M. and Meyer, T. M. (2017) 'The Radical Right as Niche Parties? The Ideological Landscape of Party Systems in Western Europe, 1980-2014', *Political Studies*, Vol. 65, Issue. 1, pp. 84-107.

Werts, H., Scheepers, P. and Lubbers, M. (2013) 'Euro-scepticism and radical right-wing voting in Europe, 2002-2008: Social cleavages, socio-political attitudes and contextual characteristics

determining voting for the radical right', *European Union Politics*, Vol. 14, No. 2, pp. 183-205.
Williams, M. H. (2006) *The Impact of Radical Right-Wing Parties in West European Democracies*, New York: Palgrave Macmillan Pub.

Appendix:

Table A1. Fixed Effects Estimates of Immigrant Shares – Additional Control Variables

Dependent Variable: Radical Right Votes Share	Model (1)	Model (2)	Model (3)	Model (4)	Model (5)	Model (6)	Model (7)
Highly-Educated Share	.006	.005	.006	.002	.008	.007	.006
	(.015)	(.015)	(.015)	(.014)	(.015)	(.015)	(.014)
Pensioners Share	.439***	.378***	.470***	.195*	.360***	.441***	.277**
	(.118)	(.121)	(.120)	(.121)	(.117)	(.122)	(.112)
Unemployment Rate	-.096	.004	-.146	.296	-.089	-.188	.179
	(.262)	(.243)	(.257)	(.225)	(.244)	(.262)	(.219)
Population Density	-.003*	-.003	-.004*	-.001	-.003	-.004*	-.001
	(.002)	(.002)	(.002)	(.002)	(.002)	(.002)	(.002)
Average House Value	-.056***	-.056***	-.056***	-.057***	-.052***	-.056***	-.046***
	(.008)	(.007)	(.008)	(.007)	(.006)	(.007)	(.006)
Crime Suspects	.005	.006	.005	.006	.004	.004	.003
	(.004)	(.004)	(.004)	(.004)	(.004)	(.004)	(.004)
Voter Turnout	.008	.002	.015	.017	-.003	.015	.021
	(.070)	(.070)	(.068)	(.068)	(.072)	(.070)	(.068)
Total Immigrants Share		-.138					
		(.112)					
Foreign-Born Share			.137				
			(.140)				
Second-Generation Share				-1.107***			
				(.249)			
Western Immigrants Share					-.763***		
					(.281)		
Non-Western Immigrants Share					.172		
					(.111)		
Foreign-Born & Western Share						-.233	
						(.313)	
Foreign-Born & Non-Western Share						.412**	
						(.189)	
Second-Gen. & Western Share							-3.762***
							(.659)
Second-Gen. & Non-Western Share							-.312
							(.200)
Constant	9.08	11.36*	7.70	16.07**	15.42**	8.68	24.70***
	(6.57)	(6.74)	(6.56)	(6.52)	(7.06)	(6.71)	(6.69)
Number of municipalities	338	338	338	338	338	338	338
Observations	1,352	1,352	1,352	1,352	1,352	1,352	1,352
R-squared	.880	.880	.880	.884	.883	.880	.892

Robust standard errors, clustered on the municipality level, in parentheses *** p<0.01, ** p<0.05, * p<0.1; two-sided t-test. All models include municipality and time fixed effects.

Table A2 Fixed Effects Estimates of Immigrant Inflows – Additional Control Variables

Dependent Variable: Radical Right Votes Share	Model (1)	Model (2)	Model (3)
Highly-Educated Share	.006	.007	.006
	(.015)	(.015)	(.015)
Pensioners Share	.439***	.487***	.470***
	(.118)	(.118)	(.117)
Unemployment Rate	-.096	-.118	-.130
	(.262)	(.263)	(.261)
Population Density	-.003*	-.003*	-.003*
	(.002)	(.002)	(.002)
Average House Value	-.056***	-.056***	-.057***
	(.008)	(.007)	(.008)
Crime Suspects	.005	.005	.005
	(.004)	(.004)	(.004)
Voter Turnout	.008	.013	.023
	(.070)	(.067)	(.067)
Total Immigrant Inflows Share		.658***	
		(.246)	
Western Immigrant Inflows Share			.065
			(.443)
Non-Western Immigrant Inflows Share			1.031**
			(.450)
Constant	9.08	7.79	7.39
	(6.57)	(6.36)	(6.26)
Number of municipalities	338	338	338
Observations	1,352	1,352	1,352
R-squared	.880	.881	.881

Robust standard errors, clustered on the municipality level, in parentheses *** $p<0.01$, ** $p<0.05$, * $p<0.1$; two-sided t-test. All models include municipality and time fixed effects.

Table A3. Fixed Effects Estimates of Immigrant Shares – Excluding the Outliers

Dependent Variable: Radical Right Votes Share	Model (1)	Model (2)	Model (3)	Model (4)	Model (5)	Model (6)	Model (7)
Highly-Educated Share	.009	.009	.009	.006	.012	.010	.012
	(.015)	(.015)	(.014)	(.014)	(.014)	(.014)	(.013)
Pensioners Share	.390***	.342***	.426***	.154	.327***	.407***	.236**
	(.118)	(.118)	(.118)	(.118)	(.113)	(.120)	(.110)
Unemployment Rate	-.076	-.012	-.143	.332	-.071	-.169	.182
	(.266)	(.238)	(.256)	(.226)	(.241)	(.263)	(.219)
Population Density	-.004*	-.003	-.004*	-.002	-.003	-.004*	-.002
	(.002)	(.002)	(.002)	(.002)	(.002)	(.002)	(.002)
Average House Value	-.055***	-.054***	-.055***	-.055***	-.051***	-.055***	-.043***
	(.008)	(.007)	(.008)	(.007)	(.006)	(.007)	(.006)
Total Immigrants Share		-.116					
		(.109)					
Foreign-Born Share			.170				
			(.126)				
Second-Generation Share				-1.103***			
				(.251)			
Western Immigrants Share					-.770**		
					(.319)		
Non-Western Immigrants Share					.183*		
					(.110)		
Foreign-Born & Western Share						-.123	
						(.333)	
Foreign-Born & Non-Western Share						.368**	
						(.185)	
Second-Gen. & Western Share							-3.922***
							(.668)
Second-Gen. & Non-Western Share							-.255
							(.201)
Constant	10.76***	12.25***	9.74***	18.31***	15.89***	10.39***	27.56***
	(3.36)	(3.79)	(3.53)	(3.98)	(4.42)	(3.79)	(4.26)
Number of municipalities	335	335	335	335	335	335	335
Observations	1,340	1,340	1,340	1,340	1,340	1,340	1,340
R-squared	.884	.885	.885	.889	.887	.888	.898

Robust standard errors, clustered on the municipality level, in parentheses *** $p<0.01$, ** $p<0.05$, * $p<0.1$; two-sided t-test. All models include municipality and time fixed effects.

Table A4. Fixed Effects Estimates of Immigrant Inflows – Excluding the Outliers

Dependent Variable: Radical Right Votes Share	Model (1)	Model (2)	Model (3)
Highly-Educated Share	.009	.011	.010
	(.015)	(.014)	(.014)
Pensioners Share	.390***	.437***	.420***
	(.118)	(.112)	(.115)
Unemployment Rate	-.076	.107	-.115
	(.266)	(.266)	(.263)
Population Density	-.004*	-.004	-.004*
	(.002)	(.002)	(.002)
Average House Value	-.055***	-.055***	-.055***
	(.008)	(.008)	(.008)
Total Immigrant Inflows Share		.653***	
		(.243)	
Western Immigrant Inflows Share			.039
			(.455)
Non-Western Immigrant Inflows Share			.974**
			(.418)
Constant	10.76***	9.94***	10.30***
	(3.36)	(3.35)	(3.36)
Number of municipalities	335	335	335
Observations	1,340	1,340	1,340
R-squared	.884	.886	.886

Robust standard errors, clustered on the municipality level, in parentheses *** $p<0.01$, ** $p<0.05$, * $p<0.1$; two-sided t-test. All models include municipality and time fixed effects.

9 781910 781852